KU-574-423

THE FUTURE OF THE WELFARE STATE: REMAKING SOCIAL POLICY

Edited by
HOWARD GLENNERSTER

Gower

© The Fabian Society 1983

All rights reserved. No part of this publication may be reproduced,
stored in a retrieval system, or transmitted in any form or by any
means, electronic, mechanical, photocopying, recording, or otherwise
without the prior permission of Gower Publishing Company Limited

First published 1983 by Heinemann Educational Books
Reprinted 1983

Reprinted 1985 by
Gower Publishing Company Limited
Gower House
Croft Road
Aldershot
Hants GU11 3HR
England

British Library Cataloguing in Publication Data

The future of the welfare state : remaking social
  policy.
  1. Public welfare–Great Britain
  I. Glennerster, Howard
  361′.941   HV245

  ISBN 0-566-05154-0

Typeset by Inforum Ltd, Portsmouth
Printed and bound in Great Britain by
Biddles Ltd, Guildford and King's Lynn

Contents

List of Contributors

Brian Abel-Smith: Professor of Social Administration London School of Economics

Geoffrey Bindman: Solicitor

Tessa Blackstone: Professor of Educational Administration London University Institute of Education

John Carrier: Lecturer in Social Administration London School of Economics

Gavyn Davies: Economist, former member of the Prime Minister's Policy Unit, 1974–79

Miriam David: Lecturer in Social Administration Bristol University

Nicholas Deakin: Professor of Social Administration Birmingham University

Howard Glennerster: Reader in Social Administration London School of Economics

Charles Greenaway: An economist interested in taxation

Hilary Land: Reader in Social Administration Bristol University

Julian Le Grand: Lecturer in Economics London School of Economics

David Piachaud: Lecturer in Social Administration London School of Economics

Chris Pond: Director, Low Pay Unit, previously Lecturer in Economics at the Civil Service College

Jennie Popay: A research officer with the Study Commission on the Family

Lesley Rimmer: Works for the Study Commission on the Family

Adrian Sinfield: Professor of Social Administration Edinburgh University

Tom Schuller: Research Director, Centre for Research in Industrial Democracy and Participation Glasgow University

David Townsend: Deputy Director of Social Services London Borough of Camden

Alan Walker: Lecturer in Social Policy Sheffield University

Malcolm Wicks: Research Director/Secretary of the Study Commission on the Family

Part I
Reappraisal

1   The Need for a Reappraisal
by *Howard Glennerster*

When the wicked Thatcher witch has been exorcised, can the social services, and social policy more generally, return to life as normal? I think not. Too much has changed in the past few years for that. Certainly the house building programme might be put together again, some of the education cuts restored, and social security benefits increased. Then there are a glittering array of new things the education and poverty lobbies would like to see done. The Labour Party has a growing policy agenda. There are many ideas that have been espoused in recent Fabian pamphlets. But it is not the purpose of this collection of essays merely to add to that list. We begin from the belief that all is not well in the welfare state as we know it – and not just because of Mrs Thatcher's cuts. 1982 was the fortieth anniversary of the publication of the Beveridge Report[1] which popularised even though it did not invent the concept of a universal welfare state, which the 1945 Labour Government partially implemented. For perhaps thirty of the succeeding forty years most of the assumptions on which those social policies were based were sustained. Services grew and adapted to new demands, social scientists criticised performance and suggested reforms, yet the structure remained recognisable and seemingly secure from attack. Then in the 1970s fewer of the old economic and social assumptions seemed to hold. The services were subjected to a great deal of hostile propaganda and more soundly based criticism. The 'welfare state', traditionally conceived, came under attack from the left and from the new voluntarists as well as from the traditional right. In September 1982 the Conservative Government seriously considered proposals that would have destroyed the Welfare State as we know it (see pages 228–30).

So it is time to take stock and consider how far the basic assumptions on which social policy has been based have to be rethought; and what, if anything, should replace them.

Economic assumptions

Full employment

The coalition government's commitment in 1944 to sustain a high and stable level of employment after the war was probably the most important social policy pronouncement of the century. Beveridge took it as one of the central assumptions in his report and the social security system ever since has been designed to function on the basis that the wage earner is only ever without a job temporarily, for a short period – hence the nature of unemployment benefit, the difference between short- and long-term benefits, and the contribution rules. As governments have come to abandon that commitment and found that their capacity to achieve full employment has been eroded, much else is called in question. 'Without full employment all else is futile', as Beveridge put it. Yet even the most radical versions of an alternative economic strategy, if they were fully implemented, would leave us with a high level of unemployment by 1990; and traditional remedies will leave us with a profound social problem. Those who would discuss social policy cannot rely on a benign economy generating full employment.

Growth and taxes

International comparisons show clearly that higher levels of growth have been associated with higher rates of development in social provision.[2] Certainly, as the economy begins to use currently idle capacity, faster income growth should occur, but it seems doubtful that rapid growth will be sustained for long. Even if it were, however, the old 1964 fallacy was to believe that it would solve our problems. In the long run, increases in earnings that follow from rising productivity in the rest of the economy affect incomes in the public sector and so the large share of costs that those incomes form forces up the cost of services. A comparable effect applies to transfer payments. Benefits have tended to rise with earnings or sometimes faster until the advent of Mrs Thatcher, so there is little room to extend the range of benefits without increasing revenue. Growth does not provide a painless way of financing social provision. However, the faltering growth rates of the 1970s and the consequent rising tax share provoked a conservative rebound that is to be found in most Western countries. That resistance takes many forms – not just voting Conservative. Corporations have used their influence and their poor profits, as well as their international mobility, to reduce their tax liabilities. Employees have avoided tax collectively by negotiating increases that pass the tax burden on in higher prices and fees, and individually by entering the black economy. All these structural constraints on the public economy have grown tighter, and sheer optimism will not wish them away. It is important to consider them before a government reaches office.

Social assumptions

The family
It is not just economic changes that call existing social policies into question. The post-war welfare state was formulated at a time when the traditional family and the traditional role of the woman in that family were largely unquestioned. The two-parent family, the stable marriage, the dependent married woman, the woman bringing up young children – all these are ingrained in the institutional and legislative fabric. There have been changes – the 1975 pensions legislation of the last Labour Government which gave women greater claims to individual pension rights, for example – but social policy still has not adapted to the changed patterns of marriage and non-marriage, women's work, women's view of themselves, or families' and neighbourhoods' capacity to undertake something called community care.

Minorities
The early post-war world that gave rise to our present institutions was also a relatively cohesive one despite class differences. There had not been significant immigration since the early part of the century. Common and undifferentiated treatment seemed a logical and desirable goal. When the new immigrant communities developed, policy towards them was continually caught between the old goals of undifferentiated treatment and the new problems of differential and discriminatory practices by society.

Intellectual assumptions
Those who influenced social policies from the 1940s to the 1960s, as well as civil servants and politicians, carried around with them an intellectual kitbag whose contents looked increasingly questionable in the 1970s.

Social policy and social change
Many protagonists in these formative years clearly believed and often argued that major changes in society could be achieved through the agency of social policy. Educational expansion and the removal of selection would promote social mobility, social cohesion and economic growth. Jencks,[3] Halsey,[4] Thurrow,[5] Goldthorpe[6] and others in the 1970s put paid to those illusions. Education research was perhaps the best example, but the data summarised in the Black Report[7] did much the same for the health services and similar doubts surround social

work's contribution. Much public housing needs no sophisticated social scientist to see that it is not working well. Part of the disillusion with social policy derives from unrealistic claims that social scientists made for it.

Social policy and equality

Despite the warnings of Titmuss and Abel-Smith[8] and other academic social administrators from the mid-1950s onwards, the equation of social service spending with benefits to the poor is still frequently made. The latest collection of evidence by Le Grand[9] and the evidence of previous Fabian surveys[10],[11] should be enough to remind us that simply to respond to pressures from the health and education lobbies on the one hand, and the Treasury on the other, will not create a fairer or more equal society. To do more than that will require much more careful attention to formulating a set of social priorities for the next Labour Government and some improved machinery of government to ensure they are not lost in the crises of day-to-day politics and departmental interests. Some of the most glaring inequalities occur at work in the access to training, fringe welfare benefits and control of people's work situation. Social policy has traditionally stopped short of this aspect of social life. It should not do so in future.

Social service bureaucracies

The traditional right, the new voluntarists and Marxists – let alone individual clients – have all made some telling criticisms of public bureaucracies and their self-interested and insular attitudes to those they are supposed to serve.[12] Audrey Harvey's Fabian pamphlet, *The Casualties of the Welfare State* (1963), was an early example. A lot of changes have taken place since, many beneficial, but on the whole departments and authorities have grown bigger and entitlements more complex. Schools are bigger; hospitals are bigger; town halls are further away; means tests are more entangled. Yet market solutions are worse than the disease. They involve more means testing, and more institutional complexity. Labour has not made simplification and local accountability a major part of its platform though it did initiate some improvements like the ombudsmen, local planning procedures and changes in governing bodies of schools to include parents.

The public service professions

Nor has the labour movement properly faced the problems presented by the growing pains of the social service professions.[13] It is precisely because the caring professions monopolise expertise and deal with vulnerable people that the market is a poor, indeed perverse vehicle. The provider is both proxy demander and supplier of the service, and it is the social worker who decides what treatment you ought to have. Yet social provision by itself will not necessarily replace the deficiencies of the dominant professional, unless we can monitor the quality of care and make those who provide the service accountable. We have singularly failed to do that at all effectively.

Value assumptions

Alongside these important reasons for rethinking some of the economic, social and intellectual assumptions that have underlain social policy in recent years have come challenges to the values on which social policy is based. If we must question the means by which social services are provided, the fundamental values need to be reasserted. The past two years have given us a glimpse of what we have in store if we abandon those values. We have seen a vision of that future and it does not work. Let us look at some of the arguments advanced by the right.

A free democratic society, imperfect though ours is, is an extraordinarily frail structure. In *Free to Choose* the Friedmans say frankly that for a free market to work efficiently our society must become more unequal than Britain or America is today.[14] The message is spelt out even more clearly in a book circulated by the Reagan administration to Congressmen, since it expressed his philosophy so well. Wealth and economic growth, it argued, required the threat of grinding poverty for those who did not work hard.[15] 'In order to succeed, the poor need most of all the spur of their poverty.' Both authors repeat the old contention that minimum government is necessary to political freedom.[16] Yet nowhere do they deal with the consequences of inequality on the support given by ordinary people to the basic institutions of a society. This is the essence of the case that Rawls made.[17] Social institutions, including those that secure individuals' liberty, will only persist if they are seen to be fair by most sections of society. Legitimacy and support derive from a perception of fairness. One does not have to accept the full panoply of Rawls' justifications or definitions of fairness to see the force of this basic proposition.

The modern economy is now so interrelated that any action of mine may produce costs for others. My decision to drive to work will increase the chances of injury to others, my choice of TV set or car may make another redundant in the Midlands, my freedom to build where I choose will destroy the amenities not merely for others but for future generations, and my failure to protest about a piece of racial intolerance at work helps damage the lives of the black community. The causes of ill-health lie deep in the living and working patterns of society. These may be old arguments but their force seems greater now than it ever did. Thus the 'liberty and fraternity' case for collective and universal policies remains at least as strong as ever it was. Indeed, as society becomes more interdependent and as social groups within it become more aware of injustice and unequal access to its benefits, those grounds become firmer. The pursuit of social justice has to be more vigorous if the perceived fairness of social institutions is to be sustained. Just how far and how fast income redistribution and the equality goal can be pursued, and what the best means of doing it is, are more debatable. Different contributors will argue on this.

Fair or socially just treatment for individuals does not always require social provision of goods or services rather than cash assistance or legal redress, but in many instances it can only be achieved by social provision. Such services are often more efficient and more responsive.

Society at large has an interest in preventive health and in the minimum of unnecessary and expensive health care. The doctor does not. He is also in a position of great power over the individual and the family, especially in a private insurance market. Prevention can only be effective as part of a comprehensive system of care with free access. Only the state as a powerful purchaser and monitor of professional practice can safeguard the individual and society from exploitation. Experience of the United States system of health care is an ample illustration of wasted resources and high public as well as private costs. Society as a whole does have an interest in ensuring that people and communities can largely fend for themselves most of the time. Adequate income support and emergency care actually do that better than the ineffective private cover the market provides. A family hit by death or disablement to one of the partners can cope if support is available, but without it the whole family becomes a casualty. A week of health care can consume a year's earnings and a year of care a lifetime's. This can set in train a whole series of breakdowns and dependencies that a more generous response could have avoided.

It is in everyone's interest to minimise 'sponging', but in fact it is the residual means tested service for the poor that breeds such an attitude. If in the end a society's moral values or its fear of the consequences will not permit it to let its poor die without care and it does step in to provide a mean level of pension, it actually encourages some people not to save for retirement and not to provide sufficient health cover. When the state is forced to intervene it is doubly resented because it is paid for by people who have both provided for themselves and are forced to pay for the 'feckless'. Even if we accept that means tests are sometimes desirable, they can only be applied very sparingly if they are not to pile up on one another and become a disincentive and an administrative nightmare. Thus the popular right wing case can in fact be turned on its head in many instances.

Remaking social policies partly means relearning some of the basic lesons. Fabians have been very ready to show up the failures of the welfare state and lay bare their disappointments, yet in contrast to many of our social and economic institutions these services have been conspicuous successes. We would do well to take a careful look at the relative successes as well as the failures of social policy.

A compromise position has been adopted by moderate Conservatives and Social Democrats. The dilemmas, they claim, can be resolved by an extension of the voluntary non-profit and private sectors of welfare. If the argument is that small and diversified organisations may on occasion provide a more varied and responsive service, for example in the care of the disabled, few would wish to argue. Most local authorities already use and encourage such developments, and if they are genuine community groups it is a welcome trend and later contributors to this book develop the idea. However, if the argument is that such developments will resolve the fiscal constraints on social spending the case is dubious. For local authorities or central government to fund such agencies is no gain unless they are very clearly cheaper. There is little evidence they are, particularly not when they are large-scale organis-ations and therefore imply large-scale funding. Where they remain small, embodying altruistic and genuine 'voluntary' help, the situation is different. Nor is there any reason why such help should not be incorporated in the range of services organised by local authorities. Yet the more widespread lay involvement and voluntary action there is, the more knowledge there tends to be about the needs of dependent groups and, in our experience, the *more* demand for services there is. If this can generate a more willing set of tax and ratepayers there may be a double gain, but that is not usually the way the argument is advanced.

In the United States, considerable sums, though still proportionately small, are raised for the personal social services from local commerce and industry and individual giving. However, this is encouraged by generous 'tax breaks' which themselves erode the tax base. They have also provided a justification for Reagan cutting many of these pro-grammes on the grounds that private charity will pick up the burden – which it has not done except in small part. It is important then to distinguish the real from the spurious in this position.

For many years Marxists have held conflicting views on social services. By many they were seen as an extension of the state's appar-atus of control. More recently, though, Marxists have developed a more convincing account. High and growing public expenditure is necessary, they argue, to sustain productivity in a capitalist economy and to contain social unrest and modify working-class demands. The welfare state outgrows the political system's capacity to finance it without undermining individualist values and incentives and running into severe inflation. This process cannot be reversed because of the working class's power to defend its gains. The system is therefore driven remorselessly to collapse, as cuts in public spending produce a working-class backlash.

The basic analysis seems flawed in several respects. Taxpayers are well able to turn off the supply of public funds. Faith in the results of industrial confrontation and class struggle betray a naive view of power in the modern state. Certainly in a highly depressed economy the signs of a working-class backlash to preserve the welfare state are difficult to discern. The common presumption of both the far left and right has been that the growth in social spending has come about because of extensions in the basic structure of welfare services. In America, where most of these theories originate, that is the case, but it has not been the case in Britain. The major factors that have caused the growth of social service spending have been demographic – the sharply rising proportion of young and elderly people in the population – and the rising relative cost of services mentioned earlier. Similarly, pensions expenditure has risen partly because of demographic factors and partly because more people became fully eligible as the scheme matured. The other major factor was the increase in benefit rates to keep pace with the rise in real wages. Taken in combination these factors account for at least two-thirds of the extra real spending. But now the demographic effect is easing, the exception being the high costs of the very elderly in the health and caring services. Both the relative price effect and the rise in benefits to keep pace with rising earnings are *caused* by economic *growth*. If growth slows, so will the importance of these factors. To a significant extent, therefore, the 'fiscal crisis' has a self-adjusting mechanism within it.

Ultimately, social institutions depend on the support they receive from ordinary people as taxpayers, parents or consumers. Social policies cannot be imposed by beneficent social administrators; people must be involved in their provision and experience them as part of their local society. Making services open and accountable to local people is in the end the best way to preserve them.

The structure of the book
That then is the agenda. We can only begin to prompt a re-evaluation of social policy. We are not trying to treat each area of social policy service by service, or merely to add more proposals to the list of desirable service developments. Other Fabian publications have done and are doing that. We are trying to discuss some of the deeper issues that run through all the service areas and the difficulties on which past governments have foundered.

First, we seek to assess the successes and failures of social policies of the traditional kind here and in other European countries. Then we look at some of the major demographic changes and developments in family patterns that have implications for many areas of policy. We look at the constraints that are imposed by the kind of economic disaster we have lived through. What economic assumptions can we make? What part can social policies play in creating fuller employment, and how should they adapt to the probability that full employment will be difficult, if not impossible, to achieve?

Having tried to rethink some of the basic assumptions we address the questions of equity and redistribution. If social policy has not been effective in achieving greater redistribution, is there any real chance it could be so in the future? What could be achieved by changing the balance of spending priorities, by changes in the tax structure or by direct attempts to control incomes at source? How can the particular inequalities that affect women and racial minorities be approached, and how should we view the services that affect the most vulnerable in the community such as the very elderly and the disabled and handicapped? How can inequalities in the workplace be reduced?

What changes are necessary in the machinery of government at national and local level if these priorities are not to be lost sight of in day-to-day crisis politics?

Notes and references

1. Beveridge Report, *Social Insurance and Allied Services*, Cmd 6404, HMSO, 1942.
2. OECD, *Public Expenditure Trends*, Paris, 1978.
3. C. Jencks, *Equality*, Basic Books, New York, 1972.
4. A.H. Halsey, *Origins and Destinations*, OUP, 1980.
5. L.C. Thurrow, *Generating Inequality*, Macmillan, 1975.
6. J.H. Goldthorpe, *Social Mobility and the Class Structure in Modern Britain*, OUP, 1980.
7. Black Report, *Report of the Working Group on Inequalities in Health*, DHSS, 1980.
8. R.M. Titmuss and B. Abel-Smith, *The Cost of the National Health Service*, OUP, 1956; also B. Abel-Smith, 'Whose Welfare State', in N. Mackenzie (ed.), *Conviction*, 1958.
9. J. Le Grand, *The Strategy of Equality*, Allen and Unwin, 1982.
10. P. Townsend and N. Bosanquet, *Labour and Inequality*, Fabian Society, 1972.
11. N. Bosanquet and P. Townsend, *Labour and Equality*, Fabian Society, 1980.
12. R. Hadley and S. Hatch, *Social Welfare and the Failure of the State*, Allen and Unwin, 1981; and E.P. Thompson, *Writing by Candlelight*, Merlin Press, 1980.
13. P. Wilding, *Socialism and the Professions*, Fabian Society, 1980.
14. M. and R. Friedman, *Free to Choose*, Penguin, 1980.
15. G. Gilder, *Wealth and Poverty*, Bantam Books, 1981.
16. M. Friedman, *Capitalism and Freedom*, Chicago University Press, 1962.
17. J. Rawls, *A Theory of Justice*, OUP, 1972.
18. Such as K. Judge in A. Walker (ed.), *Public Expenditure and Social Policy*, Heinemann, 1982; and Hadley and Hatch, *op. cit*.

2 Assessing the Balance Sheet
by Brian Abel-Smith

One of the most remarkable facts about the welfare state is how little it has changed over the last thirty-five years. Successive governments have built upon the framework introduced by the post-war Labour Government. This is when the crucial decisions were taken. Thus before we look at successes and failures we need to understand how it came to take its present shape.

The consensus on the Beveridge Report

After the Second World War the Labour Party promised to create a fairer society. The climate was right. During the war the nation had been prepared to tax itself at wholly unprecedented levels in order to win the war. Surely it would tolerate continuing high taxation to build a wholly different society after the war was won? The nation had accepted pervasive government intervention, planning and controls to achieve the war aims; would it not accept similar disciplines to achieve peace-time aims?

The war had shown that there was an alternative to the waste and degradation of high unemployment. As if by magic, the war itself brought full employment on a scale never dreamed possible before. Despite the high cost of the war effort, public expenditure was also found to improve social services. School meals and day care for children were rapidly expanded, free hospital care became extended in practice to nearly everyone. Rashly women were given pensions five years earlier than men. The labour movement was determined that there would be no return to the injustices of the 1930s – particularly the household means test and the contrasts between the prosperous South East and the rest of Britain. There had to be jobs for all and a decent standard of benefits for those unable to work.

The welfare state was built on a broad consensus. During the war the middle classes had developed a sense of guilt about how the other half lived. The process is splendidly documented in Titmuss' social history of the Second World War.[1] The first lessons came from evacuation: when children and their mothers were given temporary homes, their hosts learnt at first hand what it had been like to live in poverty and what this did to children. The second lesson came from the air raids.

Bombs did not respect social class frontiers. People of different social strata were huddled together in air raid shelters to sleep, eat and talk. The rich came to learn about the problems of the poor. Middle class wives doing 'war work' learnt the realities of the social conditions of the British people at first hand, just as did their sons and husbands when conscripted into the ranks of the armed forces.

The consensus was built around the Beveridge Report.[2] Looking back it was in some ways fortunate that the task of writing it was given to this one man, even if the reason for choosing him was to get him out of Ernie Bevin's way at the Ministry of Labour. A one-man report could be and was a remarkably quick report. Beveridge was not such a modest man that he would tolerate the narrow terms of reference given to him without stretching them far beyond the intentions of the government. Beveridge was a man of the centre, and at varying times he had had both leftist and rightist leanings, but he was never a socialist. He knew the importance of political rhetoric. Few noticed that the objectives he claimed for his social programme and the fine detail of his proposals were somewhat different. How far Beveridge himself saw the distinction is far from clear.

What however is much less fortunate is that socialists bought the rhetoric and assumed that his plan lived up to all of it. The five giants – Want, Disease, Ignorance, Squalor and Idleness – really were going to be slain. Beveridge had provided the means to dispose of Want. Poverty could be abolished by flat rate social insurance benefits provided to those legitimately off work, and family allowances for all starting from the second child. The provision of free and comprehensive health services would improve health generally, particularly the health of those who postponed going to doctors because they could not afford to pay. $8\frac{1}{2}$ per cent unemployment – the actuarial assumption underlying the Beveridge Report – was somehow presented as full employment. Beveridge's conversion to Keynesian theory had not yet taken place. The report said nothing about education and had no answer to the problem of varying housing costs, for a benefit which provided bare subsistence to those with a low rent was bound to be inadequate for those whose rent was high.

Socialists jumped on the Beveridge bandwaggon in parliament and elsewhere. In Cabinet, a reluctant Churchill was eventually forced to give it government backing in order to hold his coalition together as the war reached its critical stage.

Having won the 1945 election by an overwhelming majority, the Labour Government rushed to implement the Beveridge plan. There was no evaluation of alternatives. The Butler Act of 1944 had already established the principle of free secondary education. It was to be provided in three types of schools. This went unquestioned by the new government, if not by some within the party. Family allowances had already been introduced in 1945 by a separate Act and a separate system of financing at a level which did not accord with Beveridge's intentions. They were only increased twice in twenty-two years, despite accelerating inflation and rising living standards.

The National Health Service began in 1948 and the middle classes together with the working classes registered with a local doctor. The hospitals were taken over by central government rather than brought together under local government as previously planned. But Herbert Morrison defeated Nye Bevan in Cabinet on who should build the houses. This was given to local government and not to the national housing corporation which Bevan had proposed, thus establishing local residence rather than need as a major criterion for who should get the new homes as they were built.

National Insurance was introduced with little change from the 1944 White Paper. The scheme was launched with an inadequate level of flat rate benefits which meant that the poorest would have to claim national assistance as well, and this ensured that means-tested cash assistance would be a pervasive rather than residual feature of our post-war social security arrangements. The choice of flat rate benefits related to family size rather than earnings-related benefits created the basis for the polarisation of society into those who look mainly to occupational provision in sickness and old age and those who looked mainly to the state scheme. It also created the 'better off on benefit than at work' problem – a time bomb which finally exploded when Mrs Thatcher punished the sick and unemployed by cutting their levels of benefit. Lastly, it built in sex inequality. It was so unfair to married women who worked that they had to be allowed to opt out, which most of them naturally chose to do, thus undermining Beveridge's claim of universality.

Under the grandiloquent title of a National Health Service, there sheltered what were essentially four health insurance provisions taken over and extended from the Lloyd George Scheme of 1911 – general practice, prescribed drugs, the mandatory benefits of National Health Insurance and the main optional benefits, dentistry and spectacles. These were and still are provided by contractors in financial competition with one another – the usual pattern of health insurance. This laid the foundations for the continuing maldistribution of dentists and created barriers to the deployment of pharmacists in health centres. Although general practitioners had their rights to sell their practices bought out and barriers to entry to over-doctored areas were created, this in turn laid the foundation for the inner city problem of low standards of primary health care. In areas of population growth, new patterns of service could be created. In areas of declining population, the old kept out the new. The financial interests thus established were to become a formidable barrier to change.

Nevertheless, the legislation of 1945–8, which still underlies most of our social services today, was a major achievement realised – it should be remembered – during a time of extreme economic difficulty when real incomes were less than half of what they are today. Then, as the tax resistance grew, the consensus fell apart. The building industry rapidly became overheated with demands for houses and schools to meet the needs of the post-war birth bulge. Housing was cut back and hospitals had to be content with make do and mend. The health service cost much more than expected and became encumbered with charges. The principle of free health care lasted for only three years. The inadequate level of social security benefits was further eroded by inflation and additions for children were added on to insurance benefits to avoid incurring the cost of raising family allowances – thus abandoning the original rationale of the allowances. The road was paved for the re-discovery of poverty in the late 1950s and early 1960s.

It is, however, easy to look back and criticise the weak points of welfare state policy-making and forget how much better it all was than what had gone before. By trying to do everything all at once, the government did nothing really well. The jam was spread thinly over every service, and has been ever since. Moreover there was a lack of thinking about priorities. Who was the government most concerned to help? The free health services helped wives, children and old people not covered under the old scheme. It also benefited the higher income groups who had had to pay for their care. In the same way free grammar school and university education was of especial assistance to those on higher incomes. In some respects therefore the principle of universality was stretched unnecessarily far. In other respects (because benefits were never high enough to prevent means-tested supplements), it never got properly off the ground.

Key developments 1950–79

When the Tories returned to power they did not dismantle the welfare state. As Britain's economy recovered from the war and expenditure on defence declined, more money was spent on welfare. There was a massive investment in education in the 1950s and Macmillan hand-somely exceeded his target of 300,000 houses. Even hospitals began to be built. When Labour returned to power its highest priority was the construction of council dwellings. Its massive programme of construc-tion was cut back when Britain failed to achieve the rate of growth which had been planned. Prescription charges were removed and then restored to save the hospital building programme.

By 1964 Labour had been converted to comprehensive schools. To some this was the road to common citizenship. It would strengthen the sense of local community, and all children would be given a wider choice of curriculum. But others saw the reform as the total answer to the problem of educational opportunity. If only all children went to the same secondary school, working-class children would be able to climb the ladder of educational opportunity; it was the 11 + and the polarised school system which was holding them back. Central government started pushing local authorities in this direction. It carried through a major expansion of higher education. This was the period when the slums were bulldozed away to make room for inhuman stacks and cliffs of system-built council flats which were to fight an unequal battle against condensation. It was a period of very expensive activity, not all of which produced results its authors expected.

It was in the late 1960s that the major structural changes in the whole system of local government and of the health service began to be planned. Reorganisation was the key to comprehensive social planning and the assertion of rational priorities. This belief in structural reform was shared by the Heath government. It was the age of the 'think tank' and corporate management. Emphasis was placed on form rather than content, on method rather than objective.

With the return of the Labour Government in 1974, the comprehensive school finally came to dominate secondary education. Pensions were raised but so also were supplementary pensions. The Crossman/ Castle pension scheme finally reached the statute book but by this time the price which had to be paid for it was a partnership with occupational pensions. Child tax allowances and family allowances were finally amalgamated into a system of tax-free child benefits for every child. In housing, the potentiality of the voluntary sector was at last recognised and given substantial financial backing. But it was far too late. The territory of rented housing was already dominated by the council sector.

One of the most important innovations of the 1970s was the development of a standardised national system of housing rebates and allowances. This housing subsidy did not have a happy birth. It was introduced by the Heath government as a palliative for higher rents rather than as a practicable though imperfect way of increasing the living standards of the working poor. No one saw at the time that it was destined to grow into a unified housing benefit and replace a considerable slice of supplementary benefit payments – the additions to the basic scales intended to cover rents. Beveridge had found no solution to the large and somewhat arbitrary variations in rent levels which made it impossible to provide a standard benefit as of right, at an acceptable cost, which actually secured his planned subsistence level of income for families paying different levels of rent. Subject to the problem of take-up, a generous unified housing benefit has the potentiality to resolve this problem. The unified benefit which has been introduced is a cheap administrative simplification rather than the imaginative advance which it ought to have been.

The essence of the Beveridge social security scheme as introduced in 1948 remains substantially still in place. However, instead of the original standard rates of benefit there are now, regrettably, an indefensible and complex set of variations applying to different groups and different durations of claim. Before the war, the unemployed who were entitled to benefit were, on the whole, the most generously treated beneficiaries. Now they are the least generously treated. Only modest and inadequate provision has been introduced for disabled people who have never contributed. Little has been done for the groups which worried Beveridge in the successive drafts of his report – one-parent families other than widows.

How to assess the balance
Many criteria could be used to assess the balance. One would be the extent of public support; by this criterion the National Health Service does well and child benefit badly. Another would be the extent of democratic participation; here our centralised social security scheme scores very low. Compared to many continental countries, the involvement of representative contributors is negligible. The price paid for participation on the continent is variety. This has introduced a different type of complexity and a confusing number of entry points to obtain the various benefits about which our continental neighbours constantly complain. In terms of democratic participation, the National Health Service also gets a low rating. Theoretically housing and education have higher scores here as they are run by local authorities, but it cannot be said that the users of council houses and schools feel that provision by local government ensures that these services are responsive to their wishes.

But the criterion on which I want to concentrate here is how far the different services meet the needs of people at the bottom. If our aim is greater social equality, this is the critical measuring rod for a socialist. It helps as part of this assessment to see where we have done better or worse than other nations.

Poverty
There is no doubt that we still have a substantial problem of income poverty in Britain. Of course living standards have increased and so have the standards for judging poverty. In 1975 we still had, as a minimum, $4\frac{1}{2}$ million people living at or below the long-term supplementary benefit level, $4\frac{1}{2}$ million up to 20 per cent above and a further 5

million in the next 20 per cent band of living standards.[3] As these calculations are based on annual income they seriously underestimate poverty on a weekly basis. Moreover all these figures would be substantially higher today because of the savage growth of unemployment. There is almost certainly more relative poverty in Britain now than in 1949, the first full year after the Beveridge scheme was introduced.

The reasons why our social security system fails to provide an effective safety net are well known. The main ones are failure to take up means tested benefits, the fact that short-term benefits are now substantially below long-term benefits (and the unemployed never get this higher level), the gaps in provision for one-parent families and the chronically disabled, the absence of a minimum wage, and the failure of child benefit to meet the minimum costs of providing for children.

While we have no reason to be proud of our efforts to help the poor, nevertheless our record is better than in most countries of the EEC. A recent report by the European Economic Commission tried to put together data for the nine countries for 1975 on a comparable basis. The study used as a measuring rod half the average disposable income per adult equivalent. By this criterion we had the second lowest proportion of poor at just over 6 per cent, though Belgium and Germany were close on our heels. We came out substantially better than Denmark, France and Luxembourg with 13–15 per cent poor and much better than Italy and Ireland with 22–3 per cent poor[4] (see Table 2.1).

The country with the least poverty was the Netherlands. Nor is it hard to see why. One reason is that they have a minimum wage and put their main social security benefits for a married couple just below it, and the minimum wage and the benefit level move up in step with one another. Another reason is that the disabled get the same relatively

Table 2.1   Incidence of relative income poverty of private households

Country	Year	Percentage of households below poverty line (50 per cent of disposable income)	Number of households (1000s)
Belgium	1976	6.4	209
Denmark	1977	13.0	334
France	1975	14.8	2,630
Germany	1973	6.6	1,527
Ireland	1973	23.1	172
Italy	1978	21.8	3,823
Luxembourg	1978	14.6	16
Netherlands	1979	4.8	233
United Kingdom	1975	6.3	1,241

Source: Commission of European Communities.

generous level of benefits whatever the cause of disability. To introduce a minimum wage now with our high level of unemployment would do more harm than good by increasing the number of jobless. But if we should ever get back to relatively full employment, we should legislate for an effective minimum if only to upgrade earnings in what are primarily women's jobs, even though, taken alone, the impact on poverty would be small. We also need to raise the level of our 'short-term' benefit rates which are paradoxically and cruelly paid to the unemployed however long they have been out of work. We need to provide the same basic level of benefits to all disabled people – whether they have contributed or not. Of no less importance is the fact that we tax people into poverty by our low tax threshold and the heavy burden of social security contributions. In the Netherlands social security is paid for by what is in effect a progressive income tax. The full integration of employees' social security contributions with income tax could lighten the burden on the low earner, providing we raise the threshold and widen the tax base by phasing down allowances for mortgage interest, life insurance and occupational pensions.

Health

Despite the National Health Service, we have been falling down the international league in terms of mortality rates. This is conspicuously the case in terms of deaths of children before the age of one. As the Black Report put it, our record has been 'dismal' in this respect.[5] The most damaging data assembled in the Black Report is on the variations of health standards by social class. For example, the daughters of unskilled manual workers are four times more likely to die aged one month to one year than daughters of the managerial and professional classes. For sons, the incidence of death is five times greater. Moreover there is no evidence that the gap in health standards is narrowing. Some data suggests the reverse. Naively it was assumed that all that needed to be done to level up health standards was to remove the money barrier and provide free care.

Many of the reasons for our relative failure lie outside the health service itself, in our low provision in cash and kind for children. But the health service must take some of the blame. It is far from being an equal service when related to health need. It was shown in 1972 that the highest social classes had about 40 per cent more spent on them per reported illness than the lowest. There is evidence that doctors give their middle-class patients more time and refer them more to hospital, and that unskilled workers grossly under-use preventive services and go less to the doctor when sick[6] (see also Chapter 6).

One of the problems is that the health service waits for patients to come and ask for services; rarely does it seek out those who need help most. Moreover poor areas tend to get poor services. In general, far too little effort goes into prevention. The most important failure is in general practice. When it is good it can be very good indeed – probably the best in Europe. But standards in some areas are abysmally low – particularly in the deprived areas of inner cities.[7] General practitioners are contractors. Some do the minimum which the vaguely worded contract requires. Some do less and sanctions are largely ineffective. General practitioners have to be persuaded or bribed to work together in teams with a full range of supporting staff. Family practitioner committees are wholly outside the jurisdiction of health authorities and only nominally part of the health service.

Education

Just as in health, socialists placed excessive faith in the removal of the money barrier as a means of creating educational opportunity. When this was clearly failing to achieve the desired results, the comprehensive school was expected to do the trick. Investment in education has been vast until Mrs Thatcher cut it back. Over half our schools have been built since the war, pupil–teacher ratios have been radically improved, and the compulsory leaving age has been raised to sixteen. Though the growth of pre-school education has not been impressive, further education has been massively expanded.

Nevertheless our rate of enrolment of older students in full-time education is low by international standards. In 1977–8 we had the lowest proportion of participation in full-time education of those aged 17–22 of the ten countries in the European Economic Community, with the one exception of Ireland.[8] On the other hand we start compulsory schooling earlier than some other countries. The population aged 25–64 in Britain in 1980 had had, on average, more school years than in Denmark, France or Norway, but less than in the United States or Canada.[9]

How far have we managed to increase mobility between social classes? For socialists this is a critical test. How far have we been able to equalise educational opportunities? It has been calculated that forty years ago the son of a professional man had seven times more spent on his education than the son of an agricultural labourer. What we have managed to do is to reduce the ratio from one in seven to one in six. It is still true that a child who attends wholly private education up to the age of eighteen can have more spent on him by the state than a child wholly in the state sector who gets no higher education. While about 6 per cent of children are in fee-paying schools, 15 per cent of children in sixth forms are in private schools.

The sons and daughters of manual workers are now more likely to end up with middle-class jobs than in the past, but this is entirely because more such jobs are available. Their relative chances have not improved. In this sense we have made no progress in equalising the outcome of the educational process.[10]

On top of this we do a bad job for the child who leaves school at the age of sixteen. Compared even with countries such as Germany which has retained a selective system of education, vocational training is extremely poorly developed. Apprenticeship is in sharp decline but we have done far too little to build something effective to take its place. Over a third of boys and up to 40 per cent of girls enter jobs which offer no training opportunities.[11] Despite a century of compulsory education, it was estimated in a report published in 1974 that there were at least two million functionally illiterate adults in England and Wales – people unable to read or write at all, or at a literary level below that expected of a nine-year-old.[12] And the mentally handicapped who need educational help most do worst of all.

Housing

Over half our housing is of post-war construction and the improvements in standards have been considerable. In 1951, $7\frac{1}{2}$ million households were estimated to be living in unfit or substandard housing in England and Wales. By 1975 the figure was down to 1.7 million or 9 per cent of households. Between 1954 and 1973, one and a half million homes were demolished in Great Britain mainly in slum clearance programmes, but some were knocked down that should have been preserved. Public housing expenditure reached its peak in 1974 and has since tailed off back to the level of 50 years ago.

There are still 4 per cent of households without exclusive use of a bath or shower and 5 per cent without exclusive use of an inside WC, and 5 per cent which are overcrowded (by the bedroom standard). Only 57 per cent of households have central heating.[13] The problem of homelessness is still with us.

Yet by international standards we are better off than some of our richer neighbours. The most recent data shows that the proportion of dwellings without a fixed shower or bath is lower than in Germany, Denmark or France, though higher than in Canada or the USA. The proportion of people who express dissatisfaction with their housing is lower than in France, Italy or Ireland but higher than in every other country in the EEC.[10] It may be that our heavy concentration on local authorities as landlords is one of the reasons for our relatively poor rating in this respect. People do not choose their homes, they get allocated them. There is a limit to the number of offers one can refuse, and it is difficult to change your home once you are locked into the system. But our worst housing is undoubtedly in the private furnished sector where 54 per cent of households lack exclusive use of a bath or shower and the same proportion of an inside WC.[14] About twice the proportion of poor compared to the non-poor lack a basic amenity or are overcrowded.

The continuous shrinkage of the private sector and the time needed to get a council house have posed young people with formidable problems on trying to enter the housing market. These are made still worse by the costs of buying a house at prices inflated by the availability of mortgage interest relief. Little has been done to help the single with their housing problems. Homeless families can now get rehoused by local authorities unless they get caught on the clause which denies rights to those whose homelessness is alleged to be intentional. If rehoused, they are parked in the grottiest part of the council housing stock as are those who have got in arrears with their council rent. Homelessness is largely a problem of poverty – of what rent one can pay when supporting a wife and one or more children on one low wage. Poverty is punished by bad housing.

While the right to apply for council housing is universal, housing allocation policies have been used to concentrate problem families on particular estates. The price paid for this polarisation and also for unsuitable and impersonal architectural design has been vandalisation, mugging, and consequently 'hard to let' housing. Our post-war planners have not served us well.

Could the record have been better?

In social security, it was probably a mistake to have built our provision on flat rate benefits. This has created two nations – one which looks to employers' schemes to provide them with their main security and one which looks primarily or exclusively to the state scheme. This division could have been avoided if, as in Germany, we had instead gone for an earnings-related scheme from the start, provided an effective minimum related to a minimum wage had been built beneath it. Similarly if the Labour Government had abolished child tax allowances in 1946 and transformed family allowances into child benefit right at the start, the level of child support would probably now be higher. The whole weight of middle-class and skilled worker pressure would have been behind the development of social security. Moreover it would have been possible to have given a better flat rate benefit to those who were disabled before they were old enough to enter the labour force without endangering the hallowed principles of social insurance.

As a way of providing rights of access to health care and as an economical way of providing services, the National Health Service has been a success. If it had been better funded and we had started to rebuild our hospitals earlier, there would now be less of a challenge from the private sector. The universal health services of Denmark, run by their local authorities, have finally put all private hospitals out of business; no one is prepared to pay to use them. But as a way of helping those with the lowest health prospects, the health service has not been a success.

In housing we have been far too late in developing alternatives to local authorities as providers of housing for rent. If housing associations and co-operatives had developed earlier and acquired the strength and credibility to borrow money from the private sector, public sector borrowing for housing would not have crowded out public sector borrowing for hospitals. A national system of housing allowances introduced in 1946 would have been the key to this development. Low income people could have been offered a choice of landlord and a choice of home. Moreover the money limit on mortgage interest relief should have been introduced earlier with extra help to the first-time buyer phased out over the first ten years of the mortgage.

While there has been largely free access to the health and education services this is not the same as meeting need or securing more equal outcomes. How far should we blame the professions who have imposed their own priorities within publicly funded services? Was it a critical mistake to assume that services could be changed without fundamental reforms in the education and training of the key professions which worked in them? Why did we not build in a much wider element of consumer participation? And if we had, would this have served as an effective counterweight to professional pressures? Why were we so slow to start using financial planning mechanisms to assert priorities for the underprivileged? 'Socialism', Dick Crossman used to say, 'is about giving to the masses the privileges of the middle classes.' True up to a point. But middle-class oriented services may not be best for everybody.

In general our services have been slow to adjust to social change and to recognise the rights of women who want jobs as well as families. Compared to many other countries, our provision of child-minding services and nursery schools has been appalling, our provision of education for women – particularly women re-entering the labour force – backward, and our arrangements for social security markedly sex discriminatory. Parliament, the trade unions and management have been male-dominated.

It is now forty years since the Beveridge Report was published. How far have we succeeded in disposing of his five giants – Want, Disease, Ignorance, Squalor and Idleness? As our society has got richer, we have inevitably raised our standards of what is tolerable. With over five million people in severe relative poverty, with a dismal toll of infant mortality, with some two million illiterates, with some three million unsatisfactory homes, and on top of this with three million registered unemployed and at least another million unregistered jobless, the answer is not very far.

Three million registered unemployed are now costing government, in cash support and lost tax and social security revenue alone, some £15 billion – more than we spend on either education or health. This economic and social waste can be prevented. There is an alternative. When we put the unused resources to work, we must use them to renew the fight not only against Beveridge's five giants but also against wider forms of social injustice which he failed to recognise.

The Labour Government of 1945–50 made a great leap forward. Compared to this the record of later Labour governments in social policy have been cautious and lacking clear priorities. In 1948 we led the world. We no longer lead it. No longer do we so confidently claim to be the party of public expenditure. We act as if we had already reached the tolerable limits of public expenditure, though we tax outselves much less than other countries, as the OECD figures in Table 2.2 indicate.

The key problems are the erosion of our tax base by a whole host of generous allowances and the intolerable cost of unemployment. In the next march forward, we shall need to have clearer priorities. The

Table 2.2   Total Tax Revenue as a Percentage of Gross Domestic Product; 1979

Country	Tax as % of GDP
Sweden	52.9
Netherlands	47.2
Norway	46.7
Denmark	45.0
Belgium	44.5
Austria	41.2
France	41.0
West Germany	37.2
Finland	35.1
United Kingdom	33.8
Ireland	33.3
Italy	32.8
Switzerland	31.5
New Zealand	31.4
United States	31.3
Canada	31.2
Portugal	25.9
Spain	22.8

Source: *Economic Trends*, January 1981.

criterion underlying them should be, how far does particular expenditure help the under-privileged? Not just the poor but women, the
disabled and ethnic minorities; the decaying inner cities rather than the
plush extended suburbs; those living to the North and West rather than
those living in the relatively affluent South East. This is what socialism
is about.

Notes and references

1. R. Titmuss, *Problems of Social Policy*, HMSO, 1950.
2. *Social Insurance and Allied Services*, Cmd 6404, HMSO, 1942.
3. R. Layard, D. Piachaud and M. Stewart, *The Causes of Poverty*, Background Paper No. 5 to Report No. 6: *Lower Incomes*, Royal Commission on the Distribution of Income and Wealth, HMSO, 1978, p. 13.
4. *Final Report from the Commission to the Council on the First Programme of Pilot Schemes and Studies to Combat Poverty*, Com (81), 769 final, Commission of the European Communities, December 1981, p. 83.
5. *Inequalities in Health*, DHSS, 1980.
6. The evidence is marshalled in Julian Le Grand, *The Strategy of Equality*, Allen and Unwin, 1982, chapter 3.
7. B. Jarman, *A Survey of Primary Care in London*, Royal College of General Practitioners, 1981.
8. Central Statistical Office (CSO), *Social Trends 12*, HMSO, 1982, p. 55.
9. OECD estimates.
10. A.H. Halsey, A.F. Heath and J.M. Ridge, *Origins and Destinations*, OUP, 1980.
11. R. Berthoud and J.C. Brown, *Poverty and the Development of Anti-Poverty Policy in the UK*, Heinemann, 1982, p. 233.
12. *Ibid*. p. 237.
13. CSO, *Social Trends*, HMSO, 1982, p. 151.
14. *Ibid*. p. 151.

3 The Challenge of Change: Demographic Trends, the Family and Social Policy
by Lesley Rimmer and Malcolm Wicks

Introduction

Any attempt at 'remaking social policies' must be based on a critique of the substance of existing policy and of the policy-making process. This chapter is concerned with both specific issues raised by demographic changes and family patterns, and with the processes of government required to comprehend these changes on a continuing basis. The main contention of the chapter is that previous social policy-making has been inadequate in, firstly, not recognising the full implications of demographic changes, both in the numbers in various age groups and in the associated changes in family patterns; secondly, that the assumptions underlying policy have responded too slowly to the reality of family life; and thirdly, that mechanisms *within* the policy process have been inadequate both in assessing underlying changes in the context in which policy operates, and in failing to monitor and assess the impact of policy on families.

Population and the social services

The CPRS report, *Population and the Social Services*,[1] highlighted the extent to which policy is affected by demographic change, actual and expected, and the uncertainty which is attached to such estimates. Sheer *numbers* are crucial determinants of the demands on services and in this first part of the chapter we review the major changes in the various age groups and indicate some of their implications.

The dependency ratio

The balance between the population of working age and those above and below it is significant for policy-makers for two main reasons – firstly in its implication for the economic costs to society of financing services, and secondly as an indicator of the nature of social care. The dependency ratio is defined as the sum of the population under school leaving age, plus the population over retirement age, related to the working age population. Between the 1930s and 1971, the dependency ratio 'worsened' sharply. The ratio of dependants to working age people rose from 0.5 to 0.7, or from 50 per cent to 70 per cent, as it is sometimes expressed. This had significant economic implications.

Now that trend is past; the dependent population reached a peak of 72 per cent in 1973, and by 1980 this figure had declined to 67 per cent. In the future, though children under school leaving age and the retirement age population are expected to fluctuate in number between 1981 and the end of the century, the working age population is likely to increase steadily over this period so that the 67 per cent figure is unlikely to be exceeded.[2] This will be a significant relief. However, we need to be sensitive to the changes taking place *within* these broad categories. For example, we later highlight the increasing costly incidence of handicap and disability among the very old.

Also, the dependency ratio is based on the school leaving age and on retirement age, both of which are flexible and neither of which are necessarily the point of entry to or exit from the labour force. And equally important, the non-dependent population of working age has become increasingly 'dependent' through the rapid increases in unemployment.

We turn now to examine the changes within age groups in more detail (see Table 3.1 on page 37).

The under fives

Although there has been an almost constant decline in average family size, the actual number of births in any year tends to fluctuate quite widely. The post-war 'bulge' was followed by a smaller peak in the mid-1960s when the children of post-war babies were born. Such changes have important implications for the provision of public services, particularly the maternity and education services where there have been alternating periods of expansion and contraction. In 1974–5 the maternity services (in England) were dealing with 217,000 fewer births (or over a quarter less) than the average for 1961–5 (585,000 compared with 802,000).

The total number of children under five is likely to increase from 3.4 million in 1980 to 4.4 million in 1991. It will be returning to the levels of the 1960s and early 1970s but there is expected to be a subsequent fall to about 4 million by the end of the century. Predicting the number of under fives is hazardous. Indeed the difference between the 'central' and 'very low' birth rate projections used by the CPRS was of over one million children.[3]

During the 1970s, the proportion of children under five receiving some form of day care increased markedly. This reflects partly the slight increase in the proportion of women with a pre-school child who were working (from 25 per cent in 1973 to 28 per cent in 1979),[4] and also the increase in pre-school provision in both the school sector and the play group/day nursery sector. The proportion of children aged two to four attending nursery or primary school rose from 10 per cent in 1971 to 21 per cent in 1979 and the proportion of under fives who attended play groups or day nurseries rose from 11 per cent to 29 per cent in the same period.[5] There are substantial variations in the facilities made available by different local authorities and so there is a heavy reliance on child-minders, particularly for young children requiring full day care.[6]

There is evidence that the current levels of provision are far below those felt desirable by parents themselves; for example a survey in 1977 found that day care was desired for twice as many children as were currently using it.[7] Yet the obligation on local authorities to provide nursery education has been removed and school participation rates for under fives are projected to fall over the next five years as places fail to keep pace with rising numbers of children.[8] Indeed the most recent expenditure plans assume an absolute fall in provision for under fives as numbers in reception classes in primary schools are reduced.[9]

Clearly this is an area where the ambiguity towards the employment of women with children is greatest, made worse by a desire to cut public expenditure. The high levels of unemployment are acting as a constraint to any initiative which might increase the number of mothers able and willing to enter the labour market. But the case for better provision for the under fives does not rest solely on the more equitable treatment of mothers with young children who wish or need to take paid employment.

Children of school age

The population of school age children has fallen from 10 million in 1976 to 9.4 million in 1980. It is projected that it will fall to 8 million by 1986 and only gradually increase by the beginning of the 1990s. Primary numbers in England will reach a minimum in 1985 when they will be 30 per cent below the peak in 1973, whereas secondary school numbers will continue to decline until 1991.[10] In addition, while the total school population (in England and Wales) is likely to fall from a little under 9 million in 1979 to 8 million by 1983, with the prospect of a further fall to below 7.5 million before the end of the decade, the more recent upturn in births will mean an *increase* in the school population in the 1986–7 academic year for primary schools.[11]

Falling rolls are, for the immediate future, mainly a problem for secondary schools and sixth forms. There are local variations in the scale of the problem but the major issues are the planning of school closures and the scope of the curricula within the schools. While the 1980 Education Act was presented as a measure to strenghten parental choice, the reality is less choice as both money and pupil numbers are reduced. LEAs are being forced to consider the appropriateness of their structure of post-compulsory education, and possible alternatives – the introduction of tertiary colleges, 'mushroom' schemes or other variants. Many of these ideas are causing concern lest the worst features of the tripartite system should re-emerge.

Planning the structure of post-school education needs to be set in the context of overall provision for this age group. The total UK population of fifteen- to nineteen-year-olds has grown from 3,832,000 in 1971 to 4,638,000 in 1980.[12] About one third of young people in these age groups are still at school or in other full-time education; the rest are either seeking employment or some combination of employment and training. The number of school leavers in the UK rose from some 716,000 in 1968–9 to over 900,000 in 1978–9;[13] in response to declining employment opportunities and low levels of training, the government has now announced a 'new training initiative' which will offer a year's training to all jobless school leavers.[14] This emphasises the low level of training available to young people in comparison with our European competitors. Whereas some 80 per cent of youngsters of school leaving age in France and Germany receive further education or training, less than two-thirds do so in Britain. There is a need therefore for far greater training opportunities at work, and in parallel with work; these issues are discussed further by Tom Schuller in Chapter 13.

Provision of education and training for this group can not be separated from the question of financial support to students: educational maintenance allowances for a small minority of those who stay at school, local authority discretionary awards for those in further education, training allowances on the Youth Opportunities Programme and on the new training scheme, and supplementary benefit (or unemployment benefit) for the unemployed. The different levels of allowances available affect the choices which young people make and, as in other areas, there is a need for greater co-ordination so that 'options' are not constrained by perverse financial considerations.

The population of working age

Very recently the numbers entering the working age population have been increasing, while at the other end of the age group the number of sixty- to sixty-four-year-olds has fluctuated around the 3 million mark, and those in the pre-retirement groups (55–9) have declined and are expected to continue to do so.[15]

Even so, there can be substantial changes in the proportion of people who are economically active – that is, working or seeking work. In particular, economic activity rates of married women have increased dramatically. In 1921 less than 10 per cent of married women were in the formal labour force but the proportion rose rapidly from the Second World War onwards, so that by 1979 nearly half of all married women were 'economically active'. More recently the activity rates of men in the pre-retirement age groups have fallen quite rapidly.[16]

Elderly people

The period of rapid growth in the number of people over retirement age is now past. However, within a static or falling total population the number of the very elderly will increase. By the end of the century the number over seventy-five will increase by a fifth, and the number over eighty-five by a half. In contrast, the number of people between retirement age and seventy-five – that is the young elderly – will *decrease* by 11 per cent over the same period. There is thus a shifting balance within the elderly population, so that by the end of the century nearly 40 per cent of those over retirement age will be over seventy-five compared with just over 30 per cent in 1981.

While there is no necessary correlation between increasing age and increasing frailty, the proportion of people with some disability rises sharply over the age of seventy-five. Thus the increasing number of very elderly people poses a substantial challenge to the caring capacity of their families and to that of the community.[17] But the total number of elderly people also has implications for the cost of pensions. The new pension scheme which came into operation in 1978 will build up to maturity over a twenty-year period.

Although it is difficult to estimate the increase in pension costs implied by the scheme, some observers have suggested that these might be substantial. Fogarty, for example, has estimated that existing commitments and claims on resources by the elderly within the field of social security could 'eventually imply additional transfers from the active population to the elderly . . . equivalent to between 50 and 100 per cent of the 1980/81 budget of £9 billion (at 1979 prices), for retirement pensions, which is itself nearly 13 per cent of the 1980/81 public expenditure'.[18] However, less reliance on supplementary benefit and any reduction in the age allowance in the tax system could reduce these costs substantially. The uncertainty about these costs emphasises the importance of attempting to cost the combined 'profile' of policies more adequately. The average cost of health and personal social services for a person aged over seventy-five is seven times that of a person of working age and nearly three times the cost of a person between sixty-five and seventy-four.[19] Hence the Conservatives' White Paper, *Growing Older*, emphasises the role of non-government institutions in the care of the frail elderly: 'care *in* the community must increasingly mean care *by* the community'.[20] Just how viable such a strategy is as a way of saving money we question later.

Family patterns

Having discussed the changes in the *number* of people in the various age groups and noted some of the implications of this for social planning, we now turn to the changes which have been occurring in *patterns* of family life and the likely developments in these patterns in the coming years. We focus particularly on the issues raised by changes in family size, marital dissolution, dual worker families, and families caring for elderly dependants.

Family size

Perhaps the most significant change in family patterns to take place during the last century has been the decline in average family size. In the 1870s, two-thirds of married women would have five or more children; by the 1920s the picture had changed so that over two-thirds would have two children or fewer. Over the first fifty years of this century the proportion of families with two children has almost doubled. Today only one family in five has three or more children. These changes have, of course, had the most substantial impact on the lives of women. Halsey, for example, noted that 'in 1900 one quarter of the married women were in childbirth every year. Yet thirty years later that proportion was down by one half to one in eight.'[21] Today it is possible for women to be directly involved in childbearing and child-rearing for a relatively short period of their lives and to be able to return to the labour market after a comparatively short period.[22]

Marriage breakdown and divorce

Equally significant changes have been taking place in the nature of marriage. While in some ways marriage has never been more popular, there have been substantial increases in divorce in recent years. Over-all, it is far more likely than ever before that men and women will marry at least once during their lifetimes. But it is also more likely than ever before that their marriage will be ended by divorce. Although there have been some substantial declines in marriage rates since the beginning of the 1970s, it is still likely that nine out of ten men and women will marry. But also on the basis of current trends one in three of these marriages will end in divorce. For a teenage bride, the likelihood that her marriage will end in divorce is even greater.[23]

Separation and divorce, while obviously indicating disillusion with a particular marriage, need not indicate such disillusion with the institution of marriage itself. Indeed more than one third of all 'new' marriages involve one partner who has been married before, and in nearly one in six marriages both parties have been married before. It has been estimated that by the turn of the century one in every five men will have been married more than once. The idea of marriage as a life-long institution, therefore, needs to be tempered with an appreciation of the extent of marriage breakdown and remarriage; and the extent to which marriage can any longer be used as a criterion of entitlement to benefit in the social security system, or in defining the unit of taxation in the tax system, needs to be questioned.

The implications of divorce for the tax system, for example, are seldom recognised. For example, the recent Green Paper on *The Taxation of Husband and Wife* considers the choice of the tax unit – whether this should be the individual, the married couple or some elective combination of these two. However there is no discussion of the tax treatment of maintenance payments or any acknowledgement of the complexity of the tax treatment of marriage breakdown.[24] These issues are discussed by David and Land in Chapter 10.

Divorce may also be affecting other areas of social provision in ways that are not yet quantified. For example, one of the most striking features of the last twenty years has been the increase in the number of one-person households. Such households formed 11 per cent of all households in Great Britain in 1961 and 22 per cent in 1980. Much of this change is accounted for by the increasing number of people over retirement age who live alone. While most attention has been focused on the housing situation of lone parents with children, the housing circumstances of the 'non-custodial parent' should also be considered. Household fission as a result of divorce may be an important contributory factor to the pattern of housing demand.

One-parent families

Perhaps the most important consequence of increasing marriage breakdown and divorce has been the increasing number of one-parent families. Today nearly one million families are headed by a lone parent and they have the care of about one and a half million children. While more than one child in eight is *currently* living in a one-parent family, between one in five and one in six children will see their parents divorce during their childhood if current levels of divorce continue.[25]

The majority of one-parent families are headed by women, and their standards of living are crucially dependent both on their potential earnings and on the level of income support available. The system of income support for lone parents is complex, especially in its interaction with earnings, and future planning will need to recognise that for some parents and children a period in a one-parent family will be a relatively short transitional period between one two-parent family and a new 'reconstituted' family created by remarriage. For others, it may be a longer experience and despite some valuable data from longitudinal studies, we still know too little about the duration and consequences of lone parenthood.

Meanwhile we should be conscious of the fact that many children in one-parent families nevertheless still have two parents and it is the respective rights and obligations of both parents which are the subject of the current debate about the financial consequences of divorce. This has recently been discussed by the Law Commission which was concerned primarily with changes in the *private* law governing divorce. Its discussion was limited to the obligations of husbands and wives because 'they saw no purpose in investigating proposals which would involve a major shift from reliance on the enforcement of private law financial obligations against individuals towards a system under which social security benefits would become the primary method of making proper financial provision for families affected by divorce'.[26] Yet they acknowledged the poverty of the majority of one-parent families and the 'simple truth' that most people do not have sufficient income to maintain two families or, where a second family is not involved, two households. Despite the acknowledgement that the reform of private law could do little, if anything, to deal with the problems of poverty, it was still the Commission's view that such reform would not be irrelevant. They addressed themselves rather to the question of the sense of injustice felt by those affected by the present law, and the extent to which a greater emphasis should be given to encouraging spouses to become self-supporting.

The Law Commission's document is particularly interesting both because it focuses on the relationship of private and public law, and because it is explicitly starting to question the idea of life-long obligation to maintain being embodied in the marriage contract. Any changes in the law which follow the Commission's recommendations may well alter the way in which women view marriage, and the way in which they prepare for and follow through their own careers.

The Commission does, however, stray into areas of social security in its discussion of occupational pensions. They point out that under most pension schemes, in the event of a pensioner's death, entitlement to a widow's pension is restricted to the person to whom the deceased was married at the time of his death. Divorced wives are thus excluded from any entitlement to their ex-spouse's pension. They argue that in order to put the wife in a financial position comparable to the one in which she would have been had the marriage not broken down – the basis of the present law – the husband may have to make alternative arrangements, potentially at very heavy cost. There is however very little evidence on the extent to which husbands make such provision and it may be that the increasing complexity of occupational pensions in the wake of the 1975 Pensions Act may make the Commission's desire to 'deal with the problem of occupational pensions' difficult to achieve.

Women's capacity to work is limited by social provisions. Women with children are more likely to work part-time than other women and overall some 40 per cent of women workers in Britain work part-time.[27] The increases in women's paid employment means that an increasing number of families are dependent on two earners at some stage in the family cycle. In over half of all families with children, both husband

and wife are currently working and the earnings of one third of wives make up 30–50 per cent of family incomes.[28]

The reliance of families on two earners relates crucially to the problems of social care – whether this care is for children or for the elderly or handicapped.

Social care

On some occasions people assert that the family no longer 'cares' for elderly people in the same way that it did in some golden age gone by. It is certainly the case that an increasing proportion of households are pensioners living alone, and the proportion of the elderly who live alone has been increasing. Over a third of all elderly people do so, and the likelihood increases with advancing age. Over a quarter of all men aged eighty-five and over, and over half of all women of that age live alone. But the fact that significant proportions of elderly people live by themselves does not necessarily mean that they are not part of a family and with increasing age a greater proportion of people live with other members of their families – their children, children-in-law or other relatives. For example, in 1979–80 nearly a fifth of men and women over eighty-five lived with their children and a further tenth with their children-in-law.[29]

Even when the elderly do live alone, the family is an important source of care and support. Audrey Hunt's survey of the elderly in 1976 showed that over half those interviewed received visits from relatives at least once a week and nearly a third several times a week. Worryingly, however, Hunt's survey showed that 5 per cent of elderly people had no living relatives outside the household and that one in twenty, despite having relatives, never had visits from them.[30] Evidence from other surveys suggests that about one third of the elderly had no, or no surviving children at all. This obviously limits the availability of family care.

We have noted that the number of very elderly people will increase rapidly in the next few years and that the incidence of disability rises sharply over the age of seventy-five. One of the most obvious implications of this change in the age structure of the population is that more families, and this now usually means women in the family, will have to care for elderly dependants at some stage. Potentially the period of caring may be a long one – the expectation of life of someone aged sixty is over fifteen years for a man and twenty years for a woman; at seventy a man could still expect to live for a further ten years and a woman for a further twelve years. Indeed one survey found that 24 per cent of carers had been caring for at least ten years.[31]

In the past, the main burden of care was borne by single women, but because of the higher rates of marriage up to the 1970s in the future it will be married women who will be caring for their children, for their parents, and then perhaps for their own ageing spouses. Whereas in earlier periods, married women might have been expected to be at home and therefore in some senses 'available to care', this is no longer the case. Activity rates of married women aged 45–59 have risen from 21.5 per cent in 1951 to 46.3 per cent in 1966 and to 61 per cent in 1979.[32] While a higher proportion of women in Britain work part-time in contrast to our continental counterparts, providing continuous intensive or long-term care may well affect women's ability to work at all, or the hours or terms on which they can work. The implications of these changes for the organisation of work need to be addressed explicitly in the future.

Changing family patterns also interact here, for whereas in previous generations there would have been three or four children to share the care of elderly parents, in future there will be only one or two and the majority of these carers will have families of their own. Divorce and remarriage interact here too; we need to consider the implications of these trends for networks of family care and support.[33]

When first and second marriages are compared, about the same proportion of men (75 per cent) marry younger wives in either case, but over half of second wives were more than four years younger than their husbands compared with a quarter of first wives. At the extreme, for husbands who married again, more than ten times as many second wives as first wives were ten or more years younger than their husbands. In contrast only 6 per cent of the wives in the sample remarried people who were ten or more years their junior, whereas 10 per cent remarried those who were ten or more years their senior. Such trends can have important implications for the duration of widow(er)hood and for the probability that wives will have to care for their elderly husbands when they themselves are becoming frail.

We should also consider the impact of divorce on the children of elderly parents and whether this will affect the caring relationships between generations. Will divorced spouses return to live in parental homes or move back to or away from areas in which their parents are living? Equally we should not ignore the impact of divorce on relationships between grandparents and grandchildren and more extended family relationships which often provide crisis support.

It is clear, then, that marriage breakdown and remarriage have important implications. Our purpose in identifying them has not been to explore these implications fully – which we have done elsewhere – but to suggest that they constitute a case for the systematic monitoring of family changes in relation to social security, taxation and service provision. More than this, there is a need for some 'body' to take responsibility for such monitoring and evaluation. We have suggested that a suitably modified CPRS might take on this role, or that it could be undertaken by a body outside government.[34] But the responsibility does need to be located somewhere, so that the initial impetus is maintained. Such a body would be the stimulus for greater awareness of the implications of demographic and family change throughout the machinery of government.

We have noted (and this theme is taken up in Chapter 10) that many assumptions about the family, and of roles within it, underlie contemporary social policy. Such assumptions are normally implicit, but sometimes they come to the surface. In the early days of the modern welfare state, for example, Lloyd George explained the exclusion of all but employed men from health insurance by arguing that, since families depended on their male breadwinner, it was *his* ill health that it was important to insure against. Several decades later, Beveridge made similar assumptions about the respective roles of men and women when he noted that:

All women by marriage acquire a new economic and social status, with risks and rights different from those of the unmarried. On marriage a woman gains a legal right to maintenance by her husband as a first line of defence against the risks which fall directly on the solitary woman; she undertakes at the same time to perform vital unpaid service and becomes exposed to new risks, including the risk that her married life may be ended prematurely by widowhood or separation.[35]

There is now a growing literature on the below-the-surface 'family policy' that operates in Britain and the implications are clear. Not only should social policy take heed of certain key demographic trends and changes in family patterns in future, it should also root out the many implicit assumptions about family life which are often based on extremely conservative and sexist judgements. In their place should be some guiding principles which should be made explicit. What are these principles? While there is a need for more debate about this issue, and while there may be no easy consensus, we can note some important issues here.

Equality and the family
First, it is important to consider family questions within the wider context of equality. Together with class, race and other forms of inequality, social policy should address itself to further forms of inequality which relate to the family. In recent years, concern about vertical inequalities has been matched by a growing concern about horizontal inequalities. In particular, there is ample evidence to show the unequal treatment of families with children, compared with the single and the childless, as a result of inadequate child benefits and

taxation changes which have worked against these families. This focus of concern should be broadened to take in the position of all families with responsibility for dependants, be these children, the disabled or elderly relatives.

Second, there is increasing interest in questions relating to the distribution of income, power and opportunities *within* the family. The campaign to have child benefits paid to mothers through the post office, rather than to fathers via the pay packet, highlights the importance of this form of intra-family inequality. In principle, in order to move towards the goal of promoting wider freedoms and choices, policies should be concerned to enable adults to develop more egalitarian relationships in terms of income, work, the upbringing of children and other caring responsibilities.

Third, there is a form of inequality arising from the trend towards increasing diversity. We have suggested that the 'typical' family is in some senses far from typical. Only some 35 per cent of households fit the traditional model of a 'married couple plus two dependent children' at any one point in time. If present trends continue, a substantial proportion of children will have parents who divorce and consequently many children will spend part of their childhood in one-parent families and/or in 'reconstituted' families. Other trends, most markedly the rise of the dual worker family, but also cohabitation, represent further important departures from so-called traditional family forms.

While some of these trends call for different policy responses and possibly for positive discrimination in order to achieve equity, the guiding approach we would suggest, for families of all types, should be an egalitarian one. By this we mean that families with responsibilities for others should be treated by policies and social service agencies according to their needs, regardless of the formal nature of the relationship between the adults. In the short term this would imply the removal of the more contradictory regulations in the social welfare system which in some instances disqualify cohabitees from benefit while on other occasions they treat them as married. In the longer term it would involve a more radical reappraisal of the way individuals are grouped together for the purpose of taxation and benefits.

Fourth, there needs to be greater flexibility between family life and work; this, inevitably, involves a positive role for the state. Halsey has recently analysed current social policy developments in terms of a 'renegotiation' of the respective roles of the state, the family and the economy.[36] The need for a better integration between work and family life is made more urgent by changing family patterns, trends in employment and in patterns of care, and the goal of sex equality.

Two important examples illustrate the issue. While there is no evidence to suggest that children with employed mothers suffer, families where both parents work are often more under pressure and there are particular problems related to periods of child sickness and, more generally, daytime and after-school care. A crucial omission in post-war social policy development has been any willingness to consider the implications of dual worker families. There is no adequate framework of benefits and services to enable men and women to make rational choices about the balance between home and work responsibilities. Piachaud's recent analysis demonstrates that families with children have only been enabled to enjoy a fair share of rising living standards because many wives go out to work.[37]

The care of the frail elderly also provides an important example of the need to integrate work and family life better. Maternity and even paternity provisions are discussed but there is little consideration of the role of workers as providers of care for their elderly relatives or elderly spouses, and yet the trend towards increasing numbers of very elderly people described earlier, together with the trend towards female employment, makes this a key question for future social policy (see Chapters 10 and 11).

Policy impact and evaluation

The family trends described in this chapter raise some important and specific issues for particular areas of social policy. We have argued that, inevitably, assumptions about family life help to determine policy and it is important that in the future such assumptions are made explicit and are open to public debate. There is therefore a need for the development of a clear 'family perspective' in policy-making.[38] This should take three forms.

First, it should be based on a sound understanding of changing family patterns in Britain. Second, a family perspective within policy should involve a better understanding by government of family functions and roles and the need for a better 'partnership' between the family and the state. Thus in the fields of education, child development and health, a better understanding on the part of government as to how families affect the development of children could lead to more sensitive 'family' policies, a better relationship between parents and teachers, doctors, health visitors and other professionals, and a better mesh between family needs and service provision. Certainly within education, to take one obvious example, a growing body of research over the last two decades has shown the importance of the basic environment and parental aspirations on attainment. As the Taylor Report emphasised, 'every parent has a right to expect a school's teachers to recognise his status in the education of his child by the practical arrangements they make to communicate with him and the spirit in which they accept his interest'.[39]

A third component of the family perspective in social policy involves the monitoring and evaluation of policy. The new interest in family and policy questions springs in part from a belief that policies are not formed on the basis of a realistic evaluation of how they will affect families of different kinds. Too often policies fail to relate specific issues and objectives to other policies, do not then respond to critical questions of implementation and are not firmly based on actual family circumstances and needs. Mr Callaghan, while Prime Minister, recognised this anxiety when he stated that: 'I don't believe that the Government has done enough, hardly started to consider as a whole the impact of its policies on the family when we take our decisions in Cabinet and in government.'[40]

One firm proposal to ensure that the family perspective is taken fully into account when policy options are being discussed within Whitehall (and town hall, for the idea also has local relevance) is the introduction of family impact statements, which we have discussed elsewhere.[41] Such statements should be published and might appear at the beginning of a parliamentary Bill alongside the statements on financial implications and civil service manpower. The content of such family impact statements would vary from measure to measure, but some general issues would be addressed in all such statements. These would include the impact of the proposed policy on *different* family

Table 3.1 Trends in Population by Age Group [a]

Age group	1961	1971	1980	1986	1991	1996	2001
0–4	4.3	4.5	3.4	4.0	4.4	4.4	4.1
5–10	8.9 [b]	9.7 [b]	4.8	4.1	4.7	5.2	5.3
11–16			5.5	4.8	4.1	4.6	5.2
16–19	3.7 [c]	3.8 [c]	3.7	3.6	3.1	2.7	3.1
16–64	33.6	34.2	35.0	35.9	36.2	36.0	36.5
Over 65	6.2	7.3	8.4	8.4	8.6	8.4	8.2
Over 75	2.2	2.6	3.2	3.5	3.7	3.6	3.7
Over 85	0.3	0.5	0.6	0.7	0.8	0.8	0.9

Sources: CSO, *Annual Abstract of Statistics 1981*, HMSO, 1980; OPCS, *Population Projections 1979–2019*, Series PP2 No.11, HMSO, 1981; CSO, *Social Trends 12*, HMSO, 1981, Table 12.

[a] Millions. Figures are UK, 1979 based projections.
[b] 5–15.
[c] 15–19.

units; the policy assumptions about family life, including male and female roles; the association between the new policy proposal and existing related policies and an assessment of the combined impact of all these measures; the rights and responsibilities of families; the intelligibility of the new policy and policy goals in relation to families and how these would be achieved. They would also include procedures for monitoring and evaluation.

Given past failures and the entrenched departmentalism clearly visible within government, progress towards a family perspective within social planning is likely to be slow and faltering unless its importance is signalled from the top. And a number of shifts in attitude and procedure will be necessary. We need a clear recognition of the interdependence of areas of policy, and a positive commitment to seeing issues 'in the round'. Also there will need to be a shift in emphasis from policy 'inputs' alone to a view which encompasses policy outputs.

The case for a 'family perspective' within the policy making process is at one important level a demand for greater co-ordination within government. However, for a future Labour Government, it must mean more than this. For it is one important aspect of a strategy for equality and hence a cornerstone of a reconstituted 'welfare state'.

Notes and references

Abbreviations used

CPRS   Central Policy Review Staff
CSO   Central Statistical Office
DES   Department of Education and Science
DHSS   Department of Health and Social Security
EOC   Equal Opportunities Commission
HMSO   Her Majesty's Stationery Office
OECD   Organisation for Economic Co-operation and Development
OPCS   Office of Population Censuses and Surveys

1. CPRS, *Population and the Social Services*, HMSO, 1977.
2. CSO, *Social Trends 12*, HMSO, 1982.
3. CPRS, *op. cit*.
4. OPCS, *General Household Survey 1979*, HMSO, 1981, table 5.4.
5. *Ibid*. p. 104.
6. CSO, *Social Trends 12*, chart 3.14, p. 229.
7. M. Bone, *Pre School Children and Need for Day Care*, OPCS/HMSO, 1977, p. 59.
8. *The Government's Expenditure Plans 1982–83 to 1984–85*, Cmnd 8494, HMSO, 1982.
9. *Ibid*. p. 40.
10. Department of Education and Science, *Report on Education Number 97*, DES, 1982.
11. Department of Education and Science, *Report on Education Number 92*, DES, 1979.
12. CSO, *Annual Abstract of Statistics 1981*, HMSO, 1980.
13. Department of Education and Science, *Education Statistics for the UK*, HMSO, 1982, table 24.

14. Department of Employment, *A New Training Initiative*, Cmnd 8455, HMSO, 1981.
15. Government Actuary's Department, *Population Projections 1978–2018*, OPCS/HMSO, 1980, table appendix VI C, p. 104.
16. OPCS, *op. cit.*, table 5.1.
17. C. Rossiter and M. Wicks, *Crisis or Challenge? Family Care, Elderly People and Social Policy*, Study Commission on the Family, 1982.
18. M. Fogarty, *Retirement Age and Retirement Costs*, Policy Studies Institute, 1980, p. 88.
19. *The Government's Expenditure Plans*, Cmnd 8494, vol. II, p. 44, table 2.11.4.
20. DHSS, *Growing Older*, Cmnd 8173, HMSO, 1981.
21. A.H. Halsey, *Change in British Society*, OUP, 1978, p. 96.
22. Department of Employment, *Background Paper to the Taxation of Husband and Wife*, 1980.
23. J. Haskey, 'The Proportion of Marriages Ending in Divorce', *Population Trends 27*, OPCS/HMSO, 1982.
24. *The Taxation of Husband and Wife*, Cmnd 8093, Inland Revenue/HMSO, 1980.
25. L. Rimmer, *Families in Focus*, Study Commission on the Family, 1981.
26. Law Commission, *The Financial Consequences of Divorce: Response to the Law Commission's Discussion Paper and Recommendations on the Policy of the Law*, Law Commission No. 112, HMSO, 1981.
27. L. Rimmer and J. Popay, *Employment Trends and the Family*, Study Commission on the Family, 1982.
28. L. Hamill, *Wives as Sole and Joint Breadwinners*, Government Economic Service Working Paper No. 15, 1978, p. 38.
29. CSO, *Social Trends 12*, table 13.18.
30. A. Hunt, *The Elderly at Home: A Study of People Aged Sixty-five and Over Living in the Community in England in 1976*, HMSO, 1978.
31. EOC, *The Experience of Caring for Elderly and Handicapped Dependants*, EOC, 1980.
32. OPCS, *op. cit.*
33. R. Leete and S. Anthony, 'Divorce and Remarriage: A Record Linkage Study', *Population Trends 16*, OPCS/HMSO, 1979.
34. E. Craven, L. Rimmer and M. Wicks, *Family Issues and Public Policy*, Study Commission on the Family, 1982.
35. W. Beveridge, *Social Insurance and Allied Services*, Cmnd 6404, HMSO, 1942, p. 49.
36. OECD, *The Welfare State in Crisis*, OECD, 1981.
37. D. Piachaud, *Family Incomes since the War*, Study Commission on the Family, 1982.
38. Craven, Rimmer and Wicks, *op. cit.*
39. DHSS/Welsh Office, *A New Partnership for our Schools*, (Taylor Report), HMSO, 1979.
40. J. Callaghan, Speech at Women's Labour Conference, Southport, 14 May 1978.
41. Craven, Rimmer and Wicks, *op. cit.*

4 Social Policy and the Economy
by Gavyn Davies and David Piachaud

Five years ago, Mrs Thatcher was fond of pointing to conflicts between social and economic policy objectives: that a community which persistently increases its social expenditure relative to national income ends up paying high marginal tax rates which kill economic growth; that generous welfare provisions increase the incentive to become and remain unemployed; and that continuous attempts to cure unemployment by reflation may simply create ever-rising inflation *and* higher unemployment. She was elected on a programme to resolve these conflicts. It trebled the level of unemployment in two years, cut industrial production by a fifth (the sharpest drop in recorded history), decimated regions, eliminated entire industries – and succeeded in reducing inflation to a level only a little lower than was achieved at the bottom of the last economic cycle. It will assuredly be possible to improve on a record like that.

But the electorate recognised in the Thatcher approach some unpalatable home truths. It is not possible to pursue forever a social and economic policy mix which imposes high and increasing income taxation on working families, some of them very low down the income scale. In 1960, a typical family living on two-thirds of average earnings would have paid no income tax. Now, the same family pays 20 per cent of its income in tax and national insurance, and it may not be satisfied that it is receiving a commensurate return in the form of improved social services. There is no longer a consensus among the electorate that a better health service, higher social security payments and improved education are necessarily worth paying for. Nor is it felt that our social services are operated efficiently, with maximum concern for the needs of the sick, the unemployed and the disadvantaged. There is resentment at the pay levels and job security of public service workers. Perhaps the trend away from Labour in the past two decades can be attributed partly to our failure to deal with many of these anxieties.

The economy is indissolubly linked with social policy. Many of the social problems that we face are directly related to the workings and failings of the economic system. The present level of unemployment makes this all too clear. The resources for social provisions such as the health service and the education system are drawn from the aggregate resources available to the economy. More resources for the social services must necessarily mean less resources for something else and this remains true however rich we are and however fast the economy grows.

Goals

It is in many respects regrettable and arbitrary to make a distinction between the goals of economic policy and those of social policy. The less dismal economists are concerned with social objectives and the more realistic social policy makers recognise the importance of economic policy. Nevertheless fairly distinct goals have tended to be adopted by these two groups. In economic policy, the principal goals have been seen as: economic growth, efficiency, full employment and price stability. In social policy, the goals have been: equity, equality of opportunity and access, minimum income levels, the collective provision of social services, and social integration and cohesion.

It is evident that conflicts can arise between these goals. At the simplest level there may be conflicts between private and social spending; it is nonsense to regard the gross national product as a cake that may be carved up altogether at will, since the methods used to cut the cake can affect its size. While current tax rates may serve to increase rather than decrease the size of gross national product (through forcing people to work longer to achieve target living standards), it is absurd to suggest that there is no such thing as a level of taxes and benefits which would serve to undermine economic incentives to produce and earn more. So there will usually be conflicts between economic growth and efficiency on the one hand and redistribution and equity on the other. A second area of conflict may arise in relation to the labour supply and unemployment. Earlier retirement may reduce the labour supply thereby reducing the unemployment statistics in the short term at least; but it may be at the price of more spending on social security, lower incomes, and more isolation for the elderly. Again the expansion of the female labour force in the interests of increasing sex equality may conflict with the goal of reducing unemployment. Other conflicts may arise in relation to the method of allocating resources: in the market 'voting power' is determined by preferences and income; social provisions must be financed through taxation which ultimately depends on voters' compliance with decisions made through a bureaucratic political system. Within the public sector there may be conflicts between competing goals: there may be choices between devoting resources to industry or transport as against more conventional social needs such as education or health services.

While there are conflicts there is also correspondence between economic and social goals. Most obviously the reduction of unemployment is desirable both from an economic and social policy perspective.

Similarly rapid economic growth and technical progress is desirable providing it does not lead to increased unemployment. Some Conservative obscurantists seek to suggest that the public services have no value in wealth creation and that the only thing of any importance is the manufacturing or private sector. This is arrant nonsense. Publicly provided services such as our primary schools are of inestimable value to the community. It has yet to be explained why a private hospital is of economic value whereas a public hospital is not. Thus there can be no doubt that the social services increase the economic wealth of our society, even if there are problems in measuring their exact contribution to GNP.

Since many of our social problems and most social inequalities are attributable to, or closely related to, the workings of the economy, from a social policy perspective it would be desirable to change the economy in a variety of respects: eliminating unemployment, introducing minimum and maximum incomes, and providing secure, safe and interesting jobs for all are all desirable in themselves. But achieving such goals involves altering economic relationships and each intervention in the economy must be weighed up in terms of its merits and disadvantages.

At the macro-economic level, intervention to restore Britain to full employment is clearly the most important single requirement which serves both economic and social goals. The second goal of price stability may be desirable to avoid the arbitrary redistribution of income and wealth that results from inflation – for example from the elderly population with savings to those younger people who are net debtors – but through indexing it is possible to offset the most serious direct effects of inflation. Economic growth is important in terms of our long-term standard of living and is the ultimate determinant of the incomes of those worst off – redistribution can only do so much – but the priority that is attached to it depends on the relative weight given to absolute living standards compared with goals of reduced inequality.

At the micro-economic level it is not so straightforward. There are few interventions which simultaneously fulfil economic and social policy objectives. Market economists would argue that all interventions in the economy have costs. A minimum or a maximum wage may be desirable if considered in isolation as social policy measures but may appear less attractive if the efficiency and unemployment consequences are considered. Subsidies to transport or industry to keep down fares or preserve jobs may of themselves be attractive but it must be remembered that any subsidies are subject to the usual economic constraints. What must be assessed is the relative desirability of alternative uses of a given sum of resources.

Thus in assessing interventions at the micro-economic level the question must be asked from a social policy point of view: do they relate income to needs more efficiently than existing, or modified, social policies? How much the electorate is prepared to pay in taxes does of course depend upon what services the taxes pay for. But it is not unrealistic to think of a budget constraint fixed by the electorate. From a social policy perspective, the purpose must be to maximise the achievement of social policy goals within that budget constraint. This inevitably means that generalised forms of subsidies are inefficient and wasteful in terms of enhancing social equality. Similarly public expenditure programmes such as higher education which are predominantly used by those who have been or will be better off are inefficient in terms of enhancing social equality. The choice must be made between programmes that are cost-effective in terms of their redistributive impact and those that are not.

There are those who see the entire market system as inherently evil and seek to overthrow the mixed economy. Such an approach however ignores the costs involved. If the labour market with all its failings is eliminated it must inevitably be replaced by some form of labour direction. It is all too evident how unacceptable this would be to trade unions, and indeed to the whole community, for very good reasons. If industry is planned regardless of costs and the demand for products then some alternative set of criteria is required. Similarly those who seek to replace the mixed economy pay little regard to the problem of who is to do the controlling. Whether it is academics, civil servants, professions, unions, politicians or new forms of democratic assembly the problem remains: determining what people will and must have, and what they cannot have, involves powers which are potentially extremely dangerous. Thus we conclude that the best prospect for social policy continues to lie in a mixed economy, but an economy that is organised and run very differently from the way it has been over the past three years.

The past record
The British economy has performed poorly relative to its industrialised competitors since the war. But the post-war period has been one of the most successful eras for the British economy in historical terms. Economic growth remained consistently at 3 per cent p.a. until 1973, an unprecedented rate for the UK, and social services have expanded even faster than the economy as a whole. A substantial part of this increased social spending has been necessary to meet demographic changes and to provide rising living standards for those who work in the social services. Even allowing for this, however, there can be no doubt that social service standards are in general much higher now than they were twenty or even ten years ago. The last two years have, it is true, seen a reversal of this virtually continuous era of expansion, but even

so, levels of spending are still substantially higher than they were five years ago.

A second important feature of the past record is that the impact of the government through taxation and social policy is highly redistributive. Recent work, notably by Le Grand, may have been misunderstood and given ammunition to those who wish to suggest that the welfare state is failing. While it is certainly true that there are some services which are used to a greater extent by higher income groups (see p. 75) and there is cause for legitimate concern about the distribution of much social expenditure, when *all* social spending, including cash benefits, is considered, the broad effects are undoubtedly 'pro-poor'. We can see this in Table 4.1. It shows the redistributive effects of all social spending in relation to both income level and to household type. It can be seen that those with the lowest original incomes gain substantially from the effects of social benefits net of taxes whereas those in higher income groups are net losers. Retired households and one-parent families are net gainers as are couples with three or more children, whereas all other household types are on average losers. Thus the effects of government policy are redistributive in relation to income, in relation to life cycle, and in relation to family size. It is true that certain benefits in kind,

Table 4.1 Redistributive Effects of Taxes and Benefits by Income Level and by Household Type, 1980

Decile groups ranked by original income	Redistributive effect (%)	Household type	Redistributive effect (%) [a]
1st (lowest)	+32,040 [b]	1 adult retired	+288
2nd	+ 668	2 adults retired	+142
3rd	+ 90	1 adult non-retired	− 25
4th	+ 7	2 adults non-retired	− 29
5th	− 10	2 adults 1 child	− 21
6th	− 17	2 adults 2 children	− 14
7th	− 21	2 adults 3+ children	+ 8
8th	− 24	3+ adults 1+ child	− 10
9th	− 27	1 adult 1+ child	+ 63
10th (highest)	− 30	3+ adults	− 23
All incomes	− 11	All household types	− 11

[a] Redistributive effect = final income less original income as a percentage of original income.
[b] This figure is exceptionally large because the original income of this group was very low.

Source: The Effects of Taxes and Benefits on Household Income, 1980, *Economic Trends*, January 1982.

Table 4.2 Taxes and Social Benefits, 1980 as Percentage of Gross Income

Decile groups ranked by original income	Taxes			Benefits			Redistributive effect*
	Direct taxes	Indirect taxes	All taxes	Cash benefits	Education	National Health Service	
1st (lowest)	—	24.9	24.9	99.6	11.3	27.2	+125.3
2nd	0.7	25.9	26.6	85.3	7.0	25.4	+ 98.6
3rd	6.1	26.8	32.9	50.1	6.6	16.1	+ 45.1
4th	13.4	24.4	37.8	20.8	8.4	9.8	+ 5.5
5th	16.8	22.8	39.6	11.4	8.1	8.1	− 8.6
6th	18.8	20.9	39.7	7.3	7.5	6.3	− 15.8
7th	19.4	20.2	39.6	5.7	7.0	5.2	− 19.4
8th	20.4	19.4	39.8	4.4	6.4	4.4	− 22.6
9th	21.1	18.8	39.9	3.5	5.1	3.6	− 26.3
10th (highest)	22.8	15.9	38.7	2.1	3.7	2.6	− 29.0
All incomes	18.3	20.0	38.3	13.4	6.1	6.6	− 9.9

*Redistributive effect = final income less original income as percentage of gross income.
Source: as Table 4.1.

especially education, are worth more in *absolute* terms to those on higher than lower incomes. However as a proportion of income they are worth very much more to those at lower income levels. Broadly speaking (Table 4.2), the tax system is proportional to income whereas the value of benefits represents a higher proportion of income to the poor. This is especially true of cash benefits but it is also true of education and the National Health Service to a lesser extent. Thus it is quite clear that, taking tax and social policy together, the effect is redistributive. Indeed it is understated in these official figures because incomes are only considered in relation to the household; if income per person is taken as the basis for the analysis, the effect is even more redistributive since education is of greater benefit to larger families which, even though they may have a high income, may have a relatively low income per person.

Third, though cuts in public expenditure are often blamed for deficiencies in social policy, the facts are that social spending has consistently risen relative to the economy as a whole for most of the post-war period. Table 4.3 shows the relevant figures for the last decade, which has been undoubtedly the most difficult from an economic point of view since the 1930s. Even so, each category of social expenditure has risen as a percentage of GDP over the decade. Education expenditure has been the most stable, hovering at around $6–6\frac{1}{2}$ per cent of GDP for most of the period, though with a hump in the middle in the years 1975–76. Expenditure on the health service has shown a more persistent upward trend, rising from $4\frac{1}{2}$ per cent of GDP in 1970 to around 6 per cent in 1980. Spending on personal social services has roughly doubled over the decade, though it still takes up only 1 per cent of GDP. Benefit payments have risen from around 9 per cent of GDP in the early 1970s to $11\frac{1}{2}$ per cent now, largely because of the increase in the number of recipients. The housing programme shows a slightly different profile from the rest, starting the decade at about $2\frac{1}{2}–3$ per cent of GDP, rising to a peak of 5.6 per cent in the first year of the 1974 Labour Government, but then slowly declining to around 3.7 per cent by the end of the decade. Overall, these five programmes together have increased their share of GDP from about 23 per cent in the first three years of the 1970s to over 28 per cent now.

One interesting feature of Table 4.3 is that the apparently remorseless upward trend in social services expenditure as a percentage of GDP does not appear to have been much affected by changes of government. Even the apparently draconian Thatcher administration has presided over a sharp increase in the share of resources being devoted to the social services. But this has been mainly because of a fall in the absolute level of GDP rather than a rise in social spending. In general, the social services have *not* been starved of resources relative to the rest of the

Table 4.3   Social Expenditure as Percentage of GDP, 1970–80

Year	Education	NHS	Personal social services	Benefit payments	Housing	Total
1970	6.2	4.5	0.6	9.0	3.0	23.4
1971	6.2	4.5	0.6	8.7	2.6	22.7
1972	6.4	4.7	0.7	9.3	2.7	23.8
1973	6.5	4.6	0.8	8.6	3.6	24.1
1974	6.5	5.1	0.9	9.2	5.6	27.4
1975	7.4	5.4	1.1	9.4	4.7	28.0
1976	6.9	5.4	1.1	10.1	4.6	28.1
1977	6.5	5.3	1.0	10.4	4.0	27.2
1978	6.2	5.3	1.0	10.9	3.6	27.0
1979	6.1	5.3	1.0	11.1	3.7	27.2
1980	6.4	5.9	1.1	11.5	3.7	28.6

Source: National Income and Expenditure, 1981, HMSO.

economy, as Figure 4.1 demonstrates. Social expenditure as a percentage of personal consumption has risen from about 39 per cent at the beginning of the 1970s to about 48 per cent now, and fell only during the last three years of the previous Labour Government, when private consumption benefited from the North Sea oil boom. By contrast, general government investment fell over the same period from about 9 per cent of personal consumption to under 5 per cent. Hence, the rise in social spending – which has been mainly on current expenditure rather than on capital projects – has continued at the expense both of personal consumption and, more importantly, at the expense of general government investment. If this dramatic decline in investment is to be reversed – and it must surely be a major priority for the next government to achieve this – then social spending may come under more pressure. But it is important to recognise that in recent years there has been a major shift towards social expenditure and away from other categories of resource usage. Social policy analysts therefore cannot put all the blame for social failures on economists and the economy. Social policy must look to itself for its own defects.

Resources for social policies
The resources available for social services depend on two inter-related components: the aggregate of resources available to society as a whole, and the proportion of those resources which society is willing to allocate to the social services. In this section we shall consider each of these, first in general terms and second in more detail looking particularly at the prospects for the next five years.

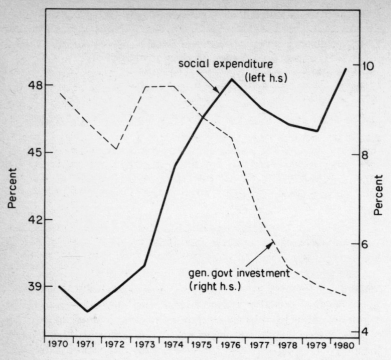

Figure 4.1   Social Expenditure and Public Investment as Percentage of Personal Consumption (%)

Source: as Table 4.3

There is no doubt that the capacity of the economy for rapid growth appears to have deteriorated sharply since the first oil price shock in 1973. Table 4.4 shows what has happened to real GDP growth in Britain and in several competitor economies in three separate periods – 1961–7, 1967–73 and 1973–9. In the first of these periods, the UK managed 2.8 per cent per annum real GDP growth, which was about two-thirds of that achieved by Germany, half of that achieved by the USA, and under one third of that achieved by Japan. Britain's growth rate was just over half of that achieved by the OECD as a whole, a relationship which has been roughly unchanged for most of this century. In the 1967–73 period, Britain achieved an average annual growth of about 3½ per cent (though this was to some extent distorted by the exceptionally high output level recorded for one year only in 1973). The general pattern continued. Britain was doing much worse than its major competitors, but much better than at any time in its history prior to 1945. However, the 1973–9 period saw a sharp deterioration in

Britain's growth performance. Average real GDP growth over this period (and it is a fair comparison since 1973 and 1979 were both years of high demand pressure) amounted to only 1.1 per cent per annum, and excluding the increase in oil production average GDP growth was less than 0.5 per cent per annum. This decline relative to past performance has been mirrored in other OECD economies, and the relationship between British and international growth rates has remained about the same as before. The story is even worse if we look at the years 1979–81, when real GDP *declined* by more than 5 per cent; the 1982 real GDP level (excluding oil) is likely to be about the same as the level achieved on average during the 1974–5 recession. Hence, if the evidence of the last two years is to be believed, the British economy (again excluding oil) has lost its capacity for long-term growth.

If we were to use the experience of the last few years as a guide, then we would conclude that there may be no additional resources available for public expenditure in the lifetime of the next government; any increase in real public spending would on this basis have to be found from reductions in the rest of the economy. However, this is almost certainly too pessimistic. Given the margin of spare labour resources in the economy at present – almost 2 million *fewer* people were unemployed as little as two years ago – a period of 'catch up' growth should be possible. Figure 4.2 shows that real GDP in 1982 is perhaps 4–5 per cent below its trend level, and if the trend level gives any indication of long-term output possibilities, then a period of above average growth is possible in the next few years. Nevertheless, it is clear from Figure 4.2 that the trend rate of growth has attenuated since 1973 (in line with the experience of other countries), and even if we argue that a large proportion of this attenuation has been due to inappropriate government policy which will be reversed by the next Labour Government, it is obviously prudent in public expenditure planning to make some allowance for the reduced trend growth rate. For there is a clear asymmetry between the consequences of public expenditure projections which are too optimistic and those which are too pessimistic.

Table 4.4   Real Annual GNP Growth (%)

Years	OECD	USA	Japan	Germany	UK
1961–7	5.1	5.0	9.6	3.7	2.8
1967–73	5.0	3.5	10.4	5.3	3.4
1973–9	2.7	2.5	4.1	2.4	1.1

Note: UK real GDP growth excluding oil averaged only 0.5% pa from 1973 to 1979.

Source: *OECD Economic Outlook*, OECD, Paris, January 1982.

As we saw in the initial years of the last Labour Government, and have seen again with the Socialist administration in France in the past two years, over-optimistic public expenditure plans can play a major part in producing foreign exchange crises, headlong depreciations in exchange rates, higher inflation and political upheaval. On the other hand, public expenditure plans which are set too low can much more easily be subsequently increased without anything like the same degree of economic and political disruption. This was certainly the experience of the last Labour Government in 1977–9, and it would be even more true if Tony Crosland's idea of a public expenditure 'shelf' were activated. This would consist of a series of reserve projects which could be very quickly activated if it became clear that the economic resources were available for additional public expenditure.

What does this imply for the public expenditure plans of the next Labour Government? First, they should initially be based on a relatively prudent assessment of growth prospects, even though the objective of the government's economic strategy would be to increase growth relative to past performance. Even if the objective of economic strategy is to achieve a growth rate of say 4 per cent per annum (which may be sufficient to reduce unemployment by some 2 million over five years), initial public expenditure exercises may be better advised to plan on a slightly lower growth rate, say $2\frac{1}{2}$ per cent per annum. This would allow for trend economic growth of some 2 per cent per annum, with some catch up over the period to allow for the fact that even in 1983 the UK is likely to be starting from an output level well below trend.

It will no doubt be argued by cold-hearted economists that a $2\frac{1}{2}$ per cent per annum growth assumption is absurdly high in the context of a world economy which, whether for policy reasons or not, is much less conducive to rapid growth that it has ever been in the post-war period. Certainly, it must be admitted that a $2\frac{1}{2}$ per cent growth assumption *could* prove too high. Even perfect British economic policy could be jeopardised by a period of high interest rates, restrictive fiscal policy and low growth in other economies. But it is surely the business of the next Labour Government to plan on the assumption that the present margin of spare capacity can be reduced, and that the Thatcher government has wantonly cut growth performance way below its real potential. Hence, an assumption of $2\frac{1}{2}$ per cent per annum growth, given Labour's social objectives, is probably prudent. A higher growth assumption – of say 4 per cent per annum – for public expenditure planning would simply be blindly optimistic in present circumstances. The 1965 national plan made a similar assumption, and came to grief over it against a much more favourable economic background.

We now turn to the second major question for social policy analysts:

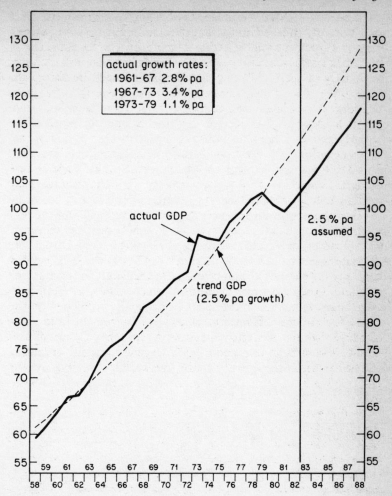

actual growth rates:
1961–67 2.8% pa
1967–73 3.4% pa
1973–79 1.1% pa

actual GDP

2.5% pa
assumed

trend GDP
(2.5% pa growth)

Figure 5.2   Actual and Trend GDP (£bn, 1975 prices)

how much of our aggregate resources should get devoted to social
services. This depends on many factors: the performance and repu-
tation of the social services, the attitude of voters to public and private
spending, the response of politicians, the pressure for more spending,
and the pressure for less tax.

The left has for many years argued that more social spending is
necessary and desirable while the right has argued for less social
spending. To justify increased social spending the left has traditionally
relied on arguments about needs and justice but more recently there has
been more emphasis on self-interest and the 'social wage'. It is argued

that more taxes would buy more services and that these additional services should be taken into account in assessing standards of living. While this argument is in aggregate undoubtedly correct, it may have only limited relevance for policy. In Tables 4.5, 4.6 and 4.7, the distribution of social spending and of high incomes are shown by household type. First, it may be noted that benefits are concentrated on particular types of household: cash benefits on retired households and education, as would be expected, on households with children. By contrast the best off households are those which are not retired *and* do not have children. Thus the dilemma arises (Table 4.7) that the households which are best off, and must be expected to bear the brunt of paying for improved social services, are the very households which benefit least from the social services. It is of course true that those who are currently members of better off households may, and probably will, benefit from the social services some time in the future, but they may not look sufficiently far ahead to realise this. So there is little correlation between those who pay for the services and those who benefit from them, and the question arises of whether the better off households will be willing to pay more taxes for more services *when those services largely benefit others*. Ultimately social spending cannot be justified purely in terms of self-interest. It must to some degree rely on altruism – enforced through the tax system – and a concern for social justice and social cohesion. Willingness to pay also depends crucially on public attitudes to the social services and to the benefits they are seen to

Table 4.5   *Distribution of Households and Benefits by Household Type, 1980*

Household type	Households	Cash benefits	National Health Service	Education	Housing subsidy
	%	%	%	%	%
1 adult retired	12.9	20.7	13.0	–	14.8
2 adults retired	9.4	22.7	15.0	0.6	9.4
1 adult non-retired	8.2	4.0	2.6	1.7	7.4
2 adults non-retired	21.6	11.2	14.7	2.1	18.2
2 adults 1 child	9.0	5.1	9.6	6.8	6.8
2 adults 2 children	12.5	7.6	13.6	24.9	11.1
2 adults 3+ children	5.2	6.0	7.4	19.6	6.5
3+ adults 1 child	8.0	8.8	10.2	28.2	9.6
1 adults 1+ child	3.0	3.9	2.2	6.4	5.0
3+ adults	10.4	10.1	11.8	10.6	11.2
All	100	100	100	100	100
Average amount		£947	£479	£448	£122

Source: as for Table 4.1

Table 4.6 *Adjusted Income Levels by Household Type, 1980*

Household type	Average All groups £	Adjusted income Top fifth of each group £	Proportion over £4000 adjusted income Of each group %	Of all groups %
1 adult retired	1,982	3,045	3.6	2.0
2 adults retired	2,173	3,701	5.7	2.3
1 adult non-retired	3,696	6,538	35.1	12.2
2 adults non-retired	4,233	7,233	47.2	43.3
2 adults 1 child	3,357	5,617	24.7	9.4
2 adults 2 children	3,179	5,211	17.8	9.4
2 adults 3+ children	2,655	4,551	10.6	2.3
3+ adults 1+ child	3,084	4,980	14.4	4.9
1 adult 1+ child	2,241	4,276	5.3	0.7
3+ adults	3,517	5,682	31.0	13.6
All	3,317	n.a.	23.6	100

Note: Adjusted income = disposable income per adult equivalent.
Adult equivalents are: 1.0 for first adult;
0.6 for second adult (usually spouse);
0.7 for only other adult;
0.3 for each child.

Source: as for Table 4.1

provide in the long run. Thus questions discussed in later chapters on the role of professionals and local communities, and the effective use of taxpayers' money, are not abstract questions but of direct political relevance to the willingness of taxpayers to finance increased social spending.

The scope for increases in social programmes

One of the first Treasury papers which will be waiting for an incoming Labour Chancellor will be an analysis of the party's public expenditure programmes, relating them to possible resources available over the period of the ensuing parliament and discussing problems of financing the planned increase in spending. Although the latter issue – finance – is extremely important, it is not directly relevant to the current argument (and is discussed by Charles Greenaway in Chapter 7).

In the first place, any expansionary public expenditure programme will be limited by its balance of payments and inflationary conse-quences. We assume here – and it is a massive assumption – that the alternative economy strategy is capable of handling balance of pay-ments difficulties through a combination of devaluation and import controls, and capable of handling inflation via price controls and incomes restraint. If these assumptions prove fallacious, or if a collapse in financial market confidence is allowed to undermine the whole economic strategy, then any scope for public expenditure increases could, in practice, be minimal. Even assuming that the economic strategy produces, say, $2\frac{1}{2}$ per cent per annum growth, there will still be severe constraints on the government's ability to increase public expenditure. These constraints are derived not so much from the laws of economics as from the laws of arithmetic – which are far more difficult to repeal by National Executive Committee fiat. Whatever the Labour Party's view of the Treasury, it cannot dispute the fact that resources are finite and cannot simultaneously be allocated to more than one use.

A growth rate of $2\frac{1}{2}$ per cent per annum over five years (taking the years 1983 to 1988 as examples) would produce about £30 billion extra resources in 1982 prices, and this would be available to be allocated between the various components of demand such as consumers' expenditure, investment, exports and public expenditure. Unlike 1974, the starting position is eased considerably by the fact that the balance of payments looks like being somewhere near to equilibrium, so the UK will not need to shift resources into the net trading sector and will be able to use them for domestic purposes instead. In the illustrations in Table 4.8 we assume that net export volume can deteriorate slightly in the course of the next parliament, freeing a further £1.4 billion (1982 prices) for use domestically. A similar amount is freed by assuming that

Table 4.7   Distribution of Benefits and High Adjusted Incomes, 1980

Household type	Average cash benefits	Average benefits in kind	Distribution of combined benefits	Distribution of households with over £4000 adjusted income
	£	£	%	%
1 adult retired	1,520	626	13.4	2.0
2 adults retired	2,285	898	14.5	2.3
1 adult non-retired	458	391	3.4	12.2
2 adults non-retired	492	533	10.7	43.3
2 adults 1 child	540	1,031	6.8	9.4
2 adults 2 children	577	1,640	13.4	9.4
2 adults 3+ children	1,090	2,703	9.5	2.3
3+ adults 1+ child	1,045	2,479	13.6	4.9
1 adult 1+ child	1,235	1,690	4.2	0.7
3+ adults	916	1,206	10.7	13.6
All	947	1,123	100	100

Source: as Table 4.1

Table 4.8   Resources Available for Public Consumption, 1983–88 (at 1982 prices)

Case A : *2.5% p.a. Growth*

	1983 [a]	1988 [b]	Extra resources	Comment
GDP (exp. based)	240.6	272.1	31.5	2.5% p.a. growth
Consumers' expenditure	169.6	187.3	17.7	2% p.a. growth
Gross domestic fixed capital formation	46.6	52.7	6.1	Maintains GDP share
Stockbuilding	4.9	3.5	−1.4	Trend level
Net exports	−7.9	−9.3	−1.4	Current a/c balance maintained
less Factor cost adjustment	29.7	31.1	1.4	In line with consumers' expenditure
Available for public consumption	57.1	69.0	11.9	4 % p.a. growth

Case B : *1% p.a. Growth*

	1983 [a]	1988 [b]	Extra resources	Comment
GDP (exp. based)	240.6	252.9	12.3	1% p.a. growth
Consumers' expenditure	169.6	178.2	8.6	1% p.a. growth
Gross domestic fixed capital formation	46.6	49.0	2.4	Maintains GDP share
Stockbuilding	4.9	3.5	−1.4	Trend level
Net exports	−7.9	−9.3	−1.4	Current a/c balance maintained
less Factor cost adjustment	29.7	31.1	1.4	In line with consumers' expenditure
Available for public consumption	57.1	62.6	5.5	1.9% p.a. growth

Sensitivity analysis :

1% extra private consumption	=	3.0% less public consumption
1% extra investment	=	0.8% less public consumption
1% worse terms of trade	=	1.4% less public consumption

[a] Forecasts.
[b] Illustration.

Source: Authors' calculations.

stock building will be able to fall slightly from its above-trend forecast 1983 level. However, other decisions are more difficult. In Table 4.8 we assume that government policy is set with the prime objective of creating room for additional public consumption – this seems a reasonable conclusion to draw from *Labour's Programme 1982*. Hence, gross domestic fixed capital formation and private consumers' expenditure are held down as far as possible. In the case of consumption, we have limited the growth rate to 2 per cent per annum over the parliament, absorbing £17.7 billion of extra resources, for reasons considered further below; anything lower than this against a background of $2\frac{1}{2}$ per cent real GDP growth would surely be unacceptable to the electorate. For total investment, we assume that its share of GDP is maintained between 1983 and 1988 (though the 1983 share would be considered by many to be unacceptably low). It would be possible to boost the total investment figures by shifting some resources away from public consumption and into public investment, though this would probably increase constraints on social expenditure which is primarily on the current rather than the capital side.

On the assumptions listed, a $2\frac{1}{2}$ per cent per annum real GDP growth rate would leave £11.9 billion of additional resources for public consumption over the period of the next parliament, implying a growth rate of 4 per cent per annum. Would this growth rate be sufficient to finance Labour's plans for social spending?

Labour's Programme 1982 (Labour Party 1982) is not a precise statement of policy. It does, however, provide an indication of what future policy a Labour Government would wish to pursue. It is therefore important to assess how the resources may be found. The emphasis throughout is on devoting a greater share of total resources to the public sector and on giving priority to the social services.

For the National Health Service, there is a firm declaration to increase the budget in real terms by at least 3 per cent per annum. Hospital building is to be stepped up and health charges are to be phased out. If all this occurred over a five-year period the extra resources required would be about £2.5 billion (including personal social services).

For education, the emphasis is on expansion particularly for under fives and the sixteen to nineteen-year-old groups. Even restoring Conservative cuts would cost £1.6 billion and a 3 per cent per annum growth rate would add up after five years to £1.9 billion. Thus Labour's programme for education would certainly require some £2 billion extra resources.

On housing, *Labour's Programme 1982* states that 'housing suffered quite disproportionately from Tory expenditure cuts. A massive house building and renovation programme has a priority claim, and restoration of the Tories' cuts in housing investment would make a substantial contribution to reflating the economy . . . A future investment programme . . . will have to be led by the public sector.' The restoration of Tory public expenditure cuts could involve some £4 billion extra resources for housing.

These then are the principal additional calls on real resources made by commitments in *Labour's Programme 1982*. They amount to some £8.5 billion (1982 prices) in five years' time, excluding cash payments which we discuss below. It should be stressed that this is by no means a complete list, nor is it necessarily a list of those commitments which will get into the election manifesto. Furthermore, many in the Labour Party have emphasised that the objectives in the 1982 programme may take more than one parliament to fulfil.

Comparing this total with the margin available for public consumption calculated in Table 4.8, it seems that (on the assumption of $2\frac{1}{2}$ per cent per annum real GDP growth) there may be real resources available to cover most of Labour's plans for increased current social expenditure, and some may be left over for additional spending in other areas such as employment and industrial policy.

If this relatively optimistic conclusion comes as something of a surprise to social policy analysts, who are used to receiving messages of gloom from the economists, then it should be remembered that several heroic assumptions have been needed to reach this conclusion. Firstly, the $2\frac{1}{2}$ per cent per annum real GDP growth rate could prove too high (see above), and if the UK were to manage only, say, 1 per cent per annum growth then the resources available for public consumption would be cut dramatically. In addition, it should be remembered that we have assumed that the next Labour Government will give priority to social policy expenditure over all other objectives. One consequence of this is that growth in consumers' expenditure is restricted to a rate of only 2 per cent per annum; another is that private fixed investment merely maintains its share of current GDP; and a third is that other public expenditure objectives take second place to social policy. As each of these assumptions is relaxed the dilemmas increase.

We now turn to the more difficult question of transfer payments. Although in principle these can be financed without limit by increasing taxation for the rest of the community, in practice it seems that no government would be willing to pursue a policy mix which involves a severe squeeze on the real living standards of people in work over the lifetime of a parliament. It follows that a major constraint could develop on transfer payments.

Labour's Programme 1982 contains extensive and expensive social security objectives. The most important of these and their current costs are:

Basic pension of one third average earnings for single pensioners and half average earnings for married couples	£8.2 billion
Lowering pension age to sixty for men	£2.6 billion
Increasing child benefit to level of short-term NI dependents addition	£1.1 billion
Comprehensive Income Scheme for disabled people	£1.5 billion
Improving unemployment benefits	£0.5 billion
Ending sex discrimination in housewives' non-contributory invalidity pension and the invalid care allowance	£0.3 billion

The gross cost of these adds up to £14 billion, although after tax the additional cost would be of the order of £10 billion.

We saw in Table 4.8 that, in order to meet the real resource requirements of Labour's programme, private consumption could grow by only about 2 per cent per annum over the next parliament. Assuming that the savings ratio remains approximately constant, this means that real personal disposable income (that is, after-tax incomes from employment, social security and so forth) can rise at only about the same rate. Translating this into 1982 prices, total disposable income could rise by only about £17.5 billion per annum by the end of five years if the real resource constraints turn out approximately as expected.

The first call on this margin for additional personal disposable income will come from those people moving out of unemployment and back into jobs. Let us assume that the 2½ per cent per annum growth rate, taken together with special job measures, increases employment by 2 million from 1983 to 1988. These 2 million workers will no longer receive sizeable social security benefits, but they will increase the wages and salaries bill. According to a recent study by the DHSS (see the *Employment Gazette*, June 1982), the median unemployed person would receive about £50 extra per week in net earnings if employed. If this average is maintained while 2 million people find extra jobs, then this will absorb approximately £5.2 billion of the £17.5 billion available for personal disposable income growth over the five-year period. This would leave £12.5 billion for other uses. Labour's plans for additional social security spending amount to an additional £10 billion. Hence, proposed extensions in social security benefits would absorb almost all the margin available after allowing for the shift back into jobs. It would mean that the real living standards of people in jobs would be virtually static over the period.

It seems unlikely that the electorate would be willing to vote for a programme which required such a prolonged freeze of the real living standards of those in work. If so, the party has some difficult choices to make before it reaches office on its priorities and the timing of its policy objectives. This conclusion is underlined if we adopt less optimistic assumptions about growth.

This is illustrated in Case B in Table 4.8. GDP grows at 1 per cent per annum, as does consumers' expenditure. On this basis, public consumption would grow by only £5.5 billion over five years, or 1.9 per cent per annum – far short of that necessary to meet the social spending plans in *Labour's Programme 1982*. Consumers' expenditure could grow by £8.6 billion which would not cover the social security plans, let alone provide *any* increase in real living standards for those in work.

An illustration of how sensitive our calculations are to the assumptions about growth and consumers' expenditure is shown in Table 4.8. For example, for every 1 per cent extra on the level of private consumption at the end of the period, public consumption needs to be reduced by 3 per cent. Similarly, an extra 1 per cent on total investment involves 0.8 per cent less for public consumption, while a deterioration of 1 per cent in the terms of trade (which means that real resources need to be moved abroad in order to maintain rough balance on the current account) would imply 1.4 per cent less for public consumption.

It therefore appears that a combination of slightly less generous assumptions on real GDP growth, the thrust of government policy, and the terms of trade would lead to a dramatic shrinking in the resources available for social policy objectives. But the calculations show that extra resources *can* be made available to improve our social services substantially in the next parliament, *provided* that Labour gives priority to this area, and *provided* that the economic strategy is not completely unsuccessful.

This discussion has focused on the last five years and on *Labour's Programme 1982*. It must be stressed that this programme has not been formulated as a five-year programme. Some of the considerations discussed here and the difficult choices they pose will have to be taken into account when the election manifesto comes to be drafted.

In conclusion:

(a) Providing the economic strategy works, and providing Labour is willing to give absolute priority to social policy commitments, then the real resource element of Labour's plans for social spending can possibly be accommodated.

(b) This would leave very limited resources for other spending areas, such as transport and industrial policy. Hence each spending programme must be evaluated in terms of the contribution it makes to the objective of reducing social inequality.

(c) The real resource commitments can only be met if private consumption is squeezed, and this puts limitations on real disposable income growth. The first call on disposable income growth will come from people moving off social security benefits back into employment. This will leave very little for anyone else – and certainly not enough over five years to finance all of Labour's plans for transfer payments increases.

(d)   Extra scope for transfer payments could be derived by increasing economic growth above the 2½ per cent per annum assumption (which seems unlikely), or by reducing commitments to increase public sector real resource spending, thus leaving more for cash benefits and personal incomes.

(e)   Therefore harsh choices cannot be avoided. The plans contained in *Labour's Programme 1982* for increased services and for larger transfer payments are not compatible. If the party does not reconcile these aims while it has time, the foreign exchange markets will do so thereafter.

Social policy can, and should, be given much higher priority than it has been in the past. But this cannot be regardless of the economic constraints.

5 The Necessity for Full Employment
by Adrian Sinfield

Full employment must be a central objective in any attempt to implement an Alternative Social Strategy. It is not only an important end in itself but a means to other social goals which cannot be omitted from a socialist programme. I do not believe we can achieve any new social objectives without first reducing unemployment significantly. It is central to any concept of full citizenship.

This is not to pretend that full employment, or even low unemployment, however defined, can be achieved quickly or painlessly. None of its advocates forty or fifty years ago believed that. Both William Beveridge and Michal Kalecki, for example, stressed the difficulties and emphasised the resistance that there would be from sections of society who would lose some of their power and control.[1] They would use all their influence on the media to convince the electorate of the inevitability of unemployment. The 'future of work' debate has had a long history of confusion. It contains too many challenges, dilemmas and pitfalls to permit easy discussion. We know from the experience of many years – and not just the 1930s or the 1980s – that unemployment damages people and limits their opportunities to participate in society.

But the labour movement is also aware of the many ways in which employment exploits workers, locking them into the class structure with its very unequal distribution of resources, power and status. People, as Tawney said, are treated as 'hands' and not people with lives of their own to lead. The recognition of the exploitative nature of much employment has led some to an acceptance of the abandonment of full employment as part of their rejection of the unscrupulous use of the 'work ethic'. This is in my view a fundamental misunderstanding which overlooks the central place of full employment as a political and social policy goal, quite apart from its economic and industrial importance.

Our mistake over the last decade and a half – if not since the war – has been to forget the political and social policy primacy of full employment and to let it become a matter for economists to discuss in largely technical terms. The objective of this chapter is to reinforce the arguments for putting full employment back among the main objectives of social planning despite the difficulty of achieving it. I wish to argue that it is also difficult, if not impossible, to achieve other basic socialist goals or even maintain the limited advances that have been gained by people dependent on their labour *without* reversing the shift in power and income brought about by sustained high unemployment.

High unemployment means more poverty and inequality

Continuing high unemployment means growing numbers of poor people and a greater degree of deprivation for the poor. This is not simply because the link between unemployment and poverty remains unbroken or because there is a dramatic increase in those suffering prolonged unemployment who are particularly vulnerable to poverty. Many other people whose resources might have been increased by part-time or occasional employment are pushed beyond the margins of the labour force. Quite apart from those pushed into early retirement, many elderly people will suffer deprivation because whole families' total resources are lowered by unemployment. Whether or not they live in the same household, the support provided in cash or kind to many elderly people is therefore reduced.

Poverty and deprivation is made all the worse by the very unequal impact of unemployment in Britain. In policy and other discussions we tend to speak of distinct categories: unemployed youth, especially school leavers; redundant workers; married women out of work or unable to return to the labour force; the early retired and so on. But because unemployment falls so unequally in class terms, the people in these categories may well be members of the same family and likely to be living in the same poorer parts of a town.

High unemployment reinforces the inequalities already so evident within our class structure. Those without capital and private resources, or cheap and easy access to them, have little real protection against a period of unemployment. A recession destroys the career expectations that would have seemed normal in better times. Harold Laski's ironic dictum that the most important thing is 'to choose one's parents wisely' gains fresh bite when school leavers have to lower their job horizons.

Greater inequality in power

The continuing lack of employment means not only a reduction in chances for individuals but a significant weakening of the power of working people, especially those on the margin of the labour force. Employers can bid 'upmarket' – as in London Transport's advertisement: 'You don't need a university background to drive a bus – but it helps' (*Guardian*, 23 June 1979). Campaigns to improve the quality of work and its rewards are largely nullified by high unemployment. It is no coincidence that the number of wages inspectors have been cut back, nor that the health and safety inspectorate has been reduced in size and restrained in its vigour.[2] Thus full employment is one vital precondition for the satisfactory achievement of other objectives, not just the reduction of poverty and inequality. Past policies to integrate groups into society and remove the barriers of disadvantage and privilege are predicated upon sustained low unemployment. If it cannot be achieved, then we need to redesign quite radically many of the programmes and strategies associated with what is popularly called the 'welfare state'.

A particularly clear example is the current foot-dragging, if not outright obstruction, by the Manpower Services Commission and other government agencies at central, regional and local level, over helping disabled people into work and assisting them once they are employed.[3] There can be no clearer illustration of Richard Titmuss' remark that those who are regarded as 'essential manpower' during periods of labour shortage are treated as 'surplus labour' during recession. The main measures to help disabled people in the labour force derive from the Disabled Persons (Employment) Acts introduced during wartime labour scarcity, and there has been a signal failure to adapt these to the very changed labour market conditions of recent years in ways that enhance the position of disabled people.

The most detailed analysis of North American and West European experience concluded: 'The maintenance of overall unemployment rates at 2 per cent or less for years at a time may be the single most important factor in minimising the number of hard to employ and motivating a programme to seek the residual group who might appear unemployable at higher levels of unemployment.'[4] This same point was brought home to me very clearly when I examined the response of some ten countries to the long-term unemployed in the mid-1960s – 'the pressure of the scarcity of labour' had led Germany and Sweden to 'push back the frontiers of unemployability' while many other countries regarded those long out of work as surplus labour rather than as essential manpower.[5]

Greater sexual and racial equality are also jeopardised by the recession. Even the limited gains in employment made by women in the early and mid-1970s already seem to have been eroded by rising unemployment.[6] These groups tend to lose out doubly amid high unemployment. They are less able to obtain jobs and also receive less public support for special measures when those long established in the labour force are in fear of their own jobs. This atmosphere is a fertile one for scapegoating those seen as 'outsiders'. Married women have experience of this but racial, ethnic and religious groups suffer the most. This is 'the misery that generates hate', as Beveridge put it at the start of his *Full Employment in a Free Society*.

The full costs of high unemployment

Continuing high unemployment is also an expensive and wasteful 'luxury' that the nation simply cannot afford. That is why even the present administration is embarrassed by official calculations of the demands on public expenditure resulting from the combination of revenues lost and benefits paid out. A Treasury minister has publicly attacked the MSC estimates as the work of 'Moscow mathematicians' – a smear quite remarkable from a government minister against civil servants. *The Times* has reported the suppression of a government report showing that even the MSC estimates so attacked now under-state the total loss of revenue to the state, and so its citizens, which should be set at £5,000,000 a year for every extra 1,000 people out of work (18 February 1982).

Virtually every recent estimate puts the cost of unemployment well above £10 billion – the total recent target for the public sector borrowing requirement. Yet discussion of the estimates fails to reveal how circumscribed the calculations are. First, they only attempt to include items in the state's official accounts and not other costs borne by those out of work or the wider society. As one clear illustration of this, it should be remembered that the abolition of earnings-related supplement and the reduction in value of other benefits actually reduces the official figures on the costs of unemployment. Second, even within the costs to the state there is no account taken of the additional demands placed on the social, health and penal services that occur with increased unemployment, even without accepting Harvey Brenner's precise claims about physical and mental illness, higher rates of imprisonment and institutional care.[7]

Persisting high unemployment deprives us all. In its demands on public expenditure it drains away funds that are desperately needed in the health and personal social services, in housing and in the provision of adequate income support for many other groups in the population.

The inequalities of a 'free market' in employment

In the past we have allowed our judgements of who and how many should be allowed a share in what employment there is to be largely dictated by the economy, or rather by its managers and mismanagers. Those already securely established in the labour force have considerable power and advantage over those trying to make their way in, whether for their first job, after giving birth, or on recovery from illness or injury. At all these stages certain groups may find themselves particularly disadvantaged, especially black and foreign workers or members of religious minorities. The formidable challenge is how we can protect all these groups equally against bearing the brunt of unemployment and help the participation and integration into society of those excluded when employment opportunities are very limited. With hindsight we can see that we have tended to place far too much reliance on a body-count battle against unemployment in contrast to ensuring the creation of, and equal opportunity to, valuable and satisfying work. The former, more limited, goal has led to strategies simply to get people 'off the register'. For those who have remained unemployed we have acquiesced in policies that offer them less financial support than other people dependent on state benefits.

If, as I am constantly told, we have to learn to live with high unemployment, it would seem only fair and proper that we should develop a *jobs policy* as well as expanding the supply of work by a *policy for jobs*. Such a rationing system would have to introduce measures to encourage or require some people to remain outside or withdraw from the labour force, and generally intervene more purposively and systematically in the allocation of jobs to those to whom it was decided to give priority rights to paid employment.

I personally believe that it is neither right nor necessary to accept that the supply of employment will continue to fall or remain well below what is needed in relation to demand, although I agree that there is an urgent need to plan policies for employment that fully recognise the enormous scale of the problem facing us. There has been very little disagreement between different economic forecasters, and the consensus now appears to be that on present policies unemployment is unlikely to fall much below 3 million registered unemployed in this decade. The latest Corporate Plan of the far-from-alarmist Manpower Services Commission has underlined the dismal nature of the forecasts among even the most cautious and 'responsible' examiners of the nation's economic entrails.

On present trends the total 'job gap' in four years' time will be about 5 million, compared with only 4 million today. That is the number of jobs needed, taking account of: (a) the increased unemployment that even the present government admits in the small print of its 1982 Budget papers; (b) the increase in unregistered unemployment as more women, more older and long-term unemployed cease registering for work; and (c) the half million extra jobseekers swelling the labour force by 1986. Even to bring registered unemployment down to 700,000 – a level approximately twice that achieved for the first twenty years after the war – would require us to create an extra 800,000 jobs a year.[8]

The lessons to be gained from past employment policies
We need measures that are designed to operate in ways that will minimise most quickly the hardships imposed on the unemployed and others suffering most severely from the recession. What lessons can be gained from past employment policies in tackling these difficulties?

There seems little evidence of more than limited success in establishing clear, generally acceptable boundaries over access to employment. Instead there has been a more dominant concern to keep a reserve army of labour available and to maintain the incentives to employment. The State has generally intervened to bring more people into, not out of, the job market.

The main explicit employment policies have been to improve the productivity of members of the labour force by training or retraining and to remove barriers of discrimination or disadvantage against women, ethnic and religious minorities, disabled workers and others. Many aspects of these policies are taken up in other chapters, but they also deserve more consideration as part of overall employment policy. Less overtly but increasingly vigorously, there has been action of varying kinds to ensure that those who are expected to work but are unemployed do in fact seek employment diligently and are not deterred from finding it by over-generous levels of benefit. These policies have been pursued more openly since the mid-1960s, and with particular energy and publicity more recently. They have tended to be directed more towards men than women, and especially towards men without specific skills. In many more ways than have generally been acknowledged, these measures represent a return to inegalitarian and pre-democratic 1834 policies. They use poverty and the principle of 'less eligibility' to maintain work discipline and launch an attack on real wages. The pursuit of these policies sabotages potentially more positive measures developed by other government departments and agencies. The deepening of deprivation and the reinforcement of stigma by the operation of the social security system in recent years has received far too little notice, let alone the outraged reaction it deserves, from the labour movement including the trade unions.

Trade unions have reacted much more vigorously to Mr Tebbit's 'New Training Initiative' with its proposed payment of £15 a week and the Young Workers Scheme which rewards employers for paying school leavers less than £45, and even more for paying less than £40, than they have done to the continuing and increasing penalisation and impoverishment of the unemployed through the social security system. Even though it was an English trade union, not Bismarck, that introduced unemployment insurance in its earliest form some 150 years ago, the solidarity of the trade unions with those out of work remains very fragile at best.[9]

While measures to drive people into the labour force under increasingly unfavourable conditions have been pursued more openly as well as vigorously, there has not however been similar official activity to restrict or discourage membership of the labour force. The Job Release Scheme is a comparatively small and fairly isolated measure, and it is too early to say how much the government will promote the opportunity for unemployed men over sixty on supplementary allowance for more than a year to convert to the more generous long-term rate on the condition that they leave the labour force. This came into effect in November 1981 but by the end of February 1982 only 27,000 people had transferred although there were very many more men eligible.

Early retirement: the creation of the undeserving worker

Changing the conditions for retirement is obviously one way to reduce the demand for jobs. In 1925 the lowering of the retirement age to 65 was, at least in part, a reaction to high unemployment. Today opinion polls have indicated that earlier retirement is the most popular policy among people of *all* ages for reducing youth unemployment. Certainly the merits of a more flexible retirement policy seem undeniable; but is this because at the present vague level of discussion it is a policy permitting infinite variety, meaning all things to all parties? As soon as we move from any uniform, standard age, we must ensure that the weight of the checks and balances are on the workers' side. People must be given greater choice and freedom to leave the workforce – sooner *or* later than the standard age, and by moving to part-time working first – not forced to continue working because of the inadequacy of pensions nor pushed and cajoled into 'volunteering' for redundancy or early retirement because others believe that age denies entitlement to a job. It would appear however that the Department of Health and Social Security and the Treasury have been convinced, at least for the moment, of the heavy demands on public expenditure this would entail, and experience in France indicates that a decent scheme is not a cheap way of reducing unemployment.

If we are to make it a deliberate policy to encourage earlier retirement, should we not offer people more to leave the labour force sooner or, at the very least, give workers their full pensions at an earlier age as in Austria? The argument that more generous treatment is not only too expensive but would remove the incentive to stay in or find work is totally inappropriate here because that is exactly the objective. Equally, accepting the reduction of one's work to part-time in order for more people to have a share of the available work merits compensation in some form because it is different from simply choosing to work shorter hours.

We have to face up to the sharp inconsistencies between two separate, and generally insulated, areas of debate. The first is concerned with the scale of unemployment and the proper distribution of a diminished amount of employment. The second focuses on the scale of unmet need and poverty among those outside the labour force, revealing the importance of employment in providing more adequate resources and enabling more active participation in society. The 'realism' of the former in urging, for example, earlier retirement must take account of the evidence of the latter that poverty grows not with age as if by some natural law but with length of time since employment.[10]

The recreation of 'two nations' among youth

The social problems and economic costs posed by early retirement indicate that at best only limited progress can be made in this direction. The difficulties at the other end of the labour force age distribution are equally great and have only been made worse by the polarisation of provision that is reinforcing the 'two nations' concept among sixteen to nineteen-year-olds just as it has been fostered amongst the older groups. In sharp contrast to some of the ideals that stimulated the move to comprehensive secondary education by rejecting segregation by social class or academic achievement,

responsibility for the 16–19 year olds has become not only segregated by institutions but by departments of state – the DES responsible for the education of the more prosperous and more able and the Department of Employment responsible for the training of the remainder. This is not a mere formal separation, for the two departments are pursuing quite different philosophies, if they can be so dignified, with totally different financial and administrative arrangements [which] provide financial incentives towards social polarisation'. (Eric Robinson in the *Times Educational Supplement*, 18 December 1981).

We have to develop strategies for egalitarian education and training policies for youth, with financial support for everyone in that age group which does not discriminate in favour of those already advantaged and widen the gulf between the employed and the unemployed. Tom Schuller discusses these issues in Chapter 13.

The opportunity for greater choice and flexibility in employment

One obvious strategy to cope with reduced employment opportunities is to ensure that more people have a share of what employment there is by deliberately making more employment positions available for part-time work.

Reduction in hours worked has been pursued by the TUC with its Campaign for Reduced Working Time. The current target of a 35-hour basic week by 1986 could be reached, it is argued, through an annual 2 per cent reduction in working time, 'through a combination of shorter weekly hours, reductions in systematic overtime, longer holidays and early retirement'.[11] The TUC recognises the importance of an expanding economy for achieving reductions in work time. So far, however, these changes have been largely a reactive device to avoid or at least delay redundancies.[12] In this respect they may be quite attractive to employers, enabling them to save the higher overtime rates and retain good workers for any expansion of demand.

Even this limited form of work sharing, however, reveals very quickly the major problem of *earnings sharing*. The peculiar achievement of much collective bargaining in Britain has been to raise overtime bonuses at the expense of basic pay which means that without their overtime payments, many jobs leave workers on or below the poverty line. The Low Pay Unit estimates that stopping overtime would increase the number of low paid men by well over half a million. While as a nation we may never have reached full employment, there has been much and harsh 'overfull employment' on an individual basis. Many are still forced to work excessive hours for inadequate wages. Others become trapped by their financial commitments and the low earnings of their main job to take on regular forms of 'moonlighting'. At any level of employment, we need to remove the pressures to overwork and increase the opportunities for leisure, but more effort could be devoted to sharing the jobs of the higher paid and salaried. People in these groups who often see work sharing as quite suitable for others are quick to point out that the current structure of occupational pensions, sick pay and many other employee benefits constitute a particularly serious obstacle as so many of these benefits are tied to status, length and continuity of service.

There are many ways in which demand for employment could be reduced temporarily to help the employment of others and could also promote other social objectives. Here I want to take just one example, the possibility of some forms of parental leave such as those which came into effect in Sweden in 1974 'to encourage men to assume a larger share of child care'.[13] An expectant mother can stop work and draw parental benefit one month before she expects to give birth but the total benefit entitlement of six months can be shared between the parents. 'Special parental benefit' at a lower rate of benefit may also be drawn for up to 180 days at any time before the end of the child's first year at school, and there is further entitlement 'for at most 60 days a year for each child' for a parent who has to stay away from work to look after a child. Either parent may claim these benefits, and most also seem available to adoptive and foster parents.[14] Within three years, one in ten fathers with newborn children were estimated to be using part of the first period, but take-up by men was much higher 'where the woman has a high level of education and income'.[13] Care would have to be taken that any such measure did not become yet one more benefit, if not privilege, more readily accessible to the better-off.

The need to improve careers and the quality of work
Measures such as these introduce greater flexibility and more choice

into workers' lives without reducing their security. It is important to extend and develop them, and to give priority to those that encourage a better distribution of employment opportunities. The need for more jobs, however, must not be allowed to diminish the long existing need to devise a comprehensive and integrated set of policies for work. At any level of employment we must seek to improve the quality of working life for the great majority of workers; to ensure a very much better, more equal distribution of the power and other rewards, both intrinsic and extrinsic, of employment; and to remove the barriers of disadvantage and discrimination facing many in the labour market. I have come to feel that the inequalities of the employment structure are embarrassing to many Fabians. They have not been subjected to the same critical, sustained and committed analysis as other inequalities – in access to or receipt of social services for example. Other chapters are taking up the inequalities of working life, but a major question is how much can be done to tackle them while unemployment remains high.

All socialists should be constantly and deeply concerned about the unrewarding and soul-destroying nature of much employment today and about the many ways in which the state encroaches upon the lives of the people. But this only reinforces the need to maintain and extend rights to legal protection and social security for those working in new, less formal, settings. Quite apart from the historical record of sweating, the increasing number of homeworkers today are 'probably the most heavily exploited and underprivileged workers in the country'.[15] They are mainly women with young children or elderly or disabled relatives to look after, others themselves disabled or prematurely retired with limited mobility, and immigrants unable to compete in the open market. The research of the Low Pay Unit shows very clearly how these people have to struggle to survive in poverty and with very little protection from the law whether in or out of work.

There are no cheap and easy solutions to high unemployment as each of these brief discussions has demonstrated. There is a wide gap between the reduction of registered unemployment by 'body count' tactics and the achievement of a more just and equal distribution of the work that is available and its rewards in ways that socialists can honourably accept.

The need to break the link between poverty and unemployment
Whatever measures we adopt, we must not allow any increase in employment opportunity to be taken up only by those who have most recently joined the unemployed or who are just entering the labour market. This will only reinforce the difficulties and disadvantages suffered by the one million people who have been registered out of work for a year or longer. The plight of these people calls attention to the

most immediate social policy objective facing any government, whatever its long-term strategy in responding to mass unemployment.

The link between unemployment, especially prolonged unemployment, and poverty must be broken. The evidence on the persistence of this link has been clear for many years to those who wished to understand it from the very earliest research after the last war.[16] Now it is not only very much more thoroughly documented but very much larger numbers of people are actually experiencing the rigours of prolonged unemployment. Successive cuts in state benefits have made the hardships worse. The abolition of earnings-related benefit, the real cut in benefits by 5 per cent, and the three reductions in the child dependant's addition can mean a cut of some £15 a week for an unemployed family of four – a severe additional penalty imposed on the government's 'conscript army' in its war against inflation and/or organised labour.

Linked to adequate benefits, we need to devise ways of countering the stigma that attaches to being out of work and demoralises the unemployed and their families. Early retirement of course might allow some to achieve what is currently seen as a more honourable status, but selective help of this type runs the danger of reinforcing the lower standing of the majority who remain unemployed. At present the government with its clear insistence on Unemployment Review Officers as a major weapon in its 'crackdown on scroungers' reinforces the stigma. This is being acknowledged by civil service unions – and also, though less openly, by senior officials – as a major threat to the civil rights of unemployed people. Any Labour Government must take the initiative to counter scrounger bashing. We must also acknowledge that the state reflects as well as shapes wider public views and prejudices against those who are seen as failing to work. At the very least, the continuing restriction of employment opportunities, whether planned or just deplored, requires that opportunities to participate in and contribute to society in ways that are properly valued and respected are available to all members of society, whether employed or not. At present many contributions are little valued and consequently appallingly rewarded, however essential they may be. But the process is circular; in our society too little is valued or respected that is not financially rewarded.

This perhaps is the central dilemma of what is called 'the work ethic', a term that has received surprisingly little analysis in recent years despite its frequent use. What I would prefer to describe as 'the *earnings* ethic' poses problems for socialists, I believe, because of the greater moral weight we placed on *earned* as opposed to *un*earned incomes. We 'work' for our living, we have 'earned' our place. Historically the labour movement has had considerable difficulty with the problem of how we support those who are not working. Those who have worked *earn* their retirement benefit, but what about those who have never been able to work? The long agonisings over disability and injury benefits have been made worse by the traditional labour movement view that injury or disability acquired at work *earns* some greater acknowledgement, and so compensation, than other disabilities, even those such as the thalidomide injuries which children have brought into the world with them. We have to devise strategies to break the 'earnings ethic' and make full citizenship possible for those who do not work. Policies to move back towards high employment need to provide resources to give workers more real freedom to choose for how many hours and how many years they wish to work; by providing them with better and more secure career structures with opportunities to train; by enabling them to change careers and obtain suitable help to retrain; and by allowing them to work and serve the community in ways other than those currently classified as employment without subjecting them to deprivation and stigma. These are all important elements of an effective socialist policy for work, *whatever* the level of employment. If high unemployment forces us to tackle these problems more vigorously and in ways that protect and enhance rights, we should seize the opportunity.

There are, as we have seen over the last decade, many varied ways of reducing formal unemployment, but few of them have enriched the lives of their 'beneficiaries' in the short or the long term. We need to give priority to achieving work for all who want it as a central social policy. Action simply to reduce unemployment is likely to emerge in practice as one more blunt weapon against the unemployed, with the costs largely borne by the more vulnerable of them and others excluded from paid work.

Socialists cannot afford not to give the attack on unemployment high priority. I have argued this not because mass unemployment may breed extremist tendencies and threaten social or political stability, but because of the many ways in which it diminishes the lives of the people.

Notes and references
1. W.H. Beveridge, *Full Employment in a Free Society*, Allen and Unwin, 1944; M. Kalecki, 'Political Aspects of Full Employment', *Political Quarterly*, 1943, pp. 322–31.
2. Adrian Sinfield, 'Social Policy Amid High Unemployment', in Catherine Jones and June Stevenson (eds), *The Yearbook of Social Policy in Britain 1980–1981*, Routledge and Kegan Paul, 1982.
3. Peter Townsend, 'Employment and Disability', in Alan Walker and Peter Townsend (eds), *Disability in Britain*, Martin Robertson, Oxford, 1981; and David Jordan, *A New Employment Programme for Disabled People*, Disability Alliance with Low Pay Unit, 1979.
4. Beatrice Reubens, *The Hard-to-Employ: European Programs*, Columbia University Press, New York, 1970, p. 384.

5.   Adrian Sinfield, *The Long Term Unemployed*, OECD, Paris, 1968, p. 36.
6.   C. Hakim, 'Job segregation: trends in the 1970s', *Employment Gazette*, December 1981.
7.   Jennie Popay, 'Unemployment: A Threat to Public Health', in Burghes and Lister (eds), *Unemployment: Who Pays the Price?*, CPAG, 1981.
8.   TUC, *Programme for Recovery: TUC Economic Review 1982*, TUC, 1982.
9.   R.A. Leeson, *Travelling Brothers*, Paladin Granada, 1979.
10. Alan Walker, 'The Social Consequences of Early Retirement', *Political Quarterly*, January 1982.
11. TUC, *op. cit*.
12. Michael White, *Case Studies of Shorter Working Time*, PSI, 1981.
13. E. Ahlqvist, 'Ready, Willing and Able – On Equality Between the Sexes on the Labor Market', in Allan Larsson (ed.), *Labor Market Reforms in Sweden*, The Swedish Institute, Stockholm, 1979, p. 81.
14. Information from The Swedish Institute, March 1981.
15. TUC, *Home Working: A TUC Statement*, TUC, 1980.
16. Peter Townsend, 'Unemployment and Social Security in Lancashire', in P. Townsend, *The Social Minority*, Allen Lane, 1973.

Additional reading

Burghes, L. and Lister, R. (eds), *Unemployment: Who Pays the Price?* CPAG 1981.

Deacon, A., 'Unemployment and Politics in Britain since 1945', in Brian Showler and Adrian Sinfield (eds), *The Workless State*, Martin Robertson, Oxford, 1981.

Dey, I., 'Making Redundancy Redundant – or How to Save Jobs Without Really Trying?', SSRC Research Workshop on Employment and Unemployment, London, 1980.

Harrington, Michael, *Full Employment: the Issue and the Movement*, Institute for Democratic Socialism, New York, 1977.

Levison, Andrew, *The Full Employment Alternative*, Coward, McCann and Geoghegan, New York, 1980.

Low Pay Unit, *Minimum Wages for Women*, LPU, 1980.

MSC, *Review of the Quota Scheme for the Employment of Disabled People: A Report*, Manpower Services Commission, 1981.

Popay, Jennie, 'Early Retirement: Its Purpose, with What Consequence for Whom?', in Colin Hines *et al.*, *Beyond Generalisation: Issues in the New Technology Debate*, Earth Resources Research and South Bank Polytechnic, London, 1981.

Part Two
The Next Steps

6 Making Redistribution Work: The Social Services
by *Julian Le Grand*

There are valid reasons for providing social services publicly and reasons for providing some free at the point of use. Howard Glennerster discusses these arguments in Chapter 1. However, it is important to rid ourselves of some false assumptions. There was a time when many people, even within the Labour Party, believed that state provision of such services as health care, education, housing, even transport, free or at heavily subsidised prices, would *in itself* be a significant contribution to redistributing income to the poorest members of the community. Inequalities would diminish and a classless society would be a little nearer attainment. These dreams were not fulfilled and it is important to understand the reasons. Some lie in the tax structure which finances these services and that is discussed in another chapter, but there is also a large amount of evidence suggesting that most of the services we have mentioned actually benefit the well off at least as much as the poor, and in many cases more than the poor. Why this is and what can be done about it is the principal theme of this chapter.

Who benefits?
We begin with a brief summary of the facts concerning the distribution of public expenditure on the principal social services. Table 6.1 divides the services into those whose distribution is pro-poor, those that are equally distributed and those that are pro-rich. The column of figures gives an indication of the relevant numbers, showing the average expenditure on people in the top fifth of the population, in income and occupational terms, expressed as a ratio of average expenditure on people in the bottom fifth. The figures refer to different groups and times. They are drawn from the author's much larger study[1] and should be taken as indicative only.

Generally they relate only to actual service spending by public authorities. With the exception of housing they exclude the benefits taxpayers receive from various tax allowances. These are even more heavily pro-rich. On the other hand, the figures exclude social security spending which is predominantly pro-poor, and spending on the personal social services which must intuitively be largely pro-poor because of the highly dependent groups served. Taxation, social security and the personal social services are discussed elsewhere in this volume. So too is redistribution in the sense of redistribution over a family life cycle or towards the elderly, children and other dependants. Here we are only concerned with the use of services by different income groups – a contentious and important enough issue on its own.

It is clear from the table that the bulk of the services listed are either distributed equally or favour the better off. Only the housing programmes aimed at council and private tenants benefit primarily the poor. The expenditure on the National Health Service is actually equally distributed in the limited sense that the average poor person receives about as much as the average rich person. But this does not take account of the fact that the poor suffer more ill health than the rich;

Table 6.1   The Distribution of Public Expenditure on the Social Services

Service	Ratio of expenditure per person in top fifth to that per person in bottom fifth
Pro-poor	
Council housing (general subsidy and rent rebates)	0.3
Rent allowances	not available
Equal	
Nursery education	not available
Primary education	0.9
Secondary education, pupils under sixteen	0.9
Pro-rich	
National Health Service	1.4 [a]
Secondary education, pupils over sixteen	1.8
Non-university higher education [b]	3.5
Bus subsidies	3.7
Universities	5.4
Tax subsidies to owner-occupiers	6.8
Rail subsidies	9.8

[a] Per person ill.
[b] Polytechnics, colleges of education and technical colleges.

Source: see text.

so per person *ill*, they receive less. State expenditure on education prior to the school leaving age is distributed equally; but expenditure on all forms of education after that age accrues largely to the better off. The subsidies that accrue to owner-occupiers through their various tax reliefs also dramatically favour the well off, with the richest group receiving nearly seven times as much on average as the poorest group. Much of public transport too is pro-rich. Indeed, the subsidies to rail travel are the most unequal of those listed.

The picture is one that many may find surprising. Of all current expenditure on the social service provision listed here, it can be estimated that only about one fifth is directed primarily at the poor. All of the rest is either distributed equally, or, more disturbingly, towards the better off.

A number of qualifications are needed to these figures. First, they show only the distribution of public expenditure in each area; they do not give the distribution of 'benefits' from that expenditure. However, it seems unlikely that the distribution of the latter would differ in any systematic way from that of the former. Second, they take no account of the taxes paid by the different groups. This perhaps needs a little more explanation.

It is often argued that the social services are redistributive because the better off pay more in taxes than they receive in services. But this proposition is incorrect. It may be true that the rich pay more in taxes for *all* the different forms of public expenditure from which they derive benefits, including defence, police and social security. But we cannot deduce from this that the social services as such are redistributive. To do so would require identifying that part of the tax system which funds the social services – an impossible task. It seems preferable to treat the overall tax system as an instrument of redistribution separate from the social services; and hence – as here – to consider the distributive effect of social service provision independently.

Is it possible to reform the social services so as to increase their redistributive impact, while preserving their essential character? The answers vary from service to service. We shall deal with each separately.

Health care

The evidence concerning the distribution of public expenditure on the National Health Service suggests that the poor do not use the service, relative to need, as much as their middle-class counterparts. The reasons for this can only be summarised here (they are discussed at length in Le Grand).[2] They include: the absence of good medical facilities in poorer areas; the poor having worse access to such facilities as do exist, due to their possessing fewer cars and telephones; manual workers, unlike the salaried middle class, losing money when they take time off to go to the doctor; and failures of communication between middle-class medical staff and working-class patients.

On the first of these, it is possible to make some progress. Following the report of the Resources Allocation Working Party,[3] the last Labour Government did make a creditable attempt to relocate health service facilities away from the medically over-endowed and wealthy South to the under-endowed and poor North and East. Partly due to the change in government, partly because the increment to distribute is so small in a barely growing service, partly because of the impassioned protests of the losers in the South, this process has now run out of steam. But it could be revived; any incoming Labour Government should make doing so one of its top priorities. However, it is difficult to be optimistic about the potential for more extensive reforms. All the other factors listed are beyond the control of the National Health Service; they are all part of wider social and economic inequalities about which there is little the NHS can do on its own. Inequality in health care, as with inequality in health itself,[4] largely reflects overall inequality in society; there is little that can be done about the former without doing something about the latter. In education, housing and transport, however, there is more scope for improving matters, as we shall now see.

Education
Education expenditure is broadly equally distributed prior to the school leaving age but subsequently it becomes highly unequal. One way to redress the balance would be to redirect education expenditure further towards schools. To some extent this has happened in the past decade. At the same time it is obviously desirable to preserve, so far as possible, the poor's access to education past the school leaving age and not to undermine university standards. The question is how best this can be done.

One proposal favoured by many on the left, including the TUC and the authors of *Manifesto*,[5] is to *expand state nursery education*. Perhaps surprisingly, nursery schools and nursery classes in primary schools are already used broadly equally by different social groups. According to the 1978 General Household Survey,[6] 38 per cent of children aged between three and four attended nursery or primary school, and there was relatively little difference in this proportion between the social classes. If this pattern were maintained following an expansion (and there seems little reason to expect it not to be), then the proportion of education expenditure that was equalising would be increased. Since the difference between the home and the school environments is likely to be greater for working-class than middle-class children, the academic and social gains for the former would be greater.

Expanding nursery provision need not be very expensive. Primary schools are already suffering from substantial over-capacity, capacity that it would be relatively easy to convert for nursery use. In 1978–9, to provide nursery classes in primary schools on a part-time basis for all children aged three to four who were not then receiving any pre-school education would have cost about £214 million, or under 3 per cent of the total education budget for that year.[7]

A more controversial proposal is to *raise the school leaving age*. This would reduce the overall inequality in public expenditure, since it would expand the period of compulsory education which is equally spread between income groups. Quite apart from this 'statistical' gain it might also contribute to reducing inequality in access to post-compulsory education, and it might even contribute to greater equality in later earnings. A group of London University economists has estimated that the raising of the school leaving age in 1972 reduced the dispersion of earnings by as much as 15 per cent in the younger age group.[8]

To be sure, the proposal has unattractive features. It would be expensive. For instance, if the leaving age had been raised by one year in 1978–9, and if the same amount per person had been spent on each of the extra people staying on as was spent on those who did in fact stay on, the cost would have been £1,200 million.[9] There would also be costs to the economy to take into account. Raising the leaving age by a year would withdraw over one million people from the labour force, with a possible loss in production, though that assumes full employment which is far from being the case in the present or medium-term prospect. Many poor households' incomes would be reduced, due to the loss of earnings from children who would have been in work (or the loss of social security payments from those who would have been unemployed). Some children and their teachers already regard the year from fifteen to sixteen as a waste of time educationally. For them, raising the leaving age might simply prolong the agony. Finally, the proposal involves an erosion of civil liberties, to which many (not least those primarily affected) might take objection.

Yet the force of these points can be exaggerated. The over-capacity already apparent in primary schools will soon appear in secondary schools. When it does the marginal resource cost of taking on extra children is likely to fall substantially below the present cost. Hence the cost to the education budget will almost certainly be less than the 1978–9 calculations suggest. Moreover, that cost is not much above that of the present government's proposed Youth Training Scheme (estimated to cost more than £1,000 million).[10] With three million people already unemployed (many of them school leavers), the loss to the economy of withdrawing even a million from the potential labour force is unlikely to be great.

The cost to poor families is a more significant problem. But this could be alleviated by an expansion of child benefit: a reform that would be desirable for other reasons as well. It could be financed at least in part by the savings in social security due to the reduction in payments to unemployed school leavers. More vocationally orientated curricula with work experience, advocated by the recent Labour Party discussion document *16–19: Learning For Life*, could be introduced. Comprehensive tertiary educational institutions, again advocated in *Learning for Life*, could make the extra period both useful educationally and more attractive to students.

An alternative which would yield some of the benefits of raising the school leaving age and impose fewer of the costs in terms of educational motivation, civil liberties and reduction in family income is the *extension of grants to sixteen- to eighteen-year-olds*. Already, local authorities provide minimal grants to students who stay on at school after sixteen. Many have advocated that these be made much more generous, and given a wider national coverage. They do have serious shortcomings nevertheless. First, in order to overcome all the financial pressures on working-class children to drop out of school, they would have to be extremely generous. Second, to ensure that they did not simply help the middle class to extract even more financial resources out of the system, they would have to be subject to a strict means test. Third, they would only have a major impact on the numbers of poor children staying on at school if the *main* reason why poor children did not stay on was the cost. For many, and possibly most, the reasons are more complex – lack of relevant information, parental distrust of the educational system and peer group pressure. None of these are likely to be affected by a system of student grants. All in all, therefore, it is a less effective option in *redistributive* terms than raising the school leaving age or extending industrial training combined with an increase in child benefit.

In the post-eighteen education sector, major redistributive gains could be achieved by *raising fees* and *switching from student grants to student loans*. If all higher and further education students were charged the marginal cost of their education and if they had to finance this, not from government grants, but via loan repayments out of their subsequent earnings, then the principal source of financial inequality in the education system would be eliminated. The consequent savings in public expenditure could be used to finance the extensions in preschool leaving age education discussed earlier. In the absence of information on the marginal costs of students' education in different institutions, it is difficult to quantify these savings; but if the result were to cut the bill for higher and further education by only half (and it might well be considerably more than that), then nearly enough would have been saved in 1978–9 to finance an increase in the school leaving age for one year *plus* an expansion of nursery education to include all children aged three to four.[11]

There are, and have been, many objections to this proposal. First, it is argued there are national economic efficiency reasons for subsidising students in higher and further education. The nation needs scientists, engineers, doctors, trained managers. Hence it should be prepared to pay for their education. But this argument is spurious. If society values good managers and engineers this will be reflected in the incomes such people can command. If people have their productivity increased by their education then, other things being equal, their employers will pay them higher wages. Only if society extracts a 'surplus' from these individuals in some way is there any case for subsidising their education. Then the subsidy should correspond only to the amount of surplus obtained.

A more powerful argument against raising fees and abolishing grants is that it would reduce the poor's access to the system. Children from working-class families would undoubtedly find it more difficult than middle-class children to find sources of finance for their education; their parents could help less and the banking system, if it offered them loans at all, would probably do so on more expensive terms. The result could be that their participation in higher education – already small – might fall yet further. Yet this is not inevitable. It will depend in part on what use is made of the money saved. If it is used to expand pre-school education and financial incentives to stay on at sixteen, the demand for higher education by working-class children might increase. Raising the cost of higher education would, other things being equal, reduce the number of aspirants relative to the number of places available. Entrance to higher education would become less competitive. This would actually improve the chances of a working-class candidate relative to a middle-class one. The reduction in subsidy to higher education, therefore, although it increases the cost to working-class students by raising their fees, simultaneously reduces the other barriers such students face.

Nonetheless, the possibility has to be faced that, on its own, such a policy would produce a decline in working-class use of the higher education system. This argues for two other variants. (1) A subsidised loan system limited to poorer students or the retention of the direct grant to cover fees of students from poorer families. (2) A way of avoiding some of the unpleasant consequences of introducing full cost charges and loans (such as the difficulties faced by graduates who may want to engage in unpaid work such as looking after their children) is to introduce a *graduate tax*. As formulated by its proponents, this generally takes the form of a percentage tax on the earnings of graduates from all publicly funded institutions of further and higher education, the rate varying with the length of course and type of institution attended. The tax would be administered by the Inland Revenue as part of the income tax collection system. It could be coupled with a flat rate student grant and a policy of zero fees for eligible students. Although it would not be as effective as a more conventional loans system (which would require full repayment from all graduates), it would substantially reduce the element of public subsidy to the better off.

Any proposal to reduce the subsidy to higher education will be politically unpopular. Moreover, as Brian Abel-Smith has pointed out, the revenue gains from either a graduate tax or from loan repayments will accrue to the government *after* the one that introduced the reform.[12] Hence it is important to consider these proposals only in conjunction with those for improving pre-school leaving age education. If all the reforms are introduced as a package, then the purpose of the whole could be better appreciated.

Housing

Housing policies are of two kinds: those designed to help owner-occupiers and those aimed at tenants (council or private). The first mostly consist of tax exemptions of one kind or another and favour the better off; the second take the form of direct grants or rebates and favour the worse off. An obvious way of improving the overall redistributive impact of housing policy is therefore to switch public expenditure from the first to the second.

By now it is commonplace among social reformers to argue for the abolition of tax subsidies to owner-occupiers. There is less agreement concerning the way in which this might be done. Some argue for the abolition of the tax relief on mortgage interest payments. Others advocate the re-introduction of taxation of the 'imputed income' on housing (imputed income, roughly, is the rent that an owner-occupied house would fetch if it were rented – and which the owner-occupier, by virtue of his ownership, can avoid paying). The two are mutually exclusive: for if imputed income is taxed, then mortgage interest payments – as part of the cost of obtaining that income – should be allowable as a deduction.

Of the two possibilities, taxing imputed income is theoretically superior, but practically and politically inferior. It would be difficult to explain to taxpayers; it would be difficult accurately to assess imputed income in every case; and it would have unfortunate transition costs (most of the initial burden would fall on the elderly, who have paid off their mortgages and hence have high imputed incomes).

Mortgage interest relief on the other hand is already widely perceived as an anomaly. Through the imposition of the £25,000 limit in 1974, it is already being reduced; that limit would now be over £60,000 if it had been raised in line with inflation. The people most affected by its withdrawal are on the whole those best able to pay: the better off with larger mortgages. Although the savings to the Exchequer might not be as great as if imputed income were taxed, they would nonetheless be sizeable: £1,110 million in 1978–9.[13]

The savings made from closing this tax loophole could be used – in whole or in part – to raise the general subsidy to council housing, and to increase the generosity of the rent rebate and allowance schemes. If they were all used for this purpose they could have a considerable impact. If, for instance in 1978–9, mortgage interest tax relief had been abolished this would have permitted a doubling of the subsidies to the rent rebate and allowance scheme without any net increase in public housing expenditure.[14]

Before we leave housing, we should comment on the redistributive effect of the most controversial aspect of current housing policy: the sale of council houses. Prospective purchasers, although certain to be among the better off council tenants, are still likely to have below average income. Hence council house sales could temporarily improve the redistributive impact of housing policy – so long as the tax subsidy to the new owner-occupiers plus any capital gain made through purchasing the house at a discount was greater than the subsidy they received as a council tenant. If the reforms just discussed were carried out, then there would be little or no tax subsidy; hence the question would depend on whether any capital gain outweighed the value of the tenant subsidy, summed appropriately over the remaining years of the tenancy. Since under our proposals this subsidy would be substantially increased, the outcome is by no means certain. One calculation suggests that, even if the level of subsidy remained the same as now, the average council tenant in 1982 would receive a larger public subsidy through remaining a tenant for twenty-five years than by buying his house at a discount of £5,000.[15]

Public transport
Public subsidies to rail users (British Rail and the London underground) massively favour the better off. The subsidies to bus travellers are more equally distributed, but even they do not benefit the poor as much as they do the rest of the population. A major reason for this is the existence of commuter services. Generally, the higher the income or occupational status, the further is the distance travelled to work. The very poor, the old, the unemployed and many single parents do not go to work at all. Manual workers often live close to their work. Professionals, employers and managers, on the other hand, usually live in the suburbs and travel into central city offices by rail, or a combination of rail and bus.

Commuter services are expensive to run. To cope effectively with the morning and evening peak periods, they need massive amounts of rolling stock and (in the case of the railways) a complex infra-structure of track and signalling. But all this capital equipment is only used intensively for about five hours out of the twenty-four; for the rest of the day, much of it lies idle. Commuter services are therefore substantial loss makers.

An obvious way to improve redistribution, therefore, would be not to increase the subsidy to commuters (as did the GLC in 1981), but substantially to reduce it. Indeed, the only way to correct the pro-rich distribution of public transport subsidies would be to eliminate them entirely, and to run public transport on a break-even basis. However, redistribution is not the only aim of social policy. The promotion of social and economic efficiency is another; and there are two important reasons why, on efficiency grounds, a break-even policy would be undesirable. The first of these is that many forms of public transport have high fixed costs (for instance, railways have high costs of installation and maintenance of track); and it is a standard proposition within economics that the efficient pricing policy for an industry with high fixed costs will be one that requires a subsidy. Secondly, the existence of public transport reduces road-use, particularly in peak hours. Eliminating the subsidy would therefore mean greater congestion and greater costs for the community as a whole.

A proposal that would reduce the need for a public transport subsidy because of the costs of congestion, and would be desirable on redistributive grounds, is the introduction of some form of pricing for road use. The reason why there is excessive congestion on the roads is because road travel, as well as public transport, is also heavily subsidised. In particular, motorists travelling in the rush hour do not have to pay directly for the costs they inflict on other travellers at that time through their contribution to traffic congestion. They will tend to over-use the road system, particularly at peak hours. An obvious remedy therefore is to levy a charge that is directly related to their use of the system. This would discourage road use, reduce congestion, increase the use (and hence the revenues) of public transport and hence reduce the need for public transport subsidies. Moreover, the cost would be borne primarily by the better off; for car ownership and use (particularly in central cities) is still far more widespread among the wealthier parts of the community than it is among the poorer.

Nor is such an idea, as many might think, quite impractical. In Singapore, a charge is levied on cars entering the central area during the morning rush hour. Its effects have been dramatic. Following its introduction, there was a 50 per cent decline in total traffic during the charge period: the volume of passenger cars alone declined by nearly three-quarters. Car pools nearly doubled, and bus ridership increased by 10 to 15 per cent. The system generated revenue at the rate of £1 million per year.[16]

Singapore is somewhat exceptional in that it is geographically compact and with relatively few entrances to the central area. But similar schemes could be – and have been – devised for larger, more spread-out cities. An elaborate, multi-price system has been proposed for Los Angeles. Nearer home, in 1974, the GLC produced an investigation into a proposed 'Supplementary Licensing Scheme' for London.[17] Motorists planning to drive within an area of about eight square miles in the city centre between 9 am and 6 pm would have to buy a licence, to be displayed on the windscreen, at a cost of approximately £1 per day. There would be special treatment for residents, commercial vehicles and disadvantaged groups such as the disabled. Enforcement would be undertaken by the police or traffic wardens in the ordinary course of their duties.

Again, the likely outcome was impressive. It was predicted that the scheme would: (a) reduce traffic in central London by one third; (b) increase public transport revenues by about £18 million (about £50 million at today's prices); and (c) generate revenue of about £45 million (about £140 million at today's prices).

The revenue raised by such a scheme would go to subsidise capital expenditure on public transport. This would overcome the problem that an efficient pricing policy might not cover the fixed costs of a public transport system, and allow the public transport operator to break-even on its operating costs.

An agenda for social services reform

Any review of the figures showing the distributional impact of the social services leaves at least one clear impression. Policies involving subsidies whose distribution is dependent upon people's decision to consume the good or use the service concerned favour the better off. Public transport, health care, continuing education and owner-occupied housing, all are subsidised, all are distributed in whole or in part according to people's decisions to use or consume them, and all have a distribution that is pro-rich.

The reasons for this are not hard to find. Unless it is one of those rare commodities whose consumption falls as income rises, the better off will always purchase more of a commodity than the worse off, and hence, if it is subsidised, obtain more of the subsidy. This will be true even of goods provided free of charge, such as continuing education or health care under the National Health Service. There is always some private expenditure involved in using even a free service, if only in the form of income foregone during the period of use: expenditure that will weigh more heavily on the poor than the rich. Moreover, the better off, being generally better educated, more articulate and more confident, will be more able to manipulate even those parts of the system ostensibly not under their control, more able to ensure that the GP refers them to the specialist, that the hospital provides them with the appropriate facilities, that their children go to the right schools and the right universities.

Any reform designed to *improve* the redistributive power of the welfare state should not involve any increase in the *subsidies* for these services, and may well involve a decrease. Instead, it should concentrate scarce fiscal resources upon those areas of policy whose distribution is determined not simply by the individual's decision whether or not to consume, but by other criteria. More specifically, there should be:

(a)   A strengthening of the RAWP process for re-allocating health care resources between regions;

(b)   An extension of state-provided nursery education to all children aged between three and four;

(c)   The raising of the school leaving age from sixteen to seventeen and/or the extension of industrial training on the lines advocated by the Labour Party;

(d)   The introduction of a graduate tax;

(e)   The gradual abolition of mortgage tax relief through the maintenance of the present £25,000 limit;

(f)   An increase in the general subsidy to council tenants, and an expansion of the rent rebate and allowance system;

(g)   A reduction in the current operating subsidies to commuter services;

(h)   The levying of charges on vehicles entering cities at peak periods and using the revenue raised to subsidise capital expenditure on public transport.

Implementation of some or all of these would remove the worse injustices of current social policy, and make the social services concerned significantly more egalitarian in their immediate impact. Cost estimates suggest that the proposals for a particular sector taken together will not necessarily involve increased expenditure on that sector. Rather they are primarily methods of re-allocating existing expenditure so as to make social policy more redistributive. The extension of nursery education and the raising of the school leaving age or other post-sixteen training plans could be financed (in the long run) by the revenue from a graduate tax. The abolition of tax relief for owner-occupiers could finance the increase in general subsidy to council tenants. And the phasing out of operating subsidies to public transport and the introduction of a road pricing system could generate enough funds to finance (probably substantial) capital expenditure on public transport.

A caveat

Desirable as many of these reforms might be for the outcomes of the social services themselves, too much should not be expected of them. In particular, they should not be seen to have much impact on poverty or on overall social and economic inequalities. There is too much evidence from too many sources that inequality in education is created by inequality in the wider society, rather than the other way around. Nor will altering the housing subsidy system eliminate inequalities in housing itself. The squalor and decay in poor areas arises not so much from deficiencies in subsidy policy, but rather from the poverty of their inhabitants. Since the poor travel relatively little, either by car or public transport, changes in the system of subsidising transport will have little impact on their lives. Rather, it is only by the direct redistribution of private income that poverty can be eliminated and overall inequality significantly reduced. That is where new spending and innovations in social policy should be primarily addressed.

Nothing in this chapter implies that the welfare state should be dismantled and its key institutions handed back to private enterprise. There are excellent reasons for maintaining state ownership and control of health services, institutions of higher education, council houses and public transport. Such control prevents exploitation by private monopolies; it permits and facilitates social and economic planning; and, by reducing the area where the profit motive is king, it helps moderate the baleful influence of greed and self-interest. But the preservation of state *control* does not necessarily imply the preservation of existing systems of state *subsidy*. It is perfectly feasible to have one without the other. The state does not *have* to provide its services free or at subsidised prices. What is being argued here, essentially, is that redistribution policy should concern itself less with subsidising services and more with 'subsidising' the *poor* – or, as I would prefer to put it, acknowledging their legitimate claim on a greater share of the nation's income and wealth.

Notes and references

1.   Most of the figures in Table 6.1 can be found in J. Le Grand, *The Strategy of Equality*, George Allen and Unwin, 1982. Specific references are: council housing and tax subsidies to owner-occupiers, pp. 88–9; National Health Service, p. 26; primary, secondary, non-university higher, and university education, p. 58; public transport subsidies, p. 109. There are no estimates for the distribution of public

expenditure on rent allowances and nursery education. However, the former are means-tested and must favour the poor; and since the use of the latter appears to be equally distributed (Office of Population Censuses and Surveys, 1980, p. 110), it is likely that public expenditure is also broadly equal.

2. *Ibid.* chapter 3.

3. Department of Health and Social Security, *Sharing Resources for Health in England*, HMSO, 1976.

4. D. Black, *Inequalities in Health*, Department of Health and Social Security, 1980, chapter 6.

5. Trades Union Congress, *Charter on Facilities for the Under-Fives*, TUC, 1979. F. Cripps, *et al.*, *Manifesto: A Radical Strategy for Britain's Future*, Pan Books, 1981.

6. Office of Population Censuses and Surveys, *General Household Survey*, 1978, HMSO, 1980, p. 110.

7. In 1978–9 there were 516,000 children attending full-time or part-time maintained nursery education in Great Britain: *The Government's Expenditure Plans, 1980–81 to 1983–84*, Cmnd 7841, HMSO, 1980, p. 94. This comprised 38 per cent of all three- and four-year-olds in the population (*ibid.*) implying that 884,000 were not attending. According to the Department of Education and Science, *Statistics of Education 1978*, vol. 5, HMSO, 1980, the cost per (full-time equivalent) pupil in nursery classes in primary schools was £508. To provide (half-time) nursery education to these children would therefore have cost £214,376,000. Total current expenditure on education in 1978–9 was £8,290 million (*The Government's Expenditure Plans*, p. 91).

8. M. Blaug, C. Dougherty and G. Psacharopoulos, 'The Distribution of Schooling and the Distribution of Earnings: Evidence from the British ROSLA of 1972', London School of Economics, 1980, *Manchester School*, forthcoming.

9. Calculated from the same sources, and in the same way as, the equivalent figure for nursery education in note 7.

10. Department of Employment, *A New Training Initiative: A Programme For Action*, Cmnd 8455, HMSO, 1981, p. 3.

11. In 1978–9, total current expenditure on further and higher education was £2,377 million (*The Government's Expenditure Plans*, p. 90). The total cost of raising the school leaving age and extending nursery education in that year as calculated earlier would have been £1,414 million: about 59 per cent of the further and higher education total.

12. Personal communication. See also Howard Glennerster, 'A Graduate Tax', *Higher Education Review*, no. 1, vol. 1, 1968.

13. Board of Inland Revenue, *Inland Revenue Statistics, 1979*, table 1.10, p. 15. Another tax loophole, the exemption of the proceeds from the sale of owner-occupied housing from capital gains tax, is now of considerably less significance than it was, due to the indexation of capital gains for tax purposes announced in the 1982 budget.

14. The rent rebate and allowance scheme cost £556 million in 1978–9.

15. R.V.F. Robinson, 'Housing Tax-Expenditures, Subsidies and the Distribution of Income', *Manchester School*, 1981, estimated the average subsidy to council tenants in 1977 as £353. In terms of 1982 prices, this would be about £550. The net present value of a stream of subsidies of £550 p.a. over a period of twenty-five years at a discount rate of 10 per cent is approximately £5,500.

16. F.R. Anderson *et al.*, *Environmental Improvement Through Economic Incentives*, Johns Hopkins Press, Baltimore, 1978.

17. Greater London Council, *Supplementary Licensing*, Greater London Council, 1974.

7   Redistribution and the Tax System
by Charles Greenaway

A high priority for the next Labour Government will be to redistribute the burden of tax away from poorer people towards the rich and better off. However, because Mrs Thatcher's government has failed to deliver its promise to reduce taxation – except for the privileged few of the wealthy and very high earners, most people now pay a higher proportion of their incomes in tax than before 1979 – carrying through this priority will be more difficult. Put simply, taking a large number of poor people out of income tax and reducing the burden for the less well off is made much more expensive (measured in terms of tax revenue foregone) by this particular Conservative failure. Even a Labour Chancellor of the Exchequer wedded to large-scale reflation of the economy will have awkward choices to offer the party when it comes to social policy objectives in the area of income redistribution.

It is the aim in this chapter to argue the case for raising tax thresholds – the level where people start paying income tax – and adjusting the rates of income tax to make the burden of tax more progressive. This chapter looks at some of the implications involved and also examines several proposals for tax reform to establish how they might fit into a socialist tax policy.[1]

I shall try to argue the case without including large amounts of supporting statistical evidence. Much of this is readily available elsewhere, and there is a good chance – in the tax area at least – that many of the details will be overtaken by events by the time of publication, let alone by the next general election which may not be held until mid-1984.

Tax policy is viewed here mainly from a social policy standpoint. Tax policy is, of course, vitally significant to economic activity, but I would suggest that it is high time that the link between tax policy and social policy was given much greater importance in economic decision-making. General economic policy may demand such and such a level of tax revenue in any given year, but the tenets and objectives of social policy should figure in how that revenue is raised.

Changing the tax burden

Conservative record

No authoritative studies will be available for some time showing the full effects of the Conservative Government's policies on the distribution of the tax burden, but from what is already known, the direction of change is certainly a transfer of the balance of taxation away from the better off towards poorer people. The 1979 budget brought in by Sir Geoffrey Howe, the Conservative Chancellor, started the process through very large cuts in the rates of income tax paid by those with top incomes. Hundreds of millions of pounds were spent on this policy with the declared object of improving financial incentives at the upper end of the income scale. The top *marginal* rate of tax – the proportion of any increase in income paid as tax – on earnings was reduced from 83 per cent to 60 per cent, and the starting points at which the higher rates of tax begin were raised substantially.

For most other people the 1979 Tory income tax changes were probably broadly neutral when account is taken of the rise in Value Added Tax to 15 per cent (from a mixed rate of 8 per cent and 12 per cent, according to expenditure category). These and other rises in indirect taxes largely offset the reduced income tax that Howe offered people: the standard rate was cut from 33 per cent to 30 per cent, and personal allowances were raised but Howe also abolished the lower 25 per cent rate of tax on the first slice of income.

Since then, however, the picture has worsened, mainly because of the failure to keep personal allowances rising as fast as inflation. Tax thresholds have now fallen to ridiculously low levels when measured against earnings. For example, in 1982 a married man or single parent began to pay income tax at a level equal to about 30 per cent of average male earnings, whilst for a single person tax began at not much more than 20 per cent of average earnings. This means that a married man or lone parent started paying tax at about £47 a week and a single person at about £30 a week. What are the effects of this?

First, and most obviously, more people are brought into tax: the very low paid and some amongst the retired and sick who would not otherwise have paid tax. This is not only an unfair burden on the poorest, but it also adds to the cost of administering the tax system.

Second, the tax burden increases on every taxpayer. Since everyone who pays tax benefits from having part of her/his income offset by personal allowances, failure to increase these in line with inflation raises everyone's tax bill. But the tax bill does not go up in equal proportion for all: the greatest rises happen to the poor who paid comparatively little or no tax before and to the better off who pay the higher marginal rates of tax. However, this latter effect has not been large enough to wipe out all the gains made by the top income earners in May 1979, and many remain significantly better off than before that date.

Third, the structure of incentives for the less well paid is worsened. A drop in the tax threshold widens the range of earnings over which both tax is payable and means tested benefits for those in work are reduced when their incomes rise. The combined effect of tax and withdrawal of benefit as incomes rise can mean that an increase in gross pay leaves a low paid person very little better off – or possibly even worse off – when increased tax and loss of benefits are taken into account. This 'poverty trap' is not caused solely by low income tax thresholds – means tested benefits and national insurance contributions are also important – and the trap existed before this government came to power, but the policy of allowing tax thresholds to fall has aggravated the position and made its cure more difficult.

Official statistics show that relatively few people are affected by the poverty trap – no more than a few per cent of families and of single people. But a few per cent still means that several hundred thousand low income people have marginal tax rates of over 50 per cent, and around 100,000 have marginal tax rates of 75 per cent or more. In addition, these estimates relate mostly to the period *before* this government came to power, and later figures are likely to show a considerable increase.

Perhaps it is more important, though, that many people who are low paid feel that the tax system operates unfairly against them. Both their incentive to increase their earnings, or to return to work if unemployed, have been seriously eroded by this present government's policies. Many low paid people acutely resent this. Cynics may say that this does not matter when several millions are unemployed, since there is a shortage of work to do; but no government should plan its tax policy on such mean calculation.

Total tax policy

In addition to the changes outlined above, the Conservative Government has pressed ahead with other tax initiatives. One of these, the taxation of single and married people, is the subject of a later chapter. The main ones to note here are various changes to capital taxation, which have greatly reduced the effective burden of the already relatively low taxes on wealth in the country, and changes in the financing of the National Insurance Fund.

National Insurance contributions have risen mainly to meet the cost of higher unemployment but partly also because the Government has cut the Treasury contribution to the Fund. Once earnings pass a certain level (£29.50 per week in 1982), all earnings – including those below that level – are subject to contributions until the 'upper earnings limit' is reached. This 'upper earnings limit' is set at about one and a half times average earnings, and people with earnings above it pay contributions only on their earnings up to that limit. The overall effect is to make employees' national insurance contributions a *regressive* source of finance, because for those earning above the upper limit national insurance contributions are a lump sum tax on being employed – like a poll tax – which declines as a proportion of income as earnings rise higher. To be progressive, the rate of national insurance contributions would have to increase, not reduce to zero, for such high earners, and possibly apply to other sources of income.

The increase in employees' national insurance contributions is a regressive change. Compared with 1977, the rate of employees' contributions has risen from $5\frac{3}{4}$ per cent of earnings (up to the upper limit) to $8\frac{3}{4}$ per cent of earnings in 1982. Since there is no equivalent to the tax free share provided by the personal allowance in the case of insurance contributions, most workers, including the lower paid, have seen their proportionate contributions rise by over a half in five years. Such an increase in income tax would surely have made headlines! Working people are being made to pay more by a different, less newsworthy, route. (Reform of national insurance contributions is discussed towards the end of the chapter.)

This emphasises that income tax is only one of several major components of total government revenue. For the socialist interested in the allocation of tax burdens this poses a considerable problem. Whilst the immediate distributional effects of changes in income tax, employee national insurance contributions and some capital taxes may usually be fairly clear, the effects of changes in 'indirect' taxes – such as VAT, corporation tax and other taxes on companies – are less certain. Much academic debate surrounds the question of who really bears the cost of, say, employers' insurance contributions or the national insurance surcharge. Is it the company itself (that is the shareholders through lower dividends), the customer (through higher prices) or the workers (through the company's need to pay lower wages)? Although there appears to be no generally valid answer to these questions, it is necessary to keep in mind developments in the whole range of tax policy when considering the distribution of income.

Future Labour Chancellors could do worse than present once a year a statement of their total tax policy outlining the goals they are seeking in each revenue-raising area, in particular where there is a desired distributional effect involved. This should include local rates.

A further difficulty to note is that some taxes, such as excise duties, may be desirable in order to limit certain activities (drinking, smoking) and may raise much revenue in doing so but be distributionally regressive. This re-emphasises the need to make the rest of those taxes where the immediate distributional effects are relatively well understood as progressive as possible. This applies especially to income tax.

Limits to action

The next Labour Government's freedom to act on tax policy will be limited by Mrs Thatcher's government's own failure to raise tax thresholds in line with inflation, by the demands of macro-economic policy and by worries about effects on work incentives. This section deals with each in turn.

Low tax thresholds

As noted earlier, one of the main effects of allowing tax thresholds to fall relative to earnings is to increase every taxpayer's tax bill. In an inflationary era this used to be an easy ploy for Chancellors of the Exchequer, since they could offer the public some rise in the money value of the personal allowances which was nevertheless less than would have been due on account of inflation. The famous 'Rooker-Wise' amendment put a stop to such activity, but in his 1981 Budget Sir Geoffrey Howe used the Conservative majority in the House of Commons to override Rooker-Wise and not only failed to raise allowances in line with inflation, but failed to raise them at all.

The additional revenue he obtained from every taxpayer may have helped to balance Howe's books for the financial year 1981/2 – and without the political embarrassment of raising the standard rate of tax – but it made the task of future reforming Chancellors exceptionally difficult. To raise tax thresholds means that all twenty-odd million taxpayers benefit because the value of everyone's personal allowance increases. This causes a large loss of revenue that must either be part of a reflationary economic policy, or be paid for by other tax changes, or be paid for by public expenditure cuts. Restoring or raising tax thresholds also has the undesirable effect of giving most benefit to the most well off, because the value of personal allowances to an individual taxpayer is directly related to the highest marginal rate of income tax that she/he pays. Those paying the highest rates of income tax benefit most from increases in allowances.

As far as cost is concerned, this has to be considered mainly in the context of macro-economic policy (see below), and a future Labour Government would not want simply to cut public spending to pay for tax cuts. But there are income tax changes that can go some way to limiting the cost of raising tax thresholds and could also offset the greater gains going to the well-to-do.

The first and most obvious is that the structure of the *rates* of tax will have to be adjusted so that the better off continue to be liable to the higher rates and, indeed, those rates are themselves increased. There is no economic law (or magic) which dictates the optimum, detailed structure of tax rates, for example that the basic rate must be 30 per cent, and a future Labour Government will have to alter them as it sees fit. In addition, there is a case for lowering the starting points of the higher tax rates to the level where national insurance contributions cease to relate to earnings. At present, there is a considerable range of earnings at relatively high levels where taxable capacity is under-used. Earnings between the contribution ceiling and the start of the higher tax rates are liable only to the basic tax of 30 per cent.

A second step is to widen the tax base, or, in plain English, to reduce the amount of income that is exempted from tax through reliefs or is not taxed because it is not reported. Changes to tax reliefs are dealt with later in the section on tax reform, but phasing them out could bring in much revenue over a period of time. Cracking down on tax evasion and reducing the scope for tax avoidance are goals that must be pursued with much greater vigour than under this Tory Government. But despite estimates indicating that the extent of the unreported, informal, or so-called 'black economy' is growing, the assessment must be that any additional revenue obtained from this source is likely to be small in comparison to total revenue collected.

A third step would be to consider switching from the use of personal allowances as the tax threshold. If a taxpayer has no other reliefs, then at present she/he begins paying tax when her/his income rises above the personal allowance. This personal allowance is used for all taxpayers whatever their income, with one major exception. For tax payers aged sixty-five and over, an 'age allowance' is given: £2,070 in 1982 compared with the ordinary personal allowance of £1,565 in the case of a single person (£3,295 compared with £2,445 for a married couple). But only less well off pensioners benefit from this higher allowance because, after their income exceeds £6,700, the excess of the age allowance over the ordinary personal allowance is phased out. Over the next band of income of an elderly person is taxed at more than the standard rate, but once the excess benefit has been withdrawn further income is taxed at the basic rate of 30 per cent. These better off pensioners in practice have only the normal personal allowances enjoyed by the rest of the population.

The suggestion is that such a system could be extended to the rest of the population. Low income earners in general could benefit from a higher preferential personal allowance, and those below this higher allowance would be removed from income tax altogether. Better off people, however, would not benefit from the higher allowance but would continue to receive the basic personal allowance (though this could be at a higher level than that now in force).

One disadvantage could lie in the clawback of the excess part of the preferential allowance over the ordinary allowance which would increase the marginal rate of tax over a certain band of earnings. Below and above this band the basic rate of tax would apply.

No doubt the Inland Revenue would complain about administrative complexity (though this looks relatively minor). Such a step might also conflict with introducing a reduced rate band which many claim would help alleviate the poverty trap. It is a matter for consideration whether a reduced rate band or a preferential allowance of the type described here would do more to relieve the less well off of tax burdens and to improve their work incentives. Depending on the level of preferential allowance that could be afforded this proposal seems a potentially attractive option.

Macro-economic policy

A future Labour Government will be committed to trying to restore full employment and to creating economic recovery. Reflation through tax cuts may be part of this policy, but it has to be recognised that any tax cuts would need to be balanced against the needs for higher public spending and that the preferred policy may be to reduce, say, VAT rather than income tax in view of its direct effects on prices. The less room that the general economic strategy leaves for income tax cuts, the more will have to be done through raising the *rates* of income tax to pay for tax reform.

Effects on work incentives

Mrs Thatcher owed not a small part of her election victory in 1979 to the feeling that income tax was too high and to her implied suggestion that it could be brought down without damaging public expenditure. Part of the accompanying charges she and her supporters made was that high tax rates were weakening British industry; it was claimed there was insufficient financial incentive for British businessmen and for their senior staff. Would the package of higher tax thresholds and higher rates of tax on the better off advocated here bring back those bad old days?

Work incentives are a contentious issue, and sadly discussion of them sometimes gives the impression of a debate between the well off, who want to pay low taxes, and the rest, who want their own taxes as low as possible and the well off to pay more. However, serious academic study has been made of the problem, and this needs to be kept in mind.

When income tax rates rise, two effects occur. The *marginal* rate of tax on any additional income rises, so that the relative incentive to earn that extra income (if it requires foregoing one's own time) is reduced. But the *average* rate of tax also rises; that is, the total tax paid on a given level of income is higher and the taxpayer is worse off than before.

Given her/his existing financial commitments and a desire to maintain a certain living standard, the taxpayer has now relatively more incentive to earn income at the expense of her/his own time. The question to be solved is whether the effect of this rise on the marginal rate of tax (called by economists the 'substitution effect' because taxpayers may prefer to substitute leisure for income at the margin) outweighs the effect of the rise in the average rate of tax (called by economists the 'income effect' because the taxpayer's income has been reduced).

There are few unambiguous answers to this problem that can be derived from economic theory, but empirical studies tend to support the view that any net disincentive effects from raising tax rates are relatively very small or non-existent for most earners, and that the income effects described above are as important as the substitution effects. A study by the Institute for Fiscal Studies concerning top earners found very little evidence indeed of any serious adverse effects on companies due to lack of financial incentives for their senior managers under the last Labour Government's pay and tax policies.[2] This suggests that the taxable capacity of many upper income people is now under-utilised by this government's tax policies, and that taxes on the better off could be increased with little harm to the economy. This lesson needs to be well learned now in opposition, because, once the party is in government and higher taxes are imposed, a repeat performance can be expected of the various stories that were trotted out last time about managers allegedly leaving the country or cutting back on their efforts because of lack of sufficient financial reward. Like last time, these stories will be either mostly myths or apply to an insignificant proportion of people.

Tax reform

So far we have concentrated mainly on changing the allowances and rates that operate within the existing income tax system. Now we turn to several proposals for major reforms to the tax system. As far as tax administration is concerned, the Inland Revenue usually warns people thinking of changes that little of major consequence could be achieved before computerisation of PAYE is completed. This may not be until late in the 1980s. It is difficult as an outsider to judge how serious an obstacle to reform carrying out computerisation need be, but budding reformers should beware this possible obstruction.

Widening the tax base

At present several thousand million pounds of income go untaxed each year because the taxpayer is able to claim certain expenses against parts of her/his income. Two of these have come regularly under attack from

Fabian writers and those of similar persuasion: mortgage interest tax relief and relief given for life assurance and superannuation contributions.

Mortgage interest tax relief

Mortgage interest tax relief falls more properly under the heading of the financial treatment of housing. Its effects and desirability (or lack of it) should be judged in the context of subsidies to housing generally. Briefly, mortgage interest tax relief is criticised for the advantages it confers on owner-occupiers relative to tenants when tenants are usually the less well off, and for the adverse effects it has on the housing market. This favourable treatment causes house prices to be higher than they need be and distorts the house and property markets.

The last Labour Government limited the amount of loan on which relief could be claimed (to £25,000), which went some way to righting the anomalies involved. Holding the £25,000 limit constant over several years has reduced its real value, but upper income earners paying the higher rates of tax still benefit more than basic rate payers because it is the highest marginal rate (or rates) paid that determines the value of a tax relief or allowance.

Governments are reluctant to proceed too fast in abolishing this relief just because it has caused house prices to be higher than they otherwise would be. (The relief has been 'capitalised' into house values, to use the jargon.) Cutting back the relief severely – or abolishing it outright – could cause house prices to fall significantly, and some – maybe a large proportion of – recent purchasers would be left with homes worth less than their mortgage, as well as having considerably higher net outgoings.

The Conservative Government has in fact made some progress in this area. It is planned in April 1983 to convert mortgage tax relief into a direct subsidy to the building societies and banks which will allow them to charge borrowers lower interest rates on house loans up to £25,000. The tax allowance for mortgage interest will disappear for most people, but gross repayments to the building society or bank will be reduced by a similar amount to the value of tax relief now received. Mortgage holders will pay more tax, but their net income after mortgage costs should be broadly unchanged.

Is this a first step towards allowing governments to be more robust in their treatment of home buyers? One could speculate that next time interest rates go up, the cash available for subsidy will be limited so that the effective value of the old tax relief falls below the 30 per cent level. Then, after interest rates go down again the new percentage of subsidy – say 25 per cent – could be retained. The process could continue for many years, but, as stated before, this is only speculation.

In case this appears to Fabian eyes too good to be true, the Conservative Government is pledged to retain the additional tax relief that benefits only higher rate taxpayers. They will still be able to claim the balance between the new subsidy and what they could have obtained under the old system of tax allowances. This featherbedding of the better off should be an early target for the next Labour Government.

Life assurance and superannuation relief

The reliefs here are worth 15 per cent of any life assurance premium (up to a limit) and 30 per cent of superannuation contributions (more if the employee pays higher rate tax). These reliefs have been justified on the grounds that they encourage people to make provision for the future. Perhaps their main effect has been to establish the life companies and pension funds as the important financial institutions that they are, owning large sections of British industry (a majority of company equities) and much else besides.

The domination of the savings market that these institutions have attained and the diversion of saving funds towards them have been criticised on economic efficiency grounds. More importantly for distributional concerns, these reliefs suffer the same disadvantage as mortgage interest relief: the better off benefit disproportionately because they can afford more of these forms of saving. In addition, it is worth noting that, when calculating the terms on which certain pension schemes can contract out of the national insurance earnings related pension, no account is taken of this tax relief. In contrast, insurance contributions do not count for tax relief. Thus, it appears that the contracted-out employee benefits from favourable treatment (relative to the employee who stays in the full state scheme) because of tax relief.

Review of the purposes of this form of relief is well overdue. There is a strong *prima facie* case for phasing it out. This could apply to new life contracts starting after a certain date, although existing contracts may have to continue benefiting from relief.

An expenditure tax

An alternative to extending the tax base is to exempt all saving from tax. Tax would be levied on the difference between income and saving – by definition on expenditure. This would encourage saving relative to spending. Progressive rates of tax could be levied depending on each person's level of expenditure.

The proposal has in recent years been given renewed force by the Meade Report from the Institute for Fiscal Studies. Whilst it may have much theoretical attraction, especially in its neutrality towards forms of saving, it would seem likely to suffer as many practical disadvantages as the present income tax. In addition, tax exemption of savings runs counter to the general socialist view that reliefs for saving tend to favour the better off. There seems no strong case for giving this proposal priority. Since Professor Meade is an SDP adviser, the idea may gain support there.

Tax credits

It is ten years since the Heath Government published their Green Paper on a tax credit system. Unfortunately for the debate on tax reform, the Green Paper presented a fraudulent prospectus. Generous giveaways were promised for the future without any clear indiction of how they would be financed. If paid for from economic growth or reduced in real value by inflation, then the value of the benefits to be conferred on the poor would have been eroded in relative terms by the end of the five years required to start the scheme. Not only was this aspect of the distributional intention unclear, but much of the proposed giveaway would have gone to above average income taxpayers. Even with the large cost involved at the time, there would have been only a small reduction in dependence on means tested benefits, and only one benefit – family income supplement – would have been partly abolished. Family income supplement was to have been retained for the self-employed because they, like many of the poorest families, were actually outside the tax credit field. To be inside the tax credit system required that one be an earner or receive a national insurance benefit.

Despite such an inauspicious start, the tax credit idea lingers on. In its 1979 manifesto the Conservative Party claimed it as one of that party's goals, when it could be afforded. More lately, some people on the left have come to consider tax credits as a possible way out of difficulties with means tested benefits. The Liberal Party has consistently supported the idea and wanted to go much further than the Tories.

The tax credit idea is attractive because it appears to offer a new automatic and direct benefit to low income people who are covered by the scheme. It would require no separate means testing as, say, family income supplement does, and would not suffer the problem of low take-up of entitlements that is endemic to means tested benefits especially for those in work.

The following example shows how the 1972 variety of tax credits would operate. At present, tax paid depends on the amount by which income exceeds the personal allowance. If income is less than the personal allowance no tax is paid at all. Under tax credits, the personal allowance is replaced by a credit which is used to offset gross tax liability. 'Gross tax' is calculated against all income received – there is no personal allowance – and is compared with the amount of credit allocated to the taxpayer, which depends on family type. Net tax to be paid is calculated as the gross tax less the credit. Usually net tax will be due to the Exchequer, but for low income people the credit may exceed the gross tax. In this case they receive the balance of their credit over the gross tax as a 'negative tax', or additional benefit.

Clearly the financial effect on low income families would depend on the value of the credits and the rate of tax. If it is assumed that the existing basic rate of tax is retained, it is possible to calculate the level of credit that would leave no existing taxpayer better or worse off. (This is given by dividing the tax allowance by the rate of tax.) Now, even back in 1972, when tax allowances were much higher relative to earnings, simply giving credits at this level would have been of very little help to the less well off who came within the scheme, and it was therefore necessary to raise the credits considerably above these levels. Given that personal allowances have fallen relatively since then, the help that could be given by converting the existing personal allowances into credits would be extremely small, and only a very large rise in credits above that level would be of much assistance to the less well off covered by the scheme.

If redistribution of income in this way is acceptable – especially if those hitherto left outside the scheme can be brought in – then the credit levels can be raised, but this benefits all taxpayers because the credits themselves are not taxable. The cost of this generosity can be met through a rise in the basic rate of tax. It was calculated that the limited 1972 scheme would have required $3\frac{1}{2}$ percentage points added to the basic rate of pay for the Green Paper credits, and probably more would be required today to achieve similar effects. Yet raising the basic rate in this way also creates substantial losses for people with average incomes and above.

Tax credits would also introduce new characteristics into the tax system that might not be desirable. First, tax credits are a form of negative income tax, and it is right to question whether 'negative tax' should be paid at all as a benefit. What looks right from an economist's equation or diagram is not necessarily correct for practical social policy. 'Negative tax' would be a means tested benefit – means tested, that is, through the income tax. It may be argued that it is better to give people more income in their own right (such as higher pensions or child benefit) and to tax that where appropriate in conjunction with other sources of income under the existing scheme. In other words, the tax credit paraphernalia is not required. This was the option chosen by the last Labour Government when it introduced child benefit to replace the old child tax allowances and in its policies to raise pension levels.

Secondly, the efficient operation of a tax credit scheme would require that a single basic rate of tax be charged over a long band of income.

Under the existing system of Pay As You Earn (PAYE), tax paid during the course of the year is automatically related to previous income in the year and takes account of most changes in earned income that may happen, due, for example, to pay rises, stoppages, etc. This applies whatever the marginal rate of tax applicable to the individual's income, and it is possible to have progressive marginal tax rates operated in this way through PAYE.

Under tax credits, existing PAYE would cease, and the credit itself would become the instrument for ensuring that tax paid was calculated to take account of changes during the year. Provided income does not move from one tax rate band to another, the credit allows the correct tax to be levied within each pay period, and there is no need for reference to income in previous pay periods. To use the jargon, tax credits are a non-cumulative system, whilst PAYE is cumulative because it has to calculate tax paid in any one pay period with reference to data on previous pay and tax since the start of the financial year.

The upshot of this is that tax credits would most likely – although not necessarily – lead to a more rigid structure of tax rates, with only a very few top tax payers at more than the basic rate. A graded structure of progressive rates across all income levels would not be possible with tax credits, unless it was also acceptable that large numbers of taxpayers would pay too much tax during the year and have to claim back over-paid tax after the end of the financial year. (Non-cumulative tax collection without a long range of basic rate tax leads to people paying too much tax as they move between tax rate bands.) This would in turn lead either to increased workload for the Inland Revenue, or to self-assessment, whereby the taxpayer makes her/his own tax assessment after the end of the year and claims back over-payments of tax. (Under-payment would be rare.)

Britain has had PAYE since the Second World War, but few other countries have a system like it. Most appear to have non-cumulative systems.

The view of this writer is that, in general, tax credits may be a sensible step forward for tax administration at some stage, but their usefulness in social policy is limited and their adoption could restrict the scope for redistributive policies because of the rigidities they could cause. However, the idea of using the tax system to deliver benefits to those with low incomes need not be totally rejected. If much higher value universal social security benefits are rejected on grounds of cost, then it is possible that the tax system could be used to identify and pay income-related benefits – or credits. As income rises, the income-related credit could be reduced at a faster rate than the basic rate of tax until it was extinguished, similar in a way to the preferential tax allowance described earlier. Socialists may not find this an attractive alternative to more generous universal benefits, but it may be the best a Labour Government could provide.

Merging national insurance and income tax

One step further down the tax credit road is the idea of merging national insurance contributions and income tax. A main criticism of national insurance contributions is their regressive effect, and a merger could allow a more progressive structure. Whether national insurance benefits would still be awarded on the basis of contribution or tax paid is a related, but separate, issue. A still further step along the road would be to abolish national insurance and other benefits as well and to have credits at levels that replace or supersede the old benefits. A new 'Department of Tax and Social Security' (DTSS) could run the scheme. scheme.

At this point one is considering very large structural changes indeed, the distributional consequences of which would require close study. Most governments are timid about even small identifiable losses that their policies induce amongst the majority of the population. Switching national insurance contributions to a tax basis with a personal allowance exemption would reduce the burden very significantly on lower paid workers, but require a considerable increase in the rate of contribution/tax. This could cause substantial losses amongst average to higher paid workers. A future Labour Government may have to face up to such a change if it is serious about redistributing the tax and contribution burden in a significant way.

Conclusion

The first main priority of the next Labour Government in tax policy must be to redistribute the tax burden away from the less well off towards the better off who are now paying too little in tax. Although most interest will be on changes to income tax where the distributional effects are usually the most clearly identifiable, the effects of all revenue sources – including national insurance contributions – need to be taken into account. However, there can be no doubt that the room for manoeuvre will be severely limited because of the Conservative Government's mismanagement of the economy and of public finance.

Amongst the recommendations considered were:

(a)   A greater role for social objectives in setting tax policy;

(b)   Raising tax thresholds and adjustments to the higher rates of tax to produce a more progressive structure;

(c)   A preferential tax allowance for all low income people that would be reduced as income rises (similar to the age allowance);

(d)   A possible extension of the income tax base by phasing out relief for life assurance and superannuation contributions and greater efforts to prevent tax evasion and tax avoidance;

(e)   Disallowing mortgage interest relief against higher rate tax;

(f)   An annual statement of total tax policy indicating the objectives for each revenue-raising area, including distributional goals where relevant.

The above seem most worthy of further consideration for a future Labour Government. Some limited development of income-related tax credits may also be advisable if the alternative of much more generous universal benefits cannot be afforded. Finally, restructuring the finances of the national insurance scheme looks desirable to place them on a more equitable and more progressive footing. The distributional consequences of such a reform would require careful assessment.

References

1. Wealth taxes have not been discussed here but should be an important element in long-term redistribution. Their contribution to the revenue needed to finance social services is less important.
2. Institute for Fiscal Studies, *Companies, Incentives and Senior Managers*, CUP, 1981.

Editor's Note

A super means test solution?

More recently the Social Democratic Party has announced its 'solution' to the complex problem of the poverty trap. (*Attacking Poverty*, SDP, 1982). The short-term answer is a new all inclusive means tested benefit, the Basic Benefit, which would replace housing benefits, free school meals and family income supplement. For pensioners and the unemployed it is essentially a renamed Supplementary Benefit. The value of the benefit would reduce as a family's income rose by 45p for each extra pound earned (30p for those without children).

Is it a solution? The benefit would have to be claimed at a local authority office for those in work but paid by the employer. Thus it would not be automatically granted, carrying many of the problems of the present means tested benefits. It would be phased out more slowly than the benefits the poor now receive as their incomes rise, but the result would be to bring far more people within the means test net, and some, notably many one-child families, would be worse off. All in all this scarcely seems the solution we have all been waiting for. In the long run we are offered an automated tax benefit which the authors admit is 'at a very tentative stage'. It raises, but does not solve, the issues discussed in this chapter.

8 Tackling Inequalities at Their Source
by Chris Pond and Jennie Popay

352 3

Introduction

In their pursuit of a fairer society, post-war Labour Governments have tended to concentrate on a twin strategy of developing the social services and using the tax and the social security system to redistribute resources from the rich to the poor. This 'Strategy of Equality', as R.H. Tawney described it,[1] allowed social and economic forces to determine the initial distribution of resources and then intervened after the event to eradicate the worst effects of those inequalities. Yet as Julian Le Grand has shown (Chapter 6), the approach has been disappointing in its results. The distribution of income and wealth is not markedly different from that which existed in the early post-war years. Poverty, measured in relative terms, remains and is, indeed, increasing. The social services, the tax system and the social security system have not resulted in a major redistribution of resources from the richer to the poorer members of society. Instead they have tended to reflect the social and economic inequalities of the society on which they were superimposed. However, the limitations of such an approach based on after-the-event redistribution suggest that any attempt to 'remake social policy' should include some element of direct intervention to influence the distribution of resources *at source*.

In this chapter we explore the possibilities of such an approach. First we examine the record on poverty and inequality since the war to assess what has been achieved. We then consider why policies directed at redistribution have not been more successful. This leads us to a third question: why, despite this lack of success, have Labour Governments preferred to concentrate on after-the-event redistribution, rather than intervening directly in the processes that generate inequality? Answers to this question are of central importance in determining future strategy. We then briefly examine the policies which might be adopted as a means of direct intervention in the determination of incomes. We do not assume that such policies will be sufficient on their own, or that they could be implemented without quite substantial changes in values and in the way our economy and our society works. They must be part of a package of policies that comprise a new social strategy. We do believe they are an essential part of that package if we are to break out of the current vicious circle in which social policy serves only to mirror, rather than to challenge, underlying social and economic inequalities.

Poverty and inequality: the post-war period record

The election of the Conservative Government in 1979 marked a significant change in the declared objectives of the state towards the distribution of resources. Previously, political parties seeking office had stressed as one of their main objectives the pursuit of a 'fairer' or more equal society. The Thatcher Government was the first post-war administration to be elected explicitly on a platform that advocated an *increase* in inequality. This change reflected a widespread belief that the previous three decades had been marked by substantial redistribution. The Conservative Party were able to exploit people's experiences of the controlling aspects of the welfare state and the increased burden of taxation by presenting these as the inevitable consequences of redistribution itself.

Writing about the decades between the Second World War and 1962, Runciman argued that there was a widespread conviction that significant redistribution had occurred.[2] That view persists today. In a recently published review of public attitudes, Peter Golding and Sue Middleton found that 'the majority of people felt the gap between rich and poor is smaller than it used to be'.[3] Such a belief does not accord with the reality.

Income

Official statistics show that over the period 1949 to 1978/9 little change occurred in the distribution of incomes. That which did occur was confined to the very richest households. The share of income enjoyed by the richest 1 per cent did halve over this period, from 11 per cent to $5\frac{1}{2}$ per cent. The rest of the top 5 per cent managed to retain most of their share (which fell from $12\frac{1}{2}$ per cent of the total in 1949 to $10\frac{3}{4}$ per cent in 1978/9). Overall, the top tenth of income recipients were left with a quarter of all personal incomes in 1978/9 – more than the poorest half had to share between them, and ten times as much as the poorest tenth. Inequalities in income were still therefore very substantial even in the late 1970s. Indeed changes in the tax system over the post-war years served to mitigate the small move towards greater equality that took place in *pre-tax* income.[4]

The later years of the period witnessed a substantial growth in capital gains and fringe benefits which are not well reflected in the official statistics. The Royal Commission on the Distribution of Income and Wealth found that between 1974 and 1978, a period in which tax and pay policies designed to reduce the share of high income groups were operating, fringe benefits proliferated. The average managing director received 12 per cent of his gross salary in fringe benefits and super-annuation in 1974, and 36 per cent in 1978. The Commission also found that the largest increases in fringe benefits were enjoyed by those at the highest salary levels. A works superintendent received fringe benefits worth 17 per cent of his salary in 1974; by 1978 still only 18 per cent of his salary came in this form.[5] As Titmuss demonstrated, 'the receipt of such benefits rises sharply with income'.[6]

Wealth

A similar picture emerges when we consider changes in the distribution of wealth. The most consistent long-term series of data on wealth inequalities are those prepared by A.B. Atkinson and A.J. Harrison.[7] They suggest that over the entire period 1923 to 1972, the share of wealth enjoyed by the richest 1 per cent declined by 0.4 per cent per year. Over that period of almost half a century, the decline in the share of the top groups was almost completely balanced by an increase in that of the slightly less well off – there was little redistribution to the poorest. Atkinson and Harrison's statistics suggest that the richest 1 per cent enjoyed just under half of the nation's wealth during the 1950s. In 1959 and 1960 there appears to have been a significant, but once and for all, fall in their share to just over one third of the total.

The collapse of the stock market in the early 1970s had a major effect on the value of the top wealth holdings. The official Inland Revenue statistics show that the share of the richest 1 per cent fell from 31 per cent in 1971 to 23 per cent in 1974, although it has remained stable since. And once again the decline in the share of the richest wealth holders has to some extent been balanced by an increase in the share of those only slightly further down the scale. The top 10 per cent of wealth holders (excluding the top 1 per cent) marginally increased their share since 1971.

By the end of the 1970s, therefore, 1 per cent of the adult population owned one quarter of all Britain's personal wealth; the top 2 per cent owned one third; the top 5 per cent owned almost half; and the top 10 per cent owned almost two-thirds. Moreover, the heaviest concentrations of wealth persisted in those forms – land, company shares and government securities – which also confer on their owners social and political power. Just 400,000 people – the richest 1 per cent – owned almost three-quarters of the private land in Britain. A similarly small group owned almost three-quarters of the listed ordinary shares and other company securities.

The growth of house ownership, building societies and bank deposits, national savings and insurance policies was an important means of extending personal wealth to a larger section of the community. But these forms of 'popular' wealth, although they provide a more comfortable standard of living and some measure of security, do not bring with them the power and influence which is attached to the ownership of land and of productive capital. This form of 'property for power' has remained heavily concentrated in the hands of the few.[8]

Why has the strategy failed?

Julian Le Grand describes the reasons why welfare expenditure has failed to be as effective as it could be in tackling inequality. The principal explanation was that these welfare services were super-imposed on an already unequal society, and these inequalities have determined, through differences in power and access, the distribution of the resources provided. The fact that the highest socio-economic groups have gained relatively more from the provision of such universal welfare services does not imply that these services have created the maldistribution, only that they have tended to reflect, rather than to eradicate, the underlying social and economic inequalities.

A similar explanation may be applied to the effects of the tax system. It can be argued that, whatever the formal incidence of taxation, changes in the effective tax burden have tended to reflect the overall balance of power amongst different groups in society. Hence, as we noted earlier, the modest movement towards equality in pre-tax incomes has been mitigated to some extent by changes in the burden of taxation. Similarly, the importance of capital taxation has been substantially reduced over the years, helping to slow down the decline in the share of personal wealth enjoyed by the richest groups.[9]

Tax evasion and avoidance

These shifts in the burden of taxation reflected changes in the structure of the tax system itself. But they were also due to an apparent increase in problems of evasion and avoidance. In evidence to the House of Commons Expenditure Committee in March 1979, the Inland Revenue reported that the problem of tax evasion had been growing over the previous decade, reaching an estimated £10 billion per annum, representing $7\frac{1}{2}$ per cent of the national income. By 1981 the Inland Revenue estimated that unreported income amounted to about £16 billion a year (still representing $7\frac{1}{2}$ per cent of GDP).[10] This implied a tax loss of about £4 billion, equivalent to about a fifth of the entire yield of income tax. And the Revenue explained to the Treasury and Civil Service Committee in 1982, 'Further up the income scale, the higher the marginal tax rate the more the taxpayer will gain from successful evasion'.[11]

The magnitude of illegal tax evasion is substantial; but so too is the extent of legal tax avoidance. More than half of all personal incomes are estimated to be exempted from tax through the operation of tax allowances, reliefs and exemptions.[12] The value of these exemptions, and the opportunity to make use of them, increases with income. Hence, by virtue of the powerful position in which they find themselves, the very richest have been able to side step attempts to reduce their share of total resources via the tax system.

The working poor

A second important reason for the failure of the post-war strategy of equality was that it was based on a misconception about the nature and distribution of poverty itself. In laying the foundations of the present social security system, Beveridge made the assumptions that full employment would be maintained and that poverty would be confined to those not currently participating fully in labour market activity. Hence, the social security system, as it was originally designed, explicitly excluded the 'working poor'. The 'rediscovery of poverty' in the late 1960s brought with it a realisation that a full-time job was no longer an insurance against poverty – if ever it was.[13] The number of families rendered poor by a combination of low pay and family responsibilities has increased substantially in recent years. By 1979 the DHSS estimated that one in five of those living on an income below the official poverty line (below the supplementary benefit entitlement) were in families where there was at least one income from *full-time* employment.[14] Next to the elderly, the working poor were then the largest single group in poverty. Many escaped poverty only through the efforts of more than one wage earner. The Central Policy Review Staff calculated that the numbers in poverty would quadruple were it not for the earnings of married women workers.[15]

The low paid are most frequently in low status, insecure jobs. They are generally in poorer health and their risk of unemployment is also particularly high. Opportunities to accumulate savings, access to pension rights and the chance for home ownership are all minimal. Not only do these factors affect present standards of living, they also help to produce poverty in old age. Low wages during an individual's working life therefore have profound implications for poverty over the life cycle.[16]

Taking account of these indirect effects, low wages may be considered the most important cause of poverty in Britain. Yet our social security system makes little provision for the working poor. Of course, increasing realisation about the problem of low wages led to adaptations to the system in the late 1960s and early 1970s. As Donnison describes it, 'because low paid workers were excluded from social assistance, and child benefits were low, a lot of new means tested benefits grew up, sometimes for the "working poor" only, and sometimes for people on social assistance as well'.[17] Most important amongst these was the introduction of family income supplement and the housing rebates and allowances. Governments once more made a conscious decision to try and alleviate the effects of low wages rather than to intervene directly in the process of wage determination. But these adaptations created their own problems. Many trade unions believe that the very existence of such benefits tended to depress wages still further, while the proliferation of means tests and the lower tax threshold created a harsh poverty trap. By 1981, it was estimated that over 90 per cent of the families considered poor enough to claim family income supplement were paying all or part of it back in income tax. An increase in gross earnings for this group (totalling 132,000 families with children in 1981) might be wholly negated by increased tax liability and reduced eligibility to means-tested benefits. Once again the social security and tax system had served to reinforce, rather than to challenge, basic wage inequalities.[18]

The challenge of change

A third reason for the failure of the post-war strategy for equality is that fiscal and social security policies have proved unable to adapt to changing social and economic circumstances. Chapter 3 described changes in the age structure of the population and in patterns of family life and dependencies. The present strategy has failed to respond to such changes or to prevent the formation of new groups of disadvantaged, for example one-parent families.

There are, as Rimmer and Wicks have argued, a number of developments which would promote increased sensitivity and flexibility. But even with improved monitoring of change and evaluation of policy impact, we would argue this failure is endemic in *post hoc* redistributive policies.

The dynamic picture painted by Rimmer and Wicks is not a recent phenomenon, though the elements may be unique. As Professor Anderson argues, family patterns have rarely been static: 'Perhaps the most basic of the de-mystifying ideas which come from improved knowledge of the past is also the most simple: change occurred before; almost no generation has got by without public crisis; most problems of our time have, in fact, also been problems in the past.'[19] For example, as our present redistributive policies creak into action in an attempt to improve the financial position of lone parents and their children (and there is no guarantee that they will) new family forms are evolving which may yet replace them. Social and economic factors interact. Change is almost continuous and to some extent unpredictable. We would argue that *post hoc* redistribution cannot match up to this 'challenge of change'.

There is no doubt that the existing policies on income maintenance and taxation could be strengthened and improved. However, by paying too little attention to the processes that generate inequalities, attempts to ameliorate their effects will continue to be frustrated.

The 'ideology of inequality'

Attempts to redistribute economic resources after the event have failed. There has been little change in the overall distribution of income or wealth during the past thirty years. This disappointing record would suggest that we should attempt to accompany future policies on redistribution – through the tax and benefit system and improvements in social services – with policies aimed at changing the distribution of economic resources directly. We must try to tackle inequality at its source. Before going on to consider, in the next section, what such policies might look like, we must first consider why, in the face of increasing evidence of failure, the emphasis of distributional policy during the post-war years has been so heavily biased towards after-the-event redistribution. Answers to such questions are important. If there are sound reasons why government cannot influence the original distribution of resources, or can only do so at an unacceptable cost, then we must content ourselves with devising more effective redistributive policies on taxation, social security and social services than those we have tried in the past. Even if there appears to be little theoretical or empirical foundation to suggestions that governments *cannot* influence inequality at source, there may be powerful social and political forces at work which effectively rule 'out of court' any attempts at such redistribution. In Chapter 4, Piachaud and Davies suggest there are limits to what can be achieved. Those concerned with the development of a realistic future programme must take such forces fully into account.

Even amongst those deeply committed to change, the dominant ideology of a market economy such as ours is a powerful influence. What Titmuss and later Le Grand have described as 'the ideology of inequality' tends to legitimise and justify the *status quo* – to suggest that change is neither feasible nor desirable. The influence of this ideology is pervasive, being made up of both social attitudes and a set of economic ideas which seem to lend objectivity to dominant values. It has been argued that successive governments have adopted the strategy of redistribution through the tax and social security system and via social services because they have accepted, either explicitly or implicitly, this 'ideology of inequality'.[20] Undoubtedly, the persistent differences in income and wealth, and in experiences of housing, education and health which have been described elsewhere, could not persist if they were not widely accepted. As Wickham argues: 'Inequality has to be justified and explained in such a way that the majority of the population (those who by definition are not privileged) accept it as morally right.'[21]

There are many variant forms of these justifications which pervade

much social and economic theory, political thought and social attitudes. They have been discussed in detail by Le Grand and Alen;[22] here
we need only sketch out some of the central elements of 'the ideology' of
particular relevance to the present discussion and illustrate the scale of
acceptance.

Attitudes to poverty

Claus Offe suggested that inequality is mainly legitimised by the
'achievement principle'. The rewards forthcoming for particular individuals are seen to depend on their contribution to the 'total social
product'. Relative income levels are believed to reflect the relative
'worth' of these contributions. It is not necessary for 'achievement' to
be measurable, merely for people to believe it to be so and for there to be
an acceptance that differential rewards according to this principle are
'fair'.[23]

The income which people 'earn' therefore comes to be seen as one to
which they have an inalienable right – their 'entitlement' as the
American philosopher Robert Novick puts it. The taxation of earnings
– particularly to provide 'cash' benefits for the poor – is therefore of
questionable legitimacy. This is reflected in the acceptance – indeed
admiration – of tax evasion, compared to the moral indignation en-
gendered by social security fraud. By the same logic the existence of
poverty is seen to arise from either an unwillingness or an innate
inability to 'achieve' or to 'contribute' to society. The ability of some
individuals may be improved by education and the provision of skills,
but for the most part the poor are viewed as 'undeserving'.

Survey evidence is limited but that which exists certainly supports
the view that large numbers of people adhere to such beliefs. However,
a note of caution should be sounded. Much of the material available
relates to periods when unemployment was not a central concern.
Attitudes towards poverty in general, and unemployment in particular,
might well have changed considerably in recent years as the recession
has deepened. But it should also be noted that in times of 'crisis'
attitudes have been shown to be as likely to harden as they are to
mellow.[24]

People do appear in general to be relatively satisfied with their
incomes.[25] In a recent survey in the EEC, 60 per cent of the UK sample
felt that society was just to them in particular. Conversely, though it
varied with income levels, almost 12 per cent of the 'high income group'
felt themselves to be victims of social injustice compared with 23 per
cent of the low income group.[26]

There would also appear to be very restricted perceptions of poverty
– at all income levels. Townsend found that fewer of those respondents
with incomes *below* the state poverty line thought that poverty existed

than those who were not 'objectively' poor (a majority in each case). He concluded that: 'Some of the poor have come to conclude that poverty does not exist. Many of those who recognise that it exists have come to conclude that it is individually caused, attributed to a mixture of ill luck, indolence and mismanagement. . . . In this they share the perceptions of the better off.'[27] Such attitudes seem if anything stronger in the UK than in other European countries. In the EEC survey noted above, 43 per cent of the UK respondents felt that poverty was caused by laziness and lack of will power and only 16 per cent looked to injustice in society. These compared with overall EEC figures of 25 per cent and 26 per cent respectively.[28]

It would be misleading, however, to suggest that the 'beliefs' outlined above are accepted by everybody.[29] As Townsend notes: 'there are significant proportions . . . who are prepared to look to the government for the blame for poverty and who are prepared to adopt expansive attitudes to their fellows'.[30]

However, as Le Grand and others have also suggested, there are many who *would* also accept the injustice of present inequalities and yet would not be prepared to see them reduced significantly. For them, it is the functional aspects of inequality which are paramount, particularly in the economic sphere.

The economics of inequality

'Orthodox economic theory', as Barbara Wootton has observed, 'has not, at least in the present century, generally found itself on the side of drastic social change.'[31] Current neo-classical theory suggests that inequalities are not only inevitable but necessary for the efficient workings of the economic system. The 'achievement principle', which we described above as having such a powerful influence in determining social attitudes to inequality, finds its counterpart in the sphere of economic theory in the notion that rewards are commensurate, within a market system, with an individual's current contribution. As Guy Routh has described it: 'There is a widely applied rationalisation: if you are paid a lot, it must be because you are worth a lot'.[32] The same rationalisation is applied, implicitly at least, to those who are paid very little. Market rewards are assumed to be commensurate with the individual's contribution to the social product.

Within the orthodox theory these rewards reflect a combination of two factors: individual ability and the prices which the market places on those abilities. Profit-maximising employers, for instance, will only pay wages which are equal to or less than an employee's contribution to total output and to the firm's revenue. If the wage rises beyond the marginal product of labour (the amount contributed by the last person employed) wages or jobs must be cut. Workers will be paid more if they have greater abilities (that is if they are more 'productive') or if the market places a higher price on those abilities.

The record of the Thatcher government is a prime example of the economic legitimisation of inequality. In April 1982 the government argued in its evidence to the Civil Service Pay Tribunal that the level of salaries of the lowest paid civil servants was a matter for supply and demand, rather than for issues of need or justice. The youngest and lowest paid civil servants were therefore offered no increase in salary at all. Others amongst the lowest grades were offered just 4 per cent. Within one month, the government announced increases of between 17 and 21 per cent for the top grades of civil servants, the judiciary and the military. Once again, arguments about market forces were employed. 'It is in the national interest', the Prime Minister told the House of Commons, 'to ensure an adequate supply of candidates of sufficient calibre for appointment to judicial office and to provide an adequate career structure and suitable differentials in the higher reaches of the civil service and armed forces.'

Neo-classical economic theory also predicts that the competitive process will tend to lead towards equality of wages (taking account of the 'non-wage' aspects of the job such as working conditions and job satisfaction) for workers who are of equal ability. Firms who pay wages below the 'going rate' will lose their workforce to better employers; those who offer wages above the 'going rate' will find themselves inundated with job applications far in excess of the number of workers they need. So any inequalities that remain must be due either to differences in the ability of the workers themselves, or to obstacles to the free operation of market forces.

The belief that ours is primarily an 'open society' reflects itself in the assumption that differences in reward reflect partly the immobility of labour. When the Secretary of State for Employment, Norman Tebbit, invoked the image of his father in the 1930s, cycling to find employment, the suggestion that this might represent a solution to unemployment today was treated with widespread ridicule. However, we must be aware of how deeply rooted in Conservative ideology is this belief.

At their extreme these ideas suggest that the pursuit of equality will result in the poor – and everyone else – having a still lower standard of living. This is a conclusion which might shake the resolve of even the most committed egalitarians. Protagonists argue that attempts by the state to intervene directly in the distribution of resources, for instance, by establishing a minimum or a maximum wage, will result in severe economic consequences, including unemployment and inflation. If we are to begin to tackle the inequalities which still characterise our economy and our society, it is necessary to challenge the ideology which supports and legitimises those inequalities.

Beyond ideology

Le Grand has argued elsewhere that many of the elements of this 'ideology of inequality' are actually empirical questions and are not supported by the evidence. To the extent that this is the case then the justifications for present inequalities may be undermined and a more favourable climate for effective redistribution created. The notion that inequalities reflect differences in individual abilities can be challenged. It is remarkable that the concept of 'the hidden hand' of market forces has retained such a firm grip on public attitudes in the absence of any substantive evidence to support it. As Barbara Wootton, again, has noted, 'It is apposite to reflect how little support can be found in economic considerations for the more conspicuous inequalities of our wage and salary system.'[33] Few would be prepared to accept that the lower rewards of women workers or those from ethnic minorities are due to a lower level of productivity; few would accept that regional and geographical income disparities are explained by a clustering together of those with high abilities in certain parts of the country. Yet these are the conclusions to which we are drawn by following the orthodox economic theories to their logical ends. The evidence is equally sparse to legitimise the rewards of the best paid individuals. Looking at the determination of the rewards of top managers, the Royal Commission on the Distribution of Income and Wealth found that:

One feature of top managerial salaries was that there were wide variations between companies in their pattern of remuneration at the highest levels. . . . If economic determinants were all important, we would expect to find some correlation between the level of salary of top managers and the profitability of their company, its rate of growth or its size, for these factors might help to determine what the senior executive is 'worth' in market terms. But the correlation is, in fact, very weak.[34]

Such arguments are most commonly applied to wage and income inequalities, but similar rationalisations are often employed to explain the extreme concentration of personal wealth. Legitimation of the wealth inequalities described in the last section are rarely challenged. The property of the rich is considered their rightful and private preserve. Underlying such attitudes once more is the belief that wealth accrues to individuals of ability and thrift, or just good fortune. Turning again to the survey of attitudes undertaken by Golding and Middleton, they found that: 'Riches are more generally seen to accrue from an unpredictable slice of good fortune. . . . Alternatively, riches could come from the due rewards for merit and effort, or from a skill with money and things financial beyond the reach of the less able.'[35]

Again the evidence provides little support for such beliefs. The Royal Commission on the Distribution of Income and Wealth examined the proposition that wealth inequalities might be explained by differences in accumulated earnings of different groups. They concluded that such an explanation would lead us to expect the richest 1 per cent of wealth holders would hold between 3 per cent and 7 per cent of the total wealth. In fact, they owned almost one quarter of the total. The extremes could not be explained by savings out of earnings. The Commission then considered the extent to which inheritance played a part in determining the fortunes of different groups. They found that, overall, about 40 per cent of all personal wealth was derived from financial windfalls, entrepreneurial fortunes and inheritances. But these sources accounted for three-quarters of the wealth enjoyed by the richest 1 per cent of wealth holders.[36]

Looking more closely at the role of inheritance, Harbury and Hitchens examined the pattern of wealth holdings of the very rich – the top 0.1 per cent who owned about one sixth of all the personal wealth. These people left the equivalent, at today's prices, of £500,000. How did they accumulate this sum? About half the men, and three-quarters of the women, had fathers who had left them the equivalent of £250,000. Even at a compound interest of only 7 per cent, this sum would double (to the amount left by the heirs themselves) in just ten years. The researchers concluded that: 'without question, the firmest conclusion to emerge from this study is that inheritance is the major determinant of wealth inequality'.[37]

The argument that inequalities can be explained by differences in individual abilities and the operation of market forces is not, therefore, wholly convincing. It might be argued, however, that inequalities represent an essential driving force of the economic system – that (whether we approve of them or not) they are functional and necessary. Here too, the evidence is inconclusive. The Thatcher government argued for an increase in inequalities on the grounds that these would increase incentives, creating more wealth for all. Yet in their evidence to the Treasury and Civil Service Select Committee, the Inland Revenue were able to point to no conclusive evidence whatsoever that the present Conservative Government's preoccupation with incentives was justified. They merely reasserted the government's *belief* that incentives were important.[38] Implicit in the economic rationale for the existing distribution of rewards is the suggestion that the operation of the market system is 'democratic', in contrast to the bureaucracy of centralised planning. People make choices on a free and individual basis and, through the price mechanism, this determines the allocation of resources. Yet this element of 'democracy' is a mirage. What the market produces, how it allocates resources, and the way in which it rewards the individuals and groups engaged in economic activity, is determined by the *existing* distribution of resources. The system is one of 'dollar voting' – those who have the most dollars have the most votes. Under socialism it is *not* necessary to discard the market mechanism itself as a means – and for some purposes an efficient means – of allocating resources. But for the market to be truly democratic – to reflect the choices of the majority – it is first necessary to ensure that resources are fairly distributed. Otherwise the market mechanism serves only to perpetuate and reinforce the inequalities which already exist.

Although it is not possible in the space available to challenge properly the empirical foundations of orthodox economic theories of inequality,[39] it is a measure of the extent to which such theories are built into dominant beliefs and values that they are sustained with such little empirical support. Again in the words of Barbara Wootton, 'Change – always, everywhere, in everything – requires justification: the strength of conservatism is that it is held to justify itself.'[40] Moreover, there are elements of the 'ideology of inequality' which are not empirically testable. There are deep-seated attitudes and values towards poverty which only time will change. However, changes in values can be facilitated by evidence and by statutory changes, and by deliberate attempts to create a more favourable climate. Townsend identified a sector of society 'prepared to adopt more expansive attitudes towards their fellows'. What is needed is the elaboration of a feasible alternative to encourage these people in their beliefs and to foster wider acceptance of them.

Towards a new strategy on redistribution

In his recent examination of the effects of post-war policies on redistribution, Julian Le Grand concluded that 'the strategy of redistribution through public provision has failed. It failed primarily because it implicitly accepted the ideology of inequality.'[41] In this chapter we have been able to discuss only briefly the reasons for this failure, and the ideology which helps to perpetuate inequalities. The reader will find these issues documented with persuasive clarity in Le Grand's own book. The conclusion, however, is clear. If we are effectively to work towards a more equal society we must be prepared to tackle inequalities at their sources, through direct intervention in the distribution of income and wealth. In part this might be achieved through the tax and social security system, although we have argued that these too tend to reflect the underlying inequalities of access and power. Such policies must be accompanied by a policy aimed at influencing the distribution of economic resources directly.

Tackling income inequalities

The greatest inequalities are those that exist between earned and property incomes, although the distribution of employment incomes is itself unacceptably wide. As we have argued, employment incomes are important in determining the living standards of most people during their working lives and beyond; low wages are a major cause of poverty. Moreover inequalities in incomes help to reinforce and perpetuate inequalities in accumulated wealth. This is where a strategy of direct intervention must begin, through a radical and comprehensive incomes policy.

To many socialists, the planned control of incomes has always been an essential element of any overall economic and social strategy. Yet the concept of an 'incomes policy' has lost the respect of many sections of the labour movement. The reason is that the concept has been abused by Labour Governments in recent years as a legitimation for more restrictive forms of wages policy. The pay policies of the past two decades have had macro-economic objectives as their central purpose. They have been intended as a means of controlling wage inflation, shifting resources from consumption to investment, and from the household to the corporate sector. These might be legitimate objectives, but in attempts to make the policies more acceptable to working people, Labour Governments have presented them as mechanisms for achieving a fairer society. The results, inevitably, have been disappointing. In accordance with their central macro-economic objectives, the policies have been directed at the control of earned incomes, rather than at the distribution of incomes overall. Indeed, they have tended to widen the inequalities between earned and property incomes as well as those between wages and salaries. By holding the entire structure of wages down (at least temporarily) while leaving their distribution unchanged, pay policies have inevitably contributed to an increase in the number of families in poverty.[42]

Recent pay policies have been characterised also by an emphasis on *annual changes* in incomes (befitting once more their macro-economic objectives) rather than on the overall distribution at any one time. Hence, even if the policies had managed to provide larger percentage increases to the lowest paid (which sadly they did not) it would have been many years before this process made a significant impact on the real distribution of earnings. In the meantime, pay policies removed from employers and trade unions the role of determining wages by negotiation without replacing this mechanism with anything more effective or sophisticated. This resulted in anomalies and feelings of injustice which quickly led to attempts to restore the *status quo* once the pay controls were lifted.

A more promising approach to incomes policy is for society to make a collective decision about the limits within which such discussions and negotiations on the wages of different groups should take place, through the establishment of a minimum and a maximum wage.

A minimum wage

The assocation with 'incomes policies' and with the regressive intervention of the state in wage determination during the late 1960s and 1970s turned many in the trade unions against the idea of a minimum wage backed by the force of law. However, the proposal is now once again winning support. David Basnett has argued the need for a 'Minimum Terms and Conditions of Employment Act' to be instituted under a future Labour Government in co-operation with the trade unions. This would include a national minimum wage, together with legislation on other basic employment rights, intended to underpin, rather than to replace, the process of collective bargaining.[43]

As we argued above, the present distribution of earnings has little functional justification. The common assumption that a minimum safety-net level of earnings would lead to an unacceptable increase in unemployment rests on the shaky foundations of orthodox economic assertions which have little empirical support. However, industries which have become geared to an abundant supply of cheap labour would inevitably face transitional problems with the introduction of a minimum wage. At the same time, there would be pressures on differentials and the development of anomalies in wage structures were the minimum to be imposed overnight. These would be made worse if a government (even a Labour Government) attempted to legislate for a minimum wage without the full co-operation of the trade unions.

Many of these difficulties could be eased if the minimum were to be phased in over a period of three to five years, allowing industries and wage structures to adjust to the change. The foundations of a minimum wage system already exist, at the time of writing, in the form of the industry-based wages boards and councils. These establish minimum rates of pay for almost 3 million of the poorest workers in shops, catering and personal services, in clothing manufacture and agriculture.[44] Since these are the industries in which private sector low wages are concentrated, the wages councils are obvious vehicles for beginning the transition to an adequate minimum wage. The Thatcher Government has undermined the wages councils by threatening their complete abolition, exerting downward pressure on their wage awards and by weakening the enforcement machinery. A future Labour Government should put these policies into reverse by recommending to the councils (which are independent bodies) an adequate minimum level of pay and ensuring proper enforcement of the minimum rates.

The appropriate level of the minimum, in wages councils and elsewhere, should be specified by the trade unions in the form of a 'minimum wage target' of the type that operated relatively successfully under the Social Contract until 1975. The target at that time was set at two-thirds average earnings and would need to be pursued with special vigour in the wages council sector, where minimum rates still hover at around 40 per cent or less of average earnings. The reintroduction of the 'fair wages laws' abolished by the present government would help, by allowing groups of workers to claim the same pay and conditions as those negotiated by better organised groups in the same industry or area. Once the target minimum wage had been achieved by a sufficient proportion of the unionised workforce, it should be backed by the force of law and extended to a national minimum. This would prevent employers in non-unionised sectors from benefiting at the expense of their competitors in better organised areas. A minimum wage, set at an adequate level, would have a disproportionate effect on the relative earnings of women workers who represent the bulk of the low paid. However, it would need still to be accompanied by more effective legislation than that which now exists on equal pay and job segregation.[45]

A maximum wage

One of the arguments often levelled against a minimum wage is that relativities and differentials would be maintained, so that the entire wage structure might be 'jacked up'. The lowest paid would be no better off in relative terms. This is one of the main reasons for the proposal for a maximum wage, which would place downward pressure on the overall distribution. Like a minimum wage, this is not a new idea. As long ago as 1965, Peter Shore introduced into parliament a Bill intended to require the disclosure by companies of the amounts paid to directors and other senior management, and to establish a Higher Incomes Council with the power to recommend controls on the salaries and other payments received by the highest income earners. Such controls would have to cover non-cash benefits as well as salary itself. During the early stages of the last Labour Government's pay policies, an upper ceiling was applied (of £8,500 p.a.) beyond which no increases in pay were allowable. However, the limit was not effectively enforced. The idea has more recently been revived. Cripps *et al.*[46] have argued for an upper income limit set at four times the average wage (about £30,000 a year at 1982 prices). Set at this level, few recipients of earned income would find their incomes actually reduced, although its existence would exert downward pressure on the upper echelons of the wage structure. Professor David Donnison has proposed a still more stringent limit, to be imposed at the level of the individual organisation: 'We should be asking whether it is morally tolerable that the highest paid groups in any industry or organisation should receive more than, say, four times what we pay to those at the bottom of the hierarchy within the same organisation.'[47]

A maximum limit to earnings of this type would not remove the need for a properly progressive system of taxation of both income and wealth, which would remain as the main mechanisms to redistribute resources at higher levels. However, the two approaches are natural accompaniments, helping to reinforce each other's effects. There is clear evidence that salaries at the highest level are determined by reference to the level of net income that the recipient, or those who formally determine his rewards, thinks appropriate. Gross salaries are then set at a level sufficient to produce this required net income. A maximum earnings limit would help to overcome this effective neutralisation of the tax system. At the same time, inequalities in wealth and inequalities in income tend to reinforce each other. High income earners are in a better position to accumulate holdings of wealth. An effective system of wealth taxation would continue to be necessary, but a maximum earnings limit would help to break this link between income and wealth inequalities.

There would be evasion of such a limit, of course. A lot would turn on the extent to which it had public support, and on the extent to which employees in firms helped to sustain it and knew all about the rewards structure in their own firms. This is where Schuller, in Chapter 13, is also relevant. But its very existence would fulfil an important function in challenging the dominant ideology of inequality. The state would no longer be condoning the assumption that high earnings reward greater ability and a more valued contribution to society. Under a system of minimum and maximum incomes, high earnings may indeed increasingly come to be associated with irresponsibility (and perhaps greed!) The Royal Commission on the Distribution of Income and Wealth found that some companies awarded lower executive and managerial salaries than their competitors in order to present a more 'responsible' company image; others awarded high salaries in order to represent their company as more successful. We need to encourage the former approach to top salaries. There will be fears, as we have shown already, that such direct controls on the highest earnings would lead to disincentive effects and to migration of those who find their salary aspirations limited. Yet most jobs at the higher levels of reward have other compensations, including job satisfaction, interest and status, which their incumbents would be relucant to forego even for reduced pecuniary reward. Some status of course is linked to earnings and with reduced differentials relative status would also change. But salary earners would certainly be insulted were it to be suggested that their principal motivation for doing their job was the high salary they received. We therefore find it difficult to share the apparent anxiety of the Prime Minister that an adequate supply of candidates for top positions in the judiciary, military and civil service would fail to appear were limits to be imposed on the financial rewards for these posts. Indeed, we would go so far as to say that we would prefer, in a democratic society, that such positions were held by people for whom pecuniary reward was *not* the principal motivation.

The case for an upper limit on earnings is perhaps strongest in the public sector, where democratically elected governments have direct control over rewards, though it is clear that the present government is pursuing the very opposite policies. Undoubtedly, market forces arguments are often applied with blatant selectivity, as was the case with the recent civil service pay awards already described. Although awarding substantial increases to the highest grade civil servants, the government was at the same time actively attempting to *reduce* their numbers. Following the logic of determining salaries according to market forces, these groups should surely have been offered zero pay rises along with the youngest and lowest paid civil servants.

Direct controls on wealth

An upper limit on earnings would help to control the additional concentration of wealth in the hands of those who were already well endowed through the accumulation of wealth. But the largest proportion of the top wealth holdings are not accumulated out of incomes; they are inherited. The tax system is probably still the most effective instrument for tackling inequalities in property incomes and wealth. But here again there is a role for a policy that incorporates an effective tax structure with direct controls of wealth. For instance, controls of the type operating in some other societies might be imposed, limiting the amount that could be inherited by any one individual. Elsewhere we have proposed the changes we feel to be necessary to improve the effectiveness of wealth taxation.[48] The case for direct controls to accompany such a strategy on wealth taxation has been argued most recently by the authors of *Manifesto*.[49] They make out the case for increased socialisation of wealth based on the transfer of private wealth into social control and common ownership. The purpose of such a policy would be to increase access for the majority of the population to the real assets which make up the concentrations of the top wealth holdings. This would represent fundamental social change, requiring the development of new and existing institutions of common ownership which it is not possible to discuss in detail here. However the proposal merits careful consideration by the labour movement as a possible means of challenging the existing distribution of wealth and power which underpins so many other elements of economic, social and political inequality.

Conclusion

We have illustrated how attempts since the war to redistribute income and wealth on any significant scale have failed. Improvements in taxation, income maintenance and the social services are both desirable and necessary, but we have also argued that failure is to some extent inherent in after-the-event redistribution policies. Whether or not one accepts the inherent weakness of such policies, it is evident that we have created an immensely complex system for redistribution where a much simpler alternative exists – direct intervention in the determination of incomes at work. We have suggested how, in broad outline, this might be achieved, but there are clear limitations on this approach too.

In particular, the proposed policies on the distribution of incomes are concerned with adequate incomes *for those in paid employment*. There are, for example, many (mostly women) whose opportunities for paid employment are restricted by caring responsibilities for children or frail and/or elderly relatives. Whilst there is a strong case for sharing such responsibilities more equally between the sexes, and providing greater community support, the responsibilities, and some of the restrictions involved, will not disappear. Certain ethnic groups, the disabled, and people with a history of ill-health are also excluded to some extent from employment, and it is also feasible that the extent of paid employment will itself be reduced significantly in the future – as it has been in the recent recession. In this context 'enlargement of access' to income is, according to Townsend, 'as important as greater equality of distribution'.[50] Also important is the payment of an 'income' as of right to those outside the formal labour market – that is, the reduction of the distinction between earners and dependants.[51]

The establishment of minimum and maximum incomes for those in employment clearly therefore cannot stand alone, but they are a vital element of any strategy to reduce inequality. There are however formidable barriers to change. Changes on the scale we are suggesting will require considerable political will and the support of large sectors of society, most notably perhaps the labour movement. Underpinning both of these however is the general tenor of public attitudes towards poverty. We have already suggested that a significant majority of people hold more generous attitudes towards the poor in our society. Any 'strategy for equality' must involve a deliberate attempt to foster this more favourable 'climate of opinion' towards redistribution. Townsend argues that such a climate would be fostered if employment and professional practices were reorganised to develop more collaborative rather than hierarchical structures.[52] Others have argued that reform of certain aspects of the mass media would at least help to place the alternative strategies for redistribution on the public agenda.[53] The role of the media in *creating* attitudes and public debate can however be exaggerated. As Golding and Middleton have recently illustrated, negative attitudes towards the poor are deeply entrenched and changes in attitudes will not easily be achieved. But at least a start could be made.

Notes and references

1. R.H. Tawney, *Equality*, George Allen and Unwin, 1964 (first published 1931), quoted in J. Le Grand, *The Strategy of Equality*, George Allen and Unwin, 1982, on which parts of this chapter draw heavily.
2. W.G. Runciman, *Relative Deprivation and Social Justice*, Penguin Books, 1972, 2nd edn.
3. P. Golding 'It's the Poor What Gets the Blame', *New Society*, 1 April 1982; see also P. Golding and S. Middleton, *Images of Welfare*, 1982.
4. Royal Commission on the Distribution of Income and Wealth Reports, and the Central Statistical Office.
5. Royal Commission on the Distribution of Income and Wealth, Report No. 7, *Fourth Report on the Standing Reference*, Cmnd 7595, HMSO, 1979, table 2.22, p. 53.
6. R.M. Titmuss, *Income Distribution and Social Change*, George Allen and Unwin, 1962, p. 171.
7. A.B. Atkinson and A.J. Harrison, *Distribution of Personal Wealth in Britain*, CUP, 1978.
8. See C. Pond, L. Burghes and B. Smith, *Taxing Wealth Inequalities*, Fabian Society, 1981.
9. L. Day and C. Pond, 'The Political Economy of Taxation and the Alternative Economic Strategy', *Socialist Economic Review 1982*, Merlin, 1982.
10. See House of Commons, Committee of Public Accounts, Twelfth Report, Session 1980–1, *Minutes of Evidence given by Board of Inland Revenue*, HMSO, June 1981, pp. 10–13.
11. House of Commons, Treasury and Civil Service Committee, Sub-committee on the Structure of Taxation and Income Support, written evidence submitted by H.M. Treasury, DHSS and Inland Revenue, mimeo, May 1982.
12. House of Commons, *Hansard*, written answers.
13. See for instance B. Abel-Smith and P. Townsend, *The Poor and the Poorest*, Bell, 1965; P. Townsend, *Poverty in the United Kingdom*, Penguin, 1979.
14. DHSS, *Low Incomes in 1979*, House of Commons Library, mimeo, 1982.
15. Central Policy Review Staff, *People and Their Families*, HMSO, 1980.
16. For a fuller discussion see A.B. Atkinson, 'Low Pay and the Cycle of Poverty', in F. Field, (ed.), *Low Pay*, Arrow Books, 1973.
17. D. Donnison, *The Politics of Poverty*, Martin Robertson, 1982, p. 11.
18. Low Pay Unit, written evidence to the House of Commons Treasury and Civil Service Committee, Sub-committee on the Structure of Taxation and Income Maintenance.
19. M. Anderson, 'The Relevance of Family History', SSRC Lecture Series, *The Family in History*, 1981.
20. Le Grand, *op. cit.*
21. J. Wickham in the translated introduction to C. Offe's *Industry and Inequality*, Edward Arnold Ltd, 1976, p. 1.
22. Golding and Middleton, Le Grand, Offee, *op. cit.*
23. Offe, *op. cit.*

24. Golding and Middleton, *op. cit*.; see also J. Popay 'Fiddlers on the Hoof: Moral Panics and Social Security Scroungers', unpublished MA paper, University of Essex, 1977.

25. Runciman, *op. cit*., p. 245.

26. Commission of the European Community, *The Perception of Poverty in Europe*, 1977, p. 48.

27. Townsend, *op. cit*., p. 429.

28. Commission of the European Community, *op. cit*., p. 70.

29. C. Hakim, in a study of occupational segregation by sex, depicts a parallel process whereby women's occupational aspirations, feelings of self-worth, perceptions of male/female abilities and level of satisfaction with, frequently lower, pay levels all reflect an acceptance of existing inequality in opportunities and rewards for women in the labour market. Women are, she suggests, to some extent 'prisoners of the mind', a powerful image mirrored in attitudes to inequality more generally. *Occupational Segregation*, Department of Employment, HMSO, 1979.

30. Townsend, *op. cit*., p. 430.

31. B. Wootton, *The Social Foundations of Wage Policy*, George Allen and Unwin, 1955, p. 163.

32. G. Routh, 'The Morals of Pay', in *The Roots of Pay Inequalities*, Low Pay Unit, Discussion Series, No. 1, 1980, p. 10.

33. B. Wootton, *op. cit*., p. 181.

34. D. Wedderburn, 'Inequalities in Pay', in *The Roots of Pay Inequalities*, p. 13.

35. Golding, *op. cit*.

36. Royal Commission on the Distribution of Income and Wealth, Report No. 7, *op. cit*., page 98.

37. C. Harbury and D. Hitchens, *Inheritance and Wealth Inequality in Britain*, Allen and Unwin, London, 1979.

38. Written evidence to the Treasury and Civil Service Committee, Sub-committee on the Structure of Income Taxation and Income Support.

39. Further discussion is to be found in Le Grand, *op. cit*.

40. Wootton, *op. cit*., p. 162.

41. Le Grand, *op. cit*., p. 157.

42. For an analysis of the effects of recent pay policies on the low paid see C. Playford, *Low Pay Policies*, Low Pay Unit.

43. D. Basnett, *The Future of Collective Bargaining*, Fabian Society, 1982.

44. For a discussion of the workings of the Wages Councils see S. Crine, *Legal Minimum Wages*, WEA, 1980, and E. MacLennan, *Minimum Wages for Women*, EOC/Low Pay Unit, 1981.

45. See P. Glucklich and M. Snell, *Women: Work and Wages*, Low Pay Unit, Discussion Series, No. 2, 1982.

46. See F. Cripps, J. Griffiths, F. Morrell, J. Reid, P. Townsend and S. Weir, *Manifesto: A Radical Strategy for Britain's Future*, Pan Books, 1981.

47. D. Donnison, in *Wage Inequalities: The Labour Movement in Response*, Low Pay Unit, 1982.

48. Pond, Burghes and Smith, *op. cit*.

49. Cripps, *et al*., *op. cit*.

50. Townsend, *op. cit*., p. 928.

51. *Ibid*. p. 926.

52. *Ibid*. p. 926–7.

53. Golding and Middleton, *op. cit*.

9 A Multi-Racial Society
by Geoffrey Bindman and John Carrier

We are already a multi-racial society. The problem is how to become a society in which members of ethnic minorities do not suffer in the distribution of benefits and opportunities. There is ample evidence that the universalist values of the welfare state have not brought equality to black and brown citizens. This situation has changed very little over the last thirty years, notwithstanding the refinement of laws against discrimination and the operation of schemes by central and local government aimed at the reduction of what is described as 'racial disadvantage'.[1]

There are thus two areas which are relevant to the goal of a just multi-racial society: the law against discrimination and policies aimed at 'racial disadvantage'.

Before 1948 and the arrival of New Commonwealth groups, British society was made up of many groups who had come to these shores seeking political and religious freedom together with economic opportunity, but there had also been large-scale emigration to empire, dominion and colony. From the arrival in the nineteenth century of Irish Catholics and Eastern European Jews to the reception and settlement immediately after the Second World War of European migrants, the absence of a black or coloured population in Britain meant that the conflicts that arose with 'newcomers' were more likely to be based on feelings of religious animosity (anti-catholicism, anti-semitism) and economic competition than on differences of skin colours. The various restrictive immigration measures, especially the 1905 and 1914 Aliens Acts, were a challenge to the pluralistic and tolerant political atmosphere of the UK, and were designed to restrict entry from Eastern Europe by using a mixture of immigration control at points of entry, work permits and stringent deportation powers.[2] As an indication of the official political response to 'the stranger at the gate', this legislation was consistently opposed by Liberal members and supported by Conservatives. However, the groups who were the targets of control were not black, and the long-term prognosis for their integration was never seriously questioned, even during some of the worst excesses of inter-war fascist activity.

The arrival of the New Commonwealth migrant in Britain coincided with two processes, the decline of empire and the development of the post-war welfare state. Serious doubts began to be raised about the political and civil level of tolerance shown by UK citizens towards immigrants from the New Commonwealth, especially from the Caribbean and the Indian sub-continent.[3] Although the UK differs from the USA in many respects (especially the absence of a written constitution and a slave-owning tradition, as well as the resort to law to solve social problems), Myrdal's famous description of the dilemma of American society in the 1940s might be applied to British society since the 1950s (and up to the present day):

There is a 'negro problem' in the United States and most Americans are aware of it although it assumes varying forms and intensity in different regions of the country and among diverse groups of the American people. Americans have to react to it, politically as citizens and where there are negroes present in the community, privately as neighbours.[4]

Given the distinctiveness of racial inequality, should 'special' social policy programmes be constructed to make equality of opportunity effective and if necessary to compensate for any condition of disadvantage that has a racial origin? Secondly, should the law be used to prevent discrimination and to enforce special programmes?

The role of the law

In a society where racial justice prevails, one would expect to see members of ethnic minorities in jobs and social positions at all levels in proportion to their numbers. Where there was any imbalance, under or over-representation of minorities, one would expect that to be the result of free choice or of chance, not the result of discriminatory pressures or actions. The present situation, falling far short of that ideal, can only have been brought about by discrimination, whether present or past, or by the failure to make special provision or allowance for cultural differences.

The changes required to move towards racial justice are sometimes within the control of private organisations – employers, landlords, or estate agents – who are unlikely to make them because it is to their individual disadvantage to do so. That is the case for legal sanctions. In other cases, government may be able to act directly, given the necessary resources and social programmes.

The majority of black migrants in the UK have come from the New Commonwealth since the early 1950s. The attitudes of government have been ambiguous. The Race Relations Acts of 1965 and 1968 were counterpointed by the Commonwealth Immigrants Acts of 1962 and 1968. The Immigration Act 1971 was followed by the 1976 Race Relations Act, perpetuating the compromise.

We need to look at the history of race relations law in more detail.

The 1965 Act made discrimination – defined as 'treating a person less favourably than another on the grounds of colour, race, or ethnic or national origins' - a civil wrong when done in relation to the facilities of certain 'places of public resort'. Effectively this covered discrimination in pubs, dance halls and hotels, but little else. It failed to touch at all on the critical areas of employment and housing. Furthermore, the sanction for breach of the law was to prove so nebulous as to be actually non-existent. In the event of a failure to conciliate a dispute by the Race Relations Board, set up to administer the law, the case could be referred to the Attorney General who had power to obtain an injunction in the County Court. But not a single case reached the court in the lifetime of the Act.

It would be a mistake to write off the Race Relations Act 1965 as worthless in improving the relative position of black people. Some functions of the law in attacking racial inequality, summarised by the Race Relations Board in its first annual report in 1966, are still valid:[5]

1. A law is an unequivocal declaration of public policy
2. A law gives support to those who do not wish to discriminate, but who feel compelled to do so by social pressure
3. A law gives protection and redress to minority groups
4. A law thus provides for the peaceful and orderly adjustment of grievances and the release of tensions
5. A law reduces prejudice by discouraging the behaviour in which prejudice finds expression (para. 65).

Undoubtedly there are many who will obey the law simply because it is there or because they are uncertain of what will happen to them if they break it, even though the penalties may be minimal. There is some evidence that the more blatant forms of colour bar in public places declined considerably following the 1965 Act. The 1968 Race Relations Act extended the coverage of the law to employment and housing and strengthened the enforcement procedure. Much of the impetus for this development came from the PEP report which showed massive discrimination against black people in employment and housing,[6] and from the report of the Street Committee on anti-discrimination legislation which had closely examined legal techniques in the United States for which a considerable measure of success was claimed.[7]

It became a civil wrong to discriminate in virtually all employment decisions on racial grounds. Discrimination in the rental and sale of housing was widely prohibited. The Board was required to investigate all complaints and could seek damages and an injunction in the County Court if it failed to resolve a complaint by conciliation. But the definition of discrimination remained as before. The burden of proving discrimination rested with the complainant, or the Board wishing to pursue a case on his or her behalf. The process was fatally defective in two major ways. First, by retaining the narrow definition of discrimination from the earlier statute, it ensured that only one of the causes of racial inequality (though admittedly the most obvious) was challenged by the law. Secondly, by concentrating entirely on individual complaints and individual redress, it failed to take account of the uniquely collective character of discrimination as contrasted with other objects of legal restraint. Although the creation of the Race Relations Board itself was a recognition that discrimination was not just a series of individual instances, the collective remedies in the United States legislation on which the Race Relations Acts purported to be modelled were absent. Even where an act of discrimination could be proved, neither the Board nor the courts had power to direct changes in practices which would avoid discrimination in the future, let alone provide actual jobs or other opportunities for black people. It was hardly surprising that the 1968 Act made only a marginal impact.

It failed to prohibit 'indirect' discrimination – the application of general criteria or rules which adversely affected racial minorities, even though not intended to discriminate. The Race Relations Act 1976 has introduced this concept into our law but it has not been fully employed.

In other, procedural, ways the US law still has many advantages over ours. By means of the 'class action' a large number of victims of discrimination may benefit from a single judicial decision. Where a practice is found to have had an unjustified adverse impact on minorities seeking employment with a firm or already employed by that firm, compensation may be awarded to those victims, however numerous, and a number of large corporations have paid out very large sums either under order of the court or, more frequently, as part of a settlement arrived at to avoid the risks and costs of a trial. More directly important in achieving the objective of greater opportunities for minorities is the power of the US courts to order the adoption and implementation of affirmative action programmes. They have provoked great controversy in the United States and more widely. They seek to promote positive discrimination in the selection of students and hiring of staff by firms and government to achieve a target representation of minority groups. The most notable case involved an appeal, as far as the Supreme Court, by a white medical student, Bakke, who claimed he was rejected by a university medical school while less qualified applicants were accepted from racial minorities. The stark situation which arose in the Bakke case, where the great majority of the applicants for places at the medical school of the University of California at Davis were chosen virtually entirely on the basis of an examination mark, but some minority members were admitted in preference to others who had higher examination marks, is unusual. The fact that a case got to the Supreme Court only in 1977 (after affirmative action programmes had been widely used for at least twenty years) indicates the rarity of the situation. More generally affirmative action programmes have set up minority recruitment targets which employers have been directed or have agreed to pursue by measures falling short of open racially based preferences. Much of the effort is directed at improving training opportunities and methods of recruitment so as to give the maximum encouragement to minority members to take advantage of the opportunities which exist, as well as creating new opportunities for minorities.

Such action, we believe, would provoke little disagreement in principle within the labour movement or more generally. The next steps may, and the issues should be squarely faced and argued through. We would argue that where claims to a job or a place in college are reasonably evenly balanced, the broader social benefit that derives from reducing discrimination in the long run argues for preferential treatment to groups previously discriminated against, up to the point where a representative balance in racial recruitment is achieved. This approach must be sufficiently sensitive to members of all groups to avoid a backlash of white opinion. Such a policy need not result in lowering employment standards. No affirmative action should require an employer to recruit or promote someone to a job they are incapable of doing, but equally the employer should not have the unlimited right to define the best candidate on racially biased criteria that ignore the broader social demands for racial justice. It is in that spirit that we argue for measures to strengthen the 1976 Act which has failed to live up to the promise of the White Paper which introduced it. Nor has it been accompanied by non-legal policies without which a comprehensive attack on discrimination is impossible. The White Paper asserted that:

the problems with which we have to deal if we are to see genuine equality of opportunity for the coloured youngsters born and educated in this country may be larger in scale and more complex than had been initially supposed. The possibility has to be faced that there is at work in this country, as elsewhere in the world, the familiar cycle of cumulative disadvantage by which relatively low paid or low status jobs for the first generation of immigrants go hand in hand with poor and overcrowded living conditions and a depressed environment. If, for example, job opportunities, education facilities, housing and environmental conditions are all poor, the next generation will grow up less well equipped to deal with the difficulties facing them. The wheel will then come full circle as the second generation find themselves trapped in poor jobs and poor housing. If, at each stage of this process, an element of racial discrimination enters in, then an entire group of people are launched on a vicious downward spiral of deprivation. They may share each of these disadvantages with some other deprived group in society; but few other groups in society display all their accumulated disadvantages.[8]

The new strategy which the government proposed in the White Paper for the first time sought to co-ordinate legal and non-legal measures. Policy consisted of the following elements:

(a) Eliminating discrimination practised by the government as employer including special training which 'may be desirable' to enable staff to realise their full potential in the civil service.

(b) Continuation of the requirement that government contractors should undertake to comply with the provisions of the Race Relations legislation with an obligation to provide information about employment policies and practices to the Department of Employment on request.

(c) Co-ordination of the race relations policies of the many government departments, local authorities and statutory bodies under the umbrella of a new Standing Advisory Council under the chairmanship of the Home Secretary.

(d) Strengthening the law already on the statute book.

The main way in which the law was strengthened was by expanding the definition of discrimination to include 'adverse impact' discrimination. Though in the United States this has been a product of judicial creativity, it was plain that in Britain the judges could never be expected to interpret the law so widely without unambiguous statutory direction. The new provision in the Race Relations Act 1976 created a new category of indirect discrimination. It covered a situation where an employer imposed a 'requirement or condition' that only a considerably smaller proportion of members of one racial group could comply with compared with other racial groups. A member of a racial minority who had suffered by the application of such a rule was treated illegally unless the person imposing the rule could show that it was 'justifiable' without regard to the colour, race, nationality or ethnic or national origins of the victim. It was hoped that this extension of the law would open up enormous opportunities for challenging industrial practices which denied employment and promotion to black people. Some of the more obvious practices which it was thought would immediately be outlawed included such injustices as the peaked cap rule of certain transport authorities which prevented turbaned Sikhs taking employment with them, or residence requirements for local authority housing which adversely affected immigrants. Of potentially more importance was the prospect of challenging both the nepotism which pervades large sections of British industry and the practice of limiting recruitment to word of mouth, an outlawed method of discrimination in the United States.

Since the 1976 Act, interpretations of the definition of indirect discrimination have been very restrictive. Even in what would seem to be the clearest cases of rules excluding Sikhs because of their traditional or religious duty to wear turbans and beards, the employment appeal tribunal and the Court of Appeal have refused to hold that such discriminatory practices are not justifiable. In one case the refusal to employ a bearded Sikh in a food factory was held justifiable notwithstanding that in seven of the eight factories operated by the same company, no prohibition of beards was thought necessary.[9] In a County Court case (upheld by the Court of Appeal) the rejection of a turbaned school boy by the headmaster of a private preparatory school was upheld on the ground that a rule barring non-standard headgear was justifiable.[10] Furthermore, a discriminatory requirement can more easily be justified than could have been intended if the US test was contemplated.[11] A discriminatory rule may be lawful even though an employer may not be able to show that it is necessary to the proper conduct of his business. In one area of major importance employers have been compelled to abandon indirectly discriminatory practices. A requirement that an employee be proficient in the English language is indirectly discriminatory except to the extent that a particular level of lanuage proficiency is validly tested and is necessary for the safe and efficient performance of the job. There is little evidence, however, that the small number of successful cases which have been brought have caused employers to pay urgent attention to the justifiability of any language criteria. Partly this is due to lack of publicity for the Race Relations Act, partly to the low level of recruiting generally, and partly to the absence of clear-cut selection criteria which makes exclusion on language grounds very difficult to identify or prove.

Five years after the Race Relations Act 1976 came into force the prevalence of indirectly discriminatory practices remains essentially unimpaired. Few individuals have brought cases alleging indirect discrimination, notwithstanding the availability of legal assistance from the Commission for Racial Equality (CRE). If the respondent can show that the indirectly discriminatory practice is not maintained for the purpose of discriminating, there can be no award of compensation. Nor does the industrial tribunal have the power to order recruitment or promotion; it can merely decide whether unlawful discrimination has taken place and make a recommendation to migitate its effect on the victim. The case which potentially has the biggest impact on language testing was that brought by seven Bangladeshi steel workers against the British Steel Corporation.[12] On reapplying after absences for jobs which they had carried out safely for many years, the applicants were faced with an English language test which they failed. It is hard to see how a language qualification can be justified for resuming a previous job, but that did not prevent the British Steel Corporation from hiring city solicitors and leading and junior counsel at a vast cost to the taxpayer to defend that claim. When offered £7,000 between them to settle the case, the applicants had a difficult choice. If they went ahead with CRE support they had virtually no hope of getting any compensation and a highly doubtful prospect of getting their jobs back because by that time the Scunthorpe plant was already laying off workers. Not surprisingly they decided to take the money coupled with a promise that BSC would carry out a study in conjunction with the CRE of the need for language testing across the whole Corporation. Three years later this study has still not been completed.

Direct discrimination too is not without its problems. The burden of proving discrimination is on the complainant and proof is often hard to find. The Race Relations Board under the earlier Act failed to overcome this problem. Since the 1976 Act came into force, individuals have been free to take their own cases to industrial tribunals with the assistance of the CRE. The CRE has been very ready to grant assistance in cases with any sign of merit. The industrial tribunals and the courts have not interpreted the law sympathetically, but some industrial tribunals have been prepared to infer discrimination more readily than others. In a number of cases, however, claims of what most people would see as blatant discrimination have been rejected because tribunals have refused to draw the necessary inference. Because the decision of the tribunal is treated as evaluation of evidence, not raising any point of law, the appeal tribunal has declined to interfere. A notable example is the case of Mr K.L. Khanna, employed by the Ministry of Defence as a photographer.[13] Although he applied for the post of head of his department after satisfactorily occupying the position on a temporary basis for several months, a white applicant with no experience was preferred, placing Mr Khanna in the embarrasing position of having to train his superior. All the objective evidence favoured the appointment of Mr Khanna, but his claim was rejected on the grounds that the members of the selection board denied any discriminatory intent and their mere denial was considered sufficient to rebut the objective evidence. Overall then the impact of the law both in relation to direct and indirect discrimination has been slight. There are a number of reforms which could be made to increase the effectiveness of the law in relation to both forms of discrimination.

So far as indirect discrimination is concerned:

(a)   Compensation should be available in all cases regardless of the absence of intent to discriminate. Indeed the whole point of indirect discrimination is to deal with cases where long-standing practices have an unintended discriminatory impact. There is

nothing unusual about imposing liability for damages on unintended acts where the person committing them has every
opportunity of avoiding them by reviewing and changing his
practices. Liability without fault has been imposed for decades
on employers whose unsafe equipment causes injury to workers.
A landlord cannot escape liability for damage resulting from his
failure to repair his premises by pleading ignorance.

(b)   The defence of justifiability can properly be restricted to cases of
necessity.

(c)   It should not be necessary to show that a discriminatory 'requirement or condition' has been imposed; any practice or
situation which leads to a discriminatory impact on minorities
should be sufficient.

So far as direct discrimination is concerned:

(a)   The burden of proof on the complainant is too heavy, as illustrated by the Khanna case. It should be sufficient to establish
that he or she was treated less favourably than a person of a
different racial group in similar circumstances. The burden
should then be on the person who has administered such treatment to prove that the reason was not racial.

(b)   Employers should be required to keep records of the reasons for
employment decisions which should be available to those who
allege discrimination. Although the courts have been reasonably
fair to complainants in ordering disclosure of information and
documents, complainants are at a disadvantage when records do
not exist and recruitment practices are subjective and arbitrary.

(c)   Although the tribunals and courts have power to award compensation in cases of direct discrimination, and to include in
such compensation payments for injury to feelings, awards of
compensation have been extremely low. Much higher awards
are needed to provide adequate compensation and to act as an
adequate deterrent. Compensation should be raised to a level
comparable with that awarded in defamation cases.

These reforms would make the law more effective but would still fall
short of the measures which are needed for a serious shift towards the
equal and uniform distribution of the benefits of society among those of
all racial groups. Is it necessary to prove discrimination at all in order to
achieve this objective? Would it not be sufficient to impose racial
quotas, as has been done in the case of disabled persons by the Disabled
Persons (Employment) Act 1944 and its successors? There may well be
merit in such a measure for some types of employment but in the field of

race relations it is doubtful whether the idea would work without the opportunity for close monitoring of the particular circumstances of each enterprise. Also, by its very crudity, a quota system could provoke a backlash. The desirable aim is a law which exerts the strongest possible pressure on employers and those in control of other institutions to take active and detailed steps to eliminate racial imbalances. There needs to be a distinct enforceable affirmative action programme for each such enterprise and the problem is how to exert that pressure.

In the United States considerable pressure has been brought about through the development of the law to the point it would be at in this country if the improvements mentioned earlier were introduced. The existence of under-representation is in itself strong evidence of direct or indirect discrimination, and US courts have been ready to draw the inference of discrimination virtually on the basis of such evidence alone. Where that situation exists an employer knows that he is vulnerable if there is an imbalance and so is likely to take steps to correct it without the need for litigation. Where he has failed to do so, legal action under Title VII of the Civil Rights Act or other appropriate legislation commonly results at an early stage in a settlement by which the employer agrees to adopt an affirmative action programme which is then embodied in an order of the court. As a result of the complex development of the law in the United States, the varying attitudes of judges and the unwillingness of some of them (including the Supreme Court in some cases) to dispense with proof of intent or at least a clearly identified practice, the system of enforcement in the United States cannot be regarded as a perfect model. There is plainly, however, much to learn from the development of the law in the United States and what is here proposed is an improved version of the American legal framework.

Wider social policies on race

The law on its own will not be enough since the disadvantages racial minorities suffer are more pervasive than those reflecting individuals' or employers' acts of discrimination. But what kind of policies should they be – those designed to combat deprivation in general or those directed at particular groups? David Smith, in his PEP report, argued that because of the very clear association between certain racial groups and deprivation status, the case for seeking to break that link was sufficiently strong on its own merits.[14] He argued that because of the small size of the population affected, and because this kind of disadvantage can be relatively easily defined, the spread of disadvantage to the next generation could be halted or at least restricted. The means of tackling such disadvantage already exists.

This report was published four years before Scarman[15] and the Fifth

Report from the Home Affairs Committee. It proposed various social policies covering the education, housing and employment opportunities of the racially disadvantaged. In the same year, the Inner City White Paper was published.[16] While devoting three short paragraphs to 'ethnic minorities', it failed to distinguish special policies to aid them. Instead, it claimed that 'where members of the ethnic minorities in inner areas suffer the kinds of disadvantage experienced by all those who live there, they should benefit directly through measures taken to improve conditions, for example, in housing, education and jobs', but 'their particular needs' would be taken into account under an enlarged urban programme. In contrast, Smith identified the need to devote additional resources to language teaching, to devise long-term policies for improving educational qualifications, to review allocation systems in council housing, and to enforce anti-discrimination measures at the workplace.

The Home Office review of ethnic minorities over a twenty-year period (published before the Brixton disorders and nine months before Scarman) suggested that the position of the black community could be viewed either more or less pessimistically.[17] The pessimistic view would be one which sees black people still trapped, after twenty years, at the bottom of the social scale, with little knowledge of their rights under legislation, with fewer opportunities for advancement and having fewer material possessions than the white majority, and with a similarly depressing future in front of them. The optimistic view would be that over these two decades there has been some adaptation by the black community to the opportunities offered by the UK and that there has been a corresponding advancement in the position of blacks, with the help of legislation.

The overall conclusion was that for the black and Asian communities housing conditions had slowly improved over the period, but that the major shortcoming was their relatively worse position in the labour market. This was attributed to the continuing existence of discrimination in employment, the concentration of black minorities in the most insecure jobs, the relative youthfulness of the black labour force (and the consequently relatively heavier unemployment rate of this age group), and the newness of the minority group which tended to make them less able to compete for jobs where academic qualifications are required.

The Home Affairs Committee Report on Racial Disadvantage (July 1981) identified four main areas of concern where action is necessary to improve the position of ethnic minorities: improved and relevant services, especially in housing, education and employment; central government machinery necessary to co-ordinate a strategy for tackling disadvantage; a review of the financial arrangements for promoting such a strategy, especially a change in the Section 11 and Urban Aid programmes; and the strong motivation of government, central and local, to implement positive discrimination policies.[18] It suggested that there was 'no effective co-ordination at minsterial level' for 'policies impinging on racial disadvantage' and recommended the creation of a Cabinet committee to remedy this. The report dismissed the Home Secretary's Council on Race Relations as 'a high powered talking shop deprived of effective power' and criticised the absence in the Home Office of 'an established mechanism for the definition of priorities or formulation of policies.[19] This had led to the ineffective monitoring of what has been happening to the black community in the past two decades. Indeed, the Home Affairs Committee suggests that although national data is available on the size of the ethnic minority population, its geographical distribution and its housing and employment opportunities, such data is not available on such crucial matters as the utilisation of health services or participation in public affairs.

Perhaps the most serious criticism of central government's response to racial disadvantage is concerned with the use of Urban Aid and Section 11. Under that section of the Local Government Act 1966, local authorities can be reimbursed by the Home Office through a grant of 75 per cent of eligible expenditure for 'special provision in the exercise of any of their functions in consequence of the presence within their areas of substantial numbers of immigrants from the Commonwealth whose language or customs differ from those of the community'.

The initiative for acting on behalf of the black population and claiming grants lies with the local authority, but the grant can only be used for the employment of staff and not for capital programmes. The major share of the grant is used for teachers' salaries, especially in schools where a significant number of pupils are from the New Commonwealth. The Home Affairs Committee was highly critical of the provisions and operation of Section 11 and in some ways echoed the criticism, made by the authors of *Colour and Citizenship* twelve years ago,[20] that 'it was left to each local authority to make expenditure claims according to its own priorities and policies'. The committee recommended that the Section 11 provision should be amended. First, it should be revised so that it can apply to non-commonwealth immigrants, thus taking into account the arrival of other immigrants since 1972, for example those from Vietnam. Secondly, the exclusion of non-salary costs from Section 11 means that capital projects cannot be supported, and the exclusion of voluntary bodies from applying is a serious shortcoming. Thirdly, the ten-year rule, limiting its operation to those here for less than ten years, should be abandoned entirely. The definition of 'substantial numbers' in an area (that is, 2 per cent of the population) should be maintained, the committee argued. Even so, the committee have unwarranted faith in a revised Section 11; there have been more far-reaching criticisms of it.

However, the will of this government to take racial disadvantage seriously may be gauged by the government's reply (Cmnd 8476, January 1982) to the report of the Home Affairs Committee. It rejected the proposal to make the Home Office the central co-ordinating department in race relations; it also rejected proposals for an inquiry into the teaching of English as a second language, the idea that central government should take responsibility for establishing a programme of teacher training for multi-cultural education, and the creation of special units to tackle racial disadvantage in the Departments of Education, Environment and Health. The formation of a body to oversee 'policy relevant' research into race relations at the Home Office and the inclusion of an ethnic question in the next census were unacceptable. The government refused to consider the idea of a new loan guarantee scheme to meet the needs of ethnic minority businesses. The only (but nonetheless important) recommendations to be accepted were the monitoring of the number of black people in the civil service and the reform of the Section 11 provisions (in consultation with the local authorities). The rejection of so many interesting and important recommendations raises serious doubts about the commitment of this government to combat racial disadvantage.

Although the main topic of Lord Scarman's report was the nature and administration of policing in multi-racial areas, Scarman's view was that the disorders could not be interpreted as a simple reaction to 'heavy' policing, but rather had to be seen within the context of complex political, social and economic factors. In particular, he identified three areas of need which are the province of social policy: the already familiar ones of inadequate housing, educational inequalities and employment (or rather severe unemployment) affecting the inner city black population. His conclusions echoed the Home Affairs Committee's findings: a review of housing policies to avoid discrimination in the public sector, rehabilitation rather than redevelopment in the inner city, provision for the under-fives, and the creation of a new awareness in teacher training of the multi-racial dimension.

However important housing and education were thought to be, Scarman identified unemployment as the crucial factor at the root of the Brixton disorders and thus pointed to one of the costs of the government's economic policy. He also agreed with the Home Affairs Committee on the need to reform Section 11:

The attack on racial disadvantage must be more direct than it has been. It must be coordinated by central government who with local authorities must ensure that the funds made available are directed to specific areas of racial disadvantage. A policy of direct coordinated attack on racial disadvantage inevitably means that the ethnic minorities will enjoy for a time a positive discrimination in their favour. But this is a price worth paying if it accelerates the elimination of the unsettling factor of racial disadvantage from the social fabric of the United Kingdom. I believe this task to be even more urgent than the task of establishing on a permanent basis good relations between the ethnic minorities and the police. Good policing will be of no avail, unless we tackle and eliminate basic flaws in our society. And, if we succeed in eliminating racial prejudice from our society, it will not be difficult to achieve good policing.[21]

The next Labour Government must set out to ensure full equality to black citizens.

Notes and references

1. 'Racial disadvantage' was the subject of the Fifth Report from the Home Affairs Committee, Session 1980–1. *Racial Disadvantage*, vol. I, Report with Minutes of Proceedings HC 424–I, July 1981. In this document it is stated (para. 12) that 'Racial disadvantage is a particular case of relative disadvantage within society. . . . But the ethnic minorities suffer such disadvantages more than the rest of the population, and more than they would if they were white.'
2. For an historical account of these measures and their impact see chapters 4, 7, 17 in Charles Husband (ed.), *Race in Britain. Continuity and Change*, Hutchinson University Library, 1982.
3. These doubts were documented in 1967 in the PEP Report, *Racial Discrimination*. See also W.W. Daniel's *Racial Discrimination in England*, Penguin Books, 1968. For a summary of these findings, see E.J.B. Rose, *et al.*, *Colour and Citizenship*, IRR, 1969, OUP, especially part IV, 'Policies and Practices'.
4. Gunnar Myrdal, *An American Dilemma*, Introduction, pp. LXIX, vol. I, McGraw Hill Paperback, 1964.
5. First Annual Report of the Race Relations Board, 1966–7, HMSO, para. 65.
6. See note 3 above.
7. H. Street, G. Howe and G. Bindman, *The Street Report on Anti-Discrimination Legislation*, PEP, 1967.
8. *Racial Discrimination*, HMSO, Cmnd 6234, 1975.
9. *Singh -v- Rowntree Mackintosh*, IRLR 199, 1979.
10. In *Mandla v Dowell-Lee* the Court of Appeal on 29 July 1982 astonishingly held that discrimination against Sikhs was outside the scope of the Race Relations Act, Sikhs not being a racial group. This decision will be reviewed by the House of Lords.
11. See *Griggs -v- Duke Power Co.*, 401 US 424, 1971.
12. *The British Steel Case*, Runnymede Trust, 1980.
13. *Khanna -v- Ministry of Defence*, IRLR 331, 1981.
14. D.J. Smith, *Racial Disadvantage in Britain*, (the PEP Report), Penguin Books, 1977.
15. *The Brixton Disorders 10–12 April 1981*, Report of an Inquiry by the Rt Hon the Lord Scarman, OBE, Cmnd 8427, November 1981.
16. *Policy for the Inner Cities*, White Paper, HMSO, Cmnd 6845, June 1977.
17. Simon Field, George Mair, Tom Rees and Philip Stevens, *Ethnic Minorities in Britain: a Study of Trends in Their Position Since 1961*, Home Office Research Study, no. 68, Home Office Research Unit, February 1981.
18. See note 1 above.
19. See note 1 above.
20. See note 3 above.
21. Scarman Report, 'Conclusion', para. 9.4, p. 135.

10 Sex and Social Policy
by *Miriam David and Hilary Land*

'There is now elaborate machinery to ensure that [women have] equal opportunity, equal pay and equal rights but I think we ought to stop and ask "where does this leave the family?" '[1]

Patrick Jenkin's question, which he raised while Secretary of State for the Social Services, is an important one to be asking at this juncture because it recognises that women's activities in the public world have to be seen in relation to their activities within the, allegedly, private world of the family. However, we would disagree with his view that women have now achieved equality with men, that this has been at the expense of their families and that in future social policies should be developed, or rather not developed, with the purpose of encouraging women to give priority to their families once again. Just what has all the equal opportunities legislation of the late 1960s and early 1970s achieved? We shall argue in this chapter that, contrary to Patrick Jenkin, the reforms of the 1970s which resulted in women being treated to a greater extent as individuals in their own right rather than in terms of their marital or familial status, have failed to reduce inequalities significantly between men and women. Indeed some women are concerned they may even have been counter-productive, for they drew attention to women without altering the basic relationships between men and women. The reforms addressed the issue of the economic dependence of women on men but ignored, and therefore left untouched, the division of labour within the family whereby women as wives, mothers and daughters, irrespective of their labour market activities, do most of the work of caring – for children, for men, for the sick and the old. The state has never taken anything but a tiny share of the responsibility for this work; women still do most of it and most of it unpaid. Indeed as a result of the public expenditure cuts since the mid-1970s, many public services which did do a little of the work of caring have been reduced or even withdrawn.

We have argued elsewhere that state social policies currently and in the past have sustained and reproduced rather than changed the division of labour between the sexes within the family and that they have *not* facilitated women's participation in activities outside the home. In future, if reducing inequalities between men and women is to be taken seriously as an objective, social policies have to be framed, administered and delivered using a different set of assumptions about the division of responsibilities for caring both within the family and between the family and the wider socio-economic system. In other words, reducing inequalities between men and women is not only a problem for women but also a problem for men. If women did change and behave like men in the public world and in particular if they adopted men's employment patterns, then – as Patrick Jenkin recognises – children, the sick and the old would indeed suffer. But the solution is not, as he sees it, to push women back into the home but to change the division of work within the family and to change the wider economic, political and social structures which currently accord so little value and priority to the work of caring and those who do it.

Our review of the equal opportunities policies will cover not only the two major pieces of legislation that are usually considered to be central, namely the Sex Discrimination Act 1975 and the Equal Pay Act 1975, but also other legislation such as the Employment Protection Act 1974, which aimed to improve women's rights at work, and policies to provide equality of opportunity in education, supported by changes in child-care policies. In the second section of the review we will look at areas of social policy, excluded from the Sex Discrimination Act, but in which similar policy changes have taken place; that is, social security, taxation and the law.

Our thesis is that all these policies reflect the particular political and legal framework in which they were formulated.[2] They were all enacted under Labour administrations, although some aspects of equal opportunities legislation were considered seriously under the Tory Government of 1970–3.[3] The framework chosen was that of extending individual legal rights or enhancing equality of opportunity to participate in economic and public life. The principle of equality of opportunity has a relatively long political history and has been used in a variety of social and economic policies.[4] It has not, however, always been applied in the same way but it certainly became central to the social democratic political ideology in the post-war era.[5] It is only in the last decade that this principle has been invoked for women's rights and has been applied in a very narrow fashion. It has been used to uphold a woman's rights as an individual to participate in public and social life, and has ignored the question of women's position in the family and in relation to men. Rendering women's marital and familial position invisible and without economic value has provoked criticism of the kind presented by Patrick Jenkin. Many are now opposed to this legislation and demand that it be rescinded. In the USA, where legislation of this kind has been more detailed, comprehensive and extensive, a greater and more vociferous opposition has been aroused, which has been labelled the 'anti-feminist backlash'[6]. In the conclusion to this paper we shall therefore try to present an alternative strategy for achieving equality between men and women both in the family and in the labour market. It is one which, we hope, will avoid the backlash that this current legislation arouses.

The policy of equality of opportunity between the sexes
The Sex Discrimination Act 1975 is the key piece of legislation in the battery of policies aimed at equality of opportunity between the sexes. In brief, as Sadie Robarts has summarised it:

The Sex Discrimination Act made it unlawful to treat women (or married people) less favourably than men (or single people) in education, training and employment and in the provision of goods, facilities and services. *The Equal Pay Act* said that women were entitled to equal pay with men if they were doing the same, or broadly similar work, or if the jobs had been rated as equivalent by a job evaluation exercise.[7]

Essentially, the legislation aimed to provide women with similar treatment to men in access to, and conditions of, employment. In addition to pronouncing the legal right to equal treatment, it set up the machinery to handle individual complaints about potentially unlawful treatment – either direct or indirect discrimination. This complaints procedure was based upon the machinery established under the Industrial Relations Act, 1971, where industrial tribunals review complaints and can be followed by appeals to the employment appeals tribunal. Ostensibly this procedure was to be informal and hence only quasi-judicial, but the tribunals were presided over by lawyers and judges. More important, the burden of proof of unfair treatment either in terms of pay or work conditions lies with the individual complainant. On the other hand, the Act also established the Equal Opportunities Commission (EOC) to monitor the workings of the two Acts and 'to promote equality of opportunity for men and women'. The Act also included provisions to achieve equal educational opportunities which would, supposedly, provide the entry qualifications to the labour market. Here the procedure was to be different, although still relying mainly on individual action. Complaints are channelled through schools, LEAs and the DES, and ultimately reach the County Courts rather than tribunals. Moreover, many types of educational institution are exempt from the provisions of the Act – such as single sex schools.[8]

In sum, the legislation is not at all concerned with removing institutional discrimination as it manifests itself in schools, places of work, banks and so forth.[9] It focuses upon discrimination, direct or indirect, as it falls on individual women. Moreover, legal redress is extremely limited, usually consisting of financial compensation. Unlike the USA, for example, upon whose legislation much of our formulation was based, an act of litigation does not create a legal precedent of compliance. In other words, it is the individual woman's grievance that is corrected, but the employer is not required to alter his future or other employment practices to comply with the law. Also unlike the USA, actions cannot be brought as what are termed 'class actions', covering groups of women in like or similar situations. Nor can corroborating evidence from other women in similar situations, what are in the USA called *amicus curiae*, be used by the complainant (or, for that matter, the defence).[10]

The liberal framework forming the backcloth to the legislation is individualistic, even more so than that on which it draws. The American legislation, formulated almost a decade prior to the British (their Equal Pay Act was passed in 1963 and the Civil Rights Act, which provided for equal employment opportunities on the grounds of sex as well as race or national origin, was enacted in 1964), has developed into a much stronger set of provisions.[11] In the USA, the emphasis has moved from what has been called being 'sex-blind' (or 'colour-blind') and providing for equality of access at the point of employment to ensuring that equality of treatment is achieved within institutional settings, such as employment or education.[12]

The Americans have developed the policy of 'affirmative action' through, initially, a series of presidential initiatives called executive orders (implemented for organisations with Federal contracts), to changes in the legislation. This policy has also become known as reverse discrimination or the method of 'statistical parity' whereby employers or educational institutions are required to set goals, targets or quotas which aim to ensure that employers attain certain proportions of women or minority groups which compare with their relative incidence in the population.[13] Although the Americans are also concerned with legal rights they do not rely on individual acts of litigation to change the situation but set out deliberately to forge a new environment for women and/or ethnic minorities. This, of course, has not been without major drawbacks and has, itself, created a huge backlash.[14] There have been many attempts in the USA to discredit the policy of affirmative action, the most famous of which is the Bakke case in the field of higher education.[15] Since the USA is, if anything, a more litigious society than Britain, the policy was ultimately decided in the Federal Supreme Court. Affirmative action was not deemed unconstitutional but the methods of applying it are strictly limited.[16]

The British legislation is also more limited than that of the EEC and the individual countries which are signatories to the Treaty of Rome. Since Britain signed the Treaty the directives issued by the EEC on equal pay and equal treatment are legally binding on the British

Government. For instance, the Equal Pay Directive (1975) says that women and men should have equal pay for work of equal value. The Equal Treatment Directive (1976), which came into force in 1978, required the elimination of sex discrimination, direct or indirect, in access to employment, promotion, training or working conditions. A number of British cases have been taken to the court in Strasbourg and been decided upon by European rather than British law, but the British have refused to implement them.[17]

The main drawback to the British legislation, notwithstanding the statutory powers given to the EOC, is that it focuses upon individual cases at the point of access to employment. The fact of the matter is that many women, perhaps the majority, are excluded from equality of access, by virtue of both their prior education and training and their familial or marital work. The weakest parts of the Act are, in fact, those promoting equality of opportunity in education. It does not require that children at school or students at college get equal or the same curricula, merely that they are not denied curricular opportunities.[18] The DES has been slow to implement the paltry provisions of the Act, and there has been no positive or affirmative action. It has been deemed sufficient to ensure that boys or girls are permitted access to courses traditionally reserved for the other sex. The HMIs, in their 1973 survey of curricular differences in secondary schools (prior to the passing of the Act), found considerable sex segregation in school offerings of both academic and non-academic subjects. There have since been few attempts to change that situation.[19] Kelly's project on 'Girls into Science and Technology' is a unique piece of action research based on ten Greater Manchester comprehensive schools and aimed at getting more girls to study both the physical sciences and also craft, design and technology.[20]

On the other hand, the DES has begun to promote, out of all keeping with practice at least since the Second World War, notions about what should be included in the school curriculum.[21] In all the documents produced there is a tension between the lip-service paid to equality of opportunity and the promotion of new subjects in the curriculum, notably moral or religious education which is to include 'family life' education.[22] At this juncture, this seems likely to espouse a traditional view of the family and especially parental responsibility, predicated upon a notion of the sexual division of responsibilities. In other words, sex difference, especially in parenting, is to be taught or preached about. Indeed, most of the courses on parent education are to be taught either to girls at school or to young mothers.[23]

This subtle shift in what is taught in schools and the contradictory emphases on sexual equality versus sex difference in adult life are mirrored in the organisation of schooling. Since the advent of comprehensive education there has, as Jenny Shaw has so clearly pointed out, been a quiet and unquestioned move towards co-education from single-sex schooling.[24]

There is much evidence to suggest that single-sex schooling, in certain contexts, provides girls with better prospects for educational achievement.[25] There is now a lively debate amongst feminists as to which is the better strategy to advocate.[26]

Two other recent policy changes signal the extent to which the organisation of schooling assumes maternal responsibility and availability for child rearing: namely the attempts in some LEAs to alter the hours of schooling to a continental school day and the very recent changes in the statutory requirements to provide school meals.[27]

Most significant of all are the contradictory efforts to extend educational opportunities to younger children, particularly those below the age of compulsory schooling.[28] Official policy is mainly concerned with promoting more equal provision for children from different social class backgrounds. There has been no concern about equality between parents in their responsibility for their children's pre-school education. Since the Plowden Report of 1967,[29] there has been a largely unquestioned assumption about the value of parental participation. This is in fact a pseudonym for maternal involvement, assuming that children's educational achievement is improved by their mother's participation in their daily schooling.[30] Moreover, participation usually means parental education rather than parental control of their children's schooling. However, as a result of the Taylor Committee's report,[31] a parent representative is now statutorily required on governing bodies. This principle, rather than that of maternal involvement, could certainly be built upon for pre-school provisions.

Various semi-official organisations have recognised the need for improvements in pre-school provision for both children and their mothers, especially those in paid employment. Governments have been slow to act but have commissioned research on which most of our knowledge of the situation is based.[32] Originally backing 'low cost' solutions, government has relied on solutions which either depend upon maternal involvement (such as playgroups) or which are based upon the maternal model of child-care (such as child-minders).[33] The nurseries that are provided by the state through the DHSS and local social service departments reach a tiny proportion of the relevant age group (less than 1 per cent) and normally exist to provide a daily substitute for 'inadequate mothers' such as those who are at risk of battering their children or who are rearing their children alone. They do not cater even for ordinary 'working mothers'.[34]

In short, virtually none of the recent legislation divests women of their responsibilities for caring for children, husbands or other members of the family; nor does it recognise that these responsibilities limit women's possibilities of achieving equality of access to employment. On the contrary, the educational service has recently tried to reinforce women's parental responsibilities and ties to the home. The government has not made it easier for mothers to take paid employment with young or even school-age children.[35] In fact, the Under-Secretary of State at the DHSS recently joined Patrick Jenkin in reasserting that it is parents' responsibility, not that of state, to make child-care arrangements.[36] In the Employment Protection Act 1975 provision 25 ensured that women, at the point of maternity, were provided with entitlements to maternity leave, pay and job reinstatement,[37] but this is of limited relevance to the majority of women if no subsequent provision is made for the care of her children until the start of compulsory schooling, and even then the daily hours restrict women's potential employment either to jobs in the education service or to part-time employment which fits with the school day.[38] If mothers do not accept these constraints and take regular full-time employment, they are often castigated for rearing 'latch-key children'.[39] The idea of the extended school day or of community schools for multiple purposes was tried only briefly in the early 1970s.[40]

Although the equal opportunities legislation has created a climate in which it is possible for individual women to take paid employment and request equal pay and conditions, it has not managed to create an infra-structure in which most women can seize these opportunities. On the contrary, the effect has been to stimulate hostility to the idea of women's equal participation in paid employment.[41] Since the Tory government returned to office, it has not only ignored the spirit of the legislation but has turned the tide back to the espousal of traditional familial values and behaviour. For example, Rhodes Boyson, junior Minister of Education, 'laid the responsibility for rioting youths, football hooligans and murderous muggings on the sins committed by the parents of today's disillusioned youth'.[42]

Although the EOC has the potential to achieve equal opportunities by its direction rather than individual complaints, it has chosen not to do so. It argues that it must proceed by persuasion and gentle behind-the-scenes debate rather than coercion.[44] It had taken up fewer formal investigations in its first three years than the Commission for Racial Equality (with the same sorts of powers) had in one year.[45] One of its most significant monitoring exercises, that on Tameside LEA's handling of its return to selective education, merely showed up both its and the legislation's ineffectiveness.[46] The fact that more girls passed the 11+ but were offered fewer selective places was deemed out of the scope of the law, because the majority of places provided were in single-sex schools – that is, boys' grammar schools.

The Equal Pay Act has been as ineffective as the Sex Discrimination Act, not only because of the drawbacks in the legislation and the interpretations put on it by the tribunal chairman,[47] but also because of the assumptions operating in the labour market that women, because of their home responsibilities, do not do the same or broadly similar work as men.[48] The labour market remains, and has become even more, rigidly sex segregated, with women tending to be offered work which mirrors the kinds of jobs they do within the home.[49]

Social security, taxation and the law

Social security

The pension system, reformed in 1975, now recognises the work of caring for the young, the sick and the old by giving credits which maintain the caretaker's entitlement to the basic state pension. This replaced Beveridge's married woman's option which, in effect, entitled every woman by virtue of being a wife to a pension (worth 60 per cent of the basic pension) on the basis of her husband's contribution record. Because of this, all men paid a higher contribution than women. Now women pay contributions on the same basis as men. Broadly speaking, the introduction of the home responsibilities credit is a subsidy to those – mainly, but not exclusively, women – who care for the young, the sick or the old on a nearly full-time basis. This is a welcome step, but women who combine their responsibilities in the home with a greater degree of participation in the labour market, together with men and women without those responsibilities, will be subsidising them. Once again, it is the traditional division of unpaid labour in the home which is being favoured.

Although the Social Security Pensions Act 1975 did attempt to put men and women on an equal footing, other remnants of the past remain. Unequal retirement ages have been incorporated into the new scheme. As a result the effects of differential mortality rates for men and women are exacerbated. Women currently outlive men by about six years. As they retire five years earlier they can expect on average to spend twice as long as men in retirement and to them survivor's pensions are important. The capital value of a flat rate pension for a woman, paid from age sixty, is about twice as much as that of the same pension for a man paid from age sixty-five.

The Trades Union Congress and the Labour Party support a common pension age of sixty years. However, they give priority to providing an adequate state contributory pension which does not require a means tested supplement. The prevailing view seems to be that it is preferable for women to withdraw from the labour market rather than for men to have to retire five years earlier.

One of the more radical features of the 1975 Act was the recognition, for the first time in the history of the British social security system, of voluntary role reversal. It was not until the regulations were published in January 1978 that it was clear that married men who stayed at home to care for children would have their pensions protected.

For the first time a married woman who paid full contributions became entitled to unemployment and sickness benefits at the same rate as her single sister. However, currently – unlike her husband – she has no automatic rights to additional dependency benefits for her children, and unless her husband is incapable of paid employment she gets no extra benefit for him either. As a result of the EEC directive requiring equal treatment for men and women in member countries' social security schemes, the British system has had to be further modified. Dependants' benefits will disappear as they are being held down until the universal child benefit catches up with them. From November 1983, married women will have the right to apply for family income supplement whereas currently only the husband in a married couple may do so. Provided the couple agree that she has been, and is, the main breadwinner, a married woman will be able to apply for means tested supplementary benefit.

Under the EEC directive, further changes will eventually have to be made in two new non-contributory benefits introduced in legislation passed in 1975. One, the non-contributory invalidity pension, is paid for those who are incapable of work and do not qualify for a contributory pension. Work is taken to be paid employment if the claimant is a man or single woman, but if she is a married or cohabiting woman then eligibility is based on her capacity to perform 'normal household duties'. The second is the invalid care allowance which is paid to men and women who give up paid employment in order to care for a sick or elderly person, not necessarily a relative. However, married or cohabiting women are not eligible in any circumstances, although all the evidence shows that they provide substantial care for the sick and elderly and that their opportunities for paid employment are thereby reduced or removed altogether. These benefits, introduced in legislation passed in the same year as the British Sex Discrimination Act, are perhaps two of the most blatant examples of the way in which married women are seen first and foremost as housewives and thus responsible for all the domestic work within the home.

None of these changes really recognise that the majority of families depend on the earnings of *both* husband and wife, even if the wife's contribution in most instances is smaller (in 1980 it averaged 28 per cent of family income). Families are still perceived as consisting of one breadwinner who only exceptionally is a woman, and of a dependent spouse whose primary responsibilities lie in the home. These families are, in fact, a minority. The General Household Survey 1979 found that only 20 per cent of economically active married men supported a dependent wife and children.[50] There is even less recognition of the needs of women who combine paid employment *and* care for their families, especially if their employment is part-time.

There are other processes which are undermining women's access to the social insurance system. Although married women have won rights to benefit which are not affected by their marital status as directly as in the recent past, more women are being pushed beyond the reaches of the scheme altogether. In 1977, 22 per cent of female part-time employees were earning less than £15 a week which at the time defined the boundary of non-employed for social insurance purposes (which means that neither they nor their employers have to pay national insurance contributions). By 1979 this had doubled.[51] National insurance contributions now constitute 9 per cent of labour costs (compared with 6 per cent in the mid-1970s), so these workers are very attractive to employers. Poor provision of income maintenance for those with part-time earnings stems from a failure to recognise that most women work part-time not because their earnings are inessential, but because their employment opportunities are severely constrained by their family commitments.

Part-time workers who earn enough to pay contributions may not qualify for unemployment benefit unless they can produce evidence that they have a 'reasonable chance' of getting part-time employment in the locality. In addition, as the responsibility for the registration of unemployment benefit is changing from Job Centres to unemployment benefit offices, pilot studies are being conducted in twenty of the latter to test new administrative procedures for establishing 'availability for work'. Women are to be asked detailed questions about their child-care arrangements, and failure to produce satisfactory answers may disqualify them from benefit. In other words, women's caring responsibilities are being used as a ground for *excluding* them from benefits.

In short, Barbara Castle's attempts to make women full citizens of the social insurance scheme, irrespective of their marital status, have had only limited success.

Income tax

The income tax system has also been the subject of review during the past decade. Some of the central pillars of the British tax system include the aggregation rule,[52] under which a wife's income is deemed to be her husband's for tax purposes, and the married tax allowance, which gives married men a personal tax allowance 40 per cent higher than a single person's. The assumption of women's dependency on men remains.

The current administration produced a Green Paper in 1980 called *The Taxation of Husband and Wife*. The Green Paper does discuss the central issues of women's dependence on their husbands and the aggregation of the incomes of husband and wife, but in a narrow and biased way. It is acknowledged that the married allowance 'recognises the special legal and moral obligations on a husband to support a wife' but that 'in recent years the tendency has been for these obligations to become reciprocal'. However it accepts, first on fiscal grounds and subsequently on social grounds, that 'where one spouse is dependent upon the other for financial support, there is a case for some recognition by the state'.[53] There is a very cursory attempt to distinguish between the reasons for that dependency. The paper therefore discusses equity in the tax system almost entirely in terms of relativities between married and single people, between one-earner and two-earner couples, and between men and women, taking little account of the existence of dependants, be they children or incapacitated relatives. There is little recognition that the care of children, the sick or the old is socially useful and necessary work and that if, as a result of doing this work, an adult cannot support herself (or himself) through paid employment, the state has some obligation to provide maintenance.

The authors of the Green Paper clearly favour replacing the married tax allowance with a system which would allow non-earning spouses to transfer their tax allowances either fully to partially to their partners. This would protect the position of the family with a married woman at home looking after children, compared with a two-earner couple. That this 'could well discourage married women from taking up work in the first place'[54] is not presented as a major problem. It is no coincidence that such a proposal is favoured at a time of high male unemployment.

The alternative approach of providing for the non-earning spouse through the social security system is given short shrift. The discussion is much influenced by 'the Government's view [that] more than accounting conventions are involved here: the distinction between cash benefits (which increase public expenditure) and tax allowances (which do not) is an important one'.[55] (When in opposition, both Sir Geoffrey Howe and Patrick Jenkin, who was Secretary of State for the Social Services at the time the Green Paper was being prepared, accepted that there was an equivalence between them.) The possibility of abolishing the married tax allowance and using the £3 billion additional tax revenue either to double child benefits and to extend the invalid care allowance to married women or to pay a special home responsibilities benefit is given a brief look and dismissed. The same argument was advanced as at the time when the Labour Government abolished the child tax allowance and translated it into a higher cash child benefit: it would transfer cash from the man's wallet to the woman's purse and this would be too unpopular. The Green Paper states that 'whereas with the child tax allowance it was not the claimant's own allowance which was at stake but only in effect an additional allowance for a dependant. with the addition of the married allowance *married men might be even more inclined to regard themselves as "losers"* particularly if their circumstances were such that the family did not stand to benefit from the additional social security provision available'[56] (our italics). This is one of, if not *the* main reason, for the statement in the Green Paper that 'In the Government's view, the arguments against provision for a dependent spouse through the social security system . . . are very weighty.'[57]

The view that this government is reluctant to alter the existing unequal economic relationship between husband and wife is supported by the Green Paper's very different approach to meeting the needs of one-parent families. In this case the equivalence of tax relief and cash benefits is acceptable. The additional personal allowance for single parents means that their personal allowance is the same as the married allowance. The Green Paper favours replacing this by increasing the already enhanced child benefit for one-parent families[58] because 'It would concentrate help for lone parents in the single form of a cash benefit, low paid working lone parents whose earnings are below the tax threshold would gain financially and their incentive to work would be improved.'[59] As a result of such a transfer it would be possible to provide financial support for lone parents much more selectively and therefore cheaply. The Board of Inland Revenue has not needed to become involved in administering cohabitation rules, and the eligibility criteria for the additional personal allowance for lone parents are very simple and are not concerned with cohabitation or financial support from the other parent. By transforming this tax relief into an even more enhanced child benefit for lone parents administered by the DHSS, cohabitation rules could be applied to *all* lone parents seeking financial assistance from the state. The message seems clear: women with children should be dependent on their husbands or the men with whom they live. If they have no claims on a man then they should be encouraged to seek paid employment.

The law

The original justification for the introduction of the married allowance in 1918 stemmed in part from a man's legal obligation to maintain his wife. As even the authors of the Green Paper acknowledge, family law has changed in this respect, especially since the Matrimonial Causes Act 1973. However, the principle of a life-long obligation to maintain which is accepted on marriage is currently under review. In 1980 the Law Commission published a discussion paper which examined alternative principles which might form the basis of future law. In December 1981, they published their recommendations.

The Law Commission explicitly confined themselves to the law governing the obligations of husband and wife to each other. The possibilities and consequences of shifting *away* from private law for the enforcement of financial obligations against individuals, and towards a system under which claims to maintenance would be met by the state through the social security system making financial provision for families affected by divorce, were not explored. Their reasons for this were partly that the Finer Committee on One Parent Families which reported in 1974 had already done so, and partly because such a shift would have implications for public expenditure. They did accept, however, that the reform of private law can have little impact on the alleviation of poverty and that hardship and deprivation were the most serious problems faced by the majority of single parents. (In 1981 there were 346,000 single parents receiving supplementary benefit, about 30 per cent of whom were divorced women.) The question addressed therefore was to what extent could or should individuals look to a former spouse for maintenance and to what extent could or should they, in particular wives, be self-sufficient.

The Law Commission's conclusions were that the objective of leaving the financial position of the parties unaffected by divorce should be abandoned. Provision of adequate financial support for children should have an overriding priority and more emphasis should be placed on the wife's earning potential, and 'any periodic financial provision ordered in favour of one spouse (usually the wife) for her own benefit – as distinct from the periodical payments made to enable her to care for the children – should be primarily directed to secure wherever possible a smooth transition from marriage to the status of independence.'[60] In February 1982, the government accepted these recommendations and announced their intention to introduce legislation 'when the opportunity occurs'.

On the face of it, this sounds quite a radical departure from the principle that once married a woman is, and should be, a life-long dependant of her husband. However, the context within which this principle would be put into practice may make 'independence' rather a sham. The Law Commission seems to have recognised this in the discussion paper when they quote the Finer Committee who said:

Since the early days of industrialisation, women have constituted both a significant proportion of the country's labour force and a main source of cheap labour. An inescapable conclusion from the many recent studies of women's experiences in trying to reconcile the claims of marriage, motherhood and work is the existence of a traditional and firmly rooted double standard of occupational morality. As a society we pay lip service to the ideal of equality for women whilst practising discrimination in the very area where it hurts most.[61]

However, what remains unacknowledged is the extent to which the inequality women experience in the labour market stems as much from the division of labour within and beyond marriage as from the 'double standard of occupational morality'. Their proposals would do little to alter this. Far more women than men continue to carry out the duties included in the marriage contract long after the legal marriage has ceased to exist. In nearly 90 per cent of divorces involving children custody is awarded to the mother and very few women cease caring for their children before they reach adulthood. They will therefore continue to experience a conflict between their family responsibilities and their paid employment for a considerable period after the marriage has ended. In contrast, marriage and the aftermath of divorce rarely disadvantages men in the labour market. In most marriages the husband's work and career is still put first and in many ways, in the services she provides for her husband, a wife is enhancing his prospects in the labour market. Given the low value our society places on the work of caring, women are, in effect, de-skilled by the experience of marriage. Men then gain in terms of their ability to be financially self-sufficient as a result of marriage; women on the whole lose. This is nowhere recognised in the discussion paper; if it were, then basing a wife's financial claims on the principle of compensation might have been considered.

In addition, men more often and more quickly break their side of the contract, namely to provide maintenance for the children and their former wife. The Finer Committee reporting in 1974 found that half of the maintenance orders made in the magistrates' courts were in arrears, half of them over £200 in arrears. In 1980, the House of Commons was told that only 6 per cent of one-parent families relied on maintenance as their sole source of support. This contrasts with over 50 per cent of lone mothers on supplementary benefit. In practice, then, the claims to maintenance which a woman has on the state are as important – and more reliable – than the claims many of them are able to make on their husbands.

The overall picture of women's position in the three interlocking areas of state policy examined in this section shows that attempts made during the last decade to alter the assumptions about the division of responsibilities within the family have met with considerable resistance. In some areas, notably social insurance, women have acquired greater rights as individuals, but these are being undermined not only by administrative practices but also by changes in the structure and boundaries of the formal labour market. Women's claims are still substantially weaker than men's. Women are discriminated against because they have caring responsibilities in the family, rather than, as in the past, just because they are married, and this affects most women. Marital status is still an important determinant of eligibility for benefit because married or cohabiting women who are prevented from being self-supporting because of their caring responsibilities do not have claims to maintenance on the state but are expected to be maintained by their husbands (or the men with whom they live). In return for her maintenance, a woman must provide domestic services for her husband. Only if she cannot because she is incapacitated does she then have claims to maintenance on the state which do not derive from her labour market activities. The assumptions about the nature of the marriage contract upon which the recent changes in policy have been based have therefore altered very little indeed.

Conclusion

We have argued that there have been contradictory processes at work during the last decade, a period normally characterised as one in which women have won equal opportunities with men. We have shown that the policies themselves were of limited relevance to the goal of achieving equal opportunities, that they focused on a narrow view of the problem and, in particular, they ignored the whole question of women's work within the family. Recently, especially under the Conservative Government, the policies have been modified and women encouraged or cajoled to return to their work within the home rather than the labour market.

If the goal of reducing inequalities between men and women is to be taken seriously, it is a problem not only for women but also for men. Women's work within the family caring for children, men, the old and the sick must be included in the calculus for change. It must be recognised not only in social policy but in economic policy. In other words, our views about what we mean by work must change.

Specifically, we would argue that, realistically, equal opportunities between men and women can only be achieved if it is recognised that men, too, may have responsibilities for caring and that they are entitled to exercise these. In this respect, the whole notion of the 'family wage' must be scrutinised and it must be made clear that the family has never been fully maintained simply through the male wage.

The wage system cannot provide for the differing needs of families as they move through the family life cycle. A shorter working week, of say twenty-five hours, would make this even more obvious. Adequate child benefits are clearly necessary and as a first step they could be doubled immediately for all children if the married man's tax allowance were abolished. In the longer term there are fundamental questions to be asked about what wages are for and how family income should be adjusted to family size. A shorter working day (rather than a shorter working week) must be one of the most immediate demands necessary to achieve this goal of equality in caring. This would acknowledge that caring cannot be done in the interstices of paid employment, but is a regular, on-going, daily responsibility. Allied to this is the need to recognise that such caring may periodically affect availability for paid employment. We would wish to see not only a shorter working day, but entitlement, through the national insurance system, as is already possible in other Western European countries such as France, to time off with cash benefits to care for sick relatives, be they dependent children, spouses, disabled or elderly relatives. This leave should be irrespective of the sex of the carer.

For those with longer-term responsibilities for the sick and disabled, there is the invalid care allowance introduced in 1976. However, currently single women and all men are eligible for this non-contributory benefit and although from June 1981 the carer no longer has to be a close relative, married women are still excluded. The EOC has calculated that this means that only 0.5 per cent of carers receive this benefit.[62] Eligibility for the invalid care allowance should be extended to married and cohabiting women.

Maternity pay and leave in Britain is not generous compared with most other European countries. We would like to see the period of paid leave extended to nine months or a year, with fathers given the option of taking some part of it. In addition we would wish parental leave to be treated as positively as leave for other reasons, for example with respect to occupational pension contributions, or entitlements to annual increments.

We would also like to see services and facilities financed by the state to enable those with caring responsibilities to exercise them adequately. We would not, however, wish to see the services and facilities of the health and personal social services necessarily managed by the state, as a central bureaucracy. Rather we would like them to be locally based, in neighbourhoods sufficiently close to home to ease the burden of care. They should be community controlled and managed by democratically elected, neighbourhood councils, which would include those most intimately involved in caring for children, the sick and the old.

In particular, we are aware of the chronic lack of services in close proximity to home not only for the sick and the elderly, but especially for pre-school children and children of school age, after school hours and in school holidays, times which do not mesh with the current hours of paid employment. Hence our demand for a shorter working day. There will, even with a shorter working day, still be a need for care for children, either full-time for those below the age of compulsory schooling or after school hours and in the holidays. We would want comprehensive community controlled day-care facilities in neighbourhood premises and after-school play centres based at the school on the lines already operating in a few local education authorities. We recognise the value of educational services and the valuable contribution already made by nursery education, and would like to see day-care combined with education. Given that nursery education is free of charge, we can see the same argument for day-care being free of charge to the direct consumer (with, of course, the exception being made for meals). This case has already been made out extremely well by the TUC's Working Party in their pamphlet, *The Under Fives*. It was also made, on slightly different grounds, by the CPRS in *Services for Children with Working Mothers*. We would not argue the case only for pre-school day-care but for day-care for school children, the disabled and the elderly. Indeed, we can see no argument against the comprehensive provision of day-care for all such groups, provided on the same terms. At present, in our system of social services, there is not only rigid sex segregation but age segregation, a system which we would dearly wish to see modified.

Our general argument has implications not only for the form of social service provision but for its administration. The trouble is that services have traditionally been provided for 'client groups' within the same categories of need and where caring has been seen as an attribute of one sex only. We would like to see modifications in the ways in which services are administered to take account of the needs of a variety of consumers. If women who have had experience of such care had more opportunities for being involved in the formulation of policies as well as the administration of such services we would develop very different kinds of systems.

In sum, we are arguing that, if our goal is equal opportunities between men and women, our views and assumptions about not only social policies but also economic policies and family relationships must be radically changed. We might eventually reach a situation in which sex was not the main criterion by which we allocated care and maintenance in our society. Men and women would have equal claims on the labour market, the state and the family, while care would be work of central value in our society.

Notes and references

1. Quoted in J. Coussins and A. Coote, *The Family in the Firing Line: A Discussion Document on Family Policy*, Poverty Pamphlet 51, CPAG and NCCL, 1981, p. 7.
2. M.E. David, *The State, the Family and Education*, Routledge and Kegan Paul, 1980, chapter 1.
3. A. Sachs and J. Hoff Wilson, *Sexism and the Law*, Martin Robertson, 1978.
4. J. Parker, *Social Policy and Citizenship*, Macmillan, 1976.
5. Centre for Contemporary Cultural Studies, *Unpopular Education*, Hutchinson, 1981.

6. R.P. Petchesky, 'Anti-abortion Anti-feminism and the Rise of the New Right', *Feminist Studies*, 7, 2, summer 1981.
7. Sadie Roberts, *Positive Action for Women: The Next Step*, NCCL, 1981, p. 7.
8. Harriet Harman, *Sex Discrimination in Schools – How to Fight It*, NCCL, 1978.
9. Roberts, *op. cit.*
10. *Ibid.*
11. M.E. David, 'Sex, Education and Social Policy: Towards a new Moral Economy', in J. Lewis (ed.), *Women and Public Policy*, Croom Helm, 1982.
12. N. Glazer, *Affirmative Discrimination*, Basic Books, 1976.
13. *Ibid.*
14. Z. Eisenstein, 'Anti-feminism in the Politics and Election of 1980', *Feminist Studies*, 7, 2, summer 1981.
15. R. Dworkin, *Taking Rights Seriously*, Duckworth, 1978.
16. *Ibid.*
17. Roberts, *op. cit.*
18. David, *op. cit.*
19. M.E. David, *The State, the Family and Education*, Routledge and Kegan Paul, 1980, chapter 12.
20. Alison Kelly's personal communication, Department of Sociology, University of Manchester.
21. David, 'Sex, Education and Social Policy'.
22. *Ibid.*
23. *Ibid.*
24. Jenny Shaw, 'Mixed Schooling – A Mixed Blessing?', in R. Deem (ed.), *Women and Schooling*, Routledge and Kegan Paul, 1980.
25. R.R. Dale, *Single Sex or Mixed Schools*, vols 1–3, Routledge and Kegan Paul, 1975.
26. M. Arnot, 'Coeducation', in L. Barton and S. Walker (eds), *Gender, Class and Education*, Falmer Press, 1982.
27. David, *The State, the Family and Education*.
28. M.E. David, 'Day Care Policies and Parenting', *Journal of Social Policy*, 1982, vol 11, 1, pp. 81–92.
29. Central Council on Education, *Children and Their Primary Schools*, Plowden, HMSO, 1967.
30. David, 'Day Care Policies and Parenting'.
31. *Ibid.*
32. M. Bone, *Preschool Services and the Need for Day Care*, OPCS/HMSO, 1977.
33. David, 'Day Care Policies and Parenting'.
34. M. Hughes *et al.*, *Nurseries Now*, Penguin, 1980.
35. *Ibid.*
36. M.E. David, 'Sexual Morality, Sex Education and the New Right, A New "Policy of Restriction" ', paper given at BSA Conference, Manchester University, 6 April 1982.
37. J. Coussins, *Maternity Provisions for Working Women*, NCCL, 1981.
38. David, 'Day Care Policies and Parenting'.
39. *Ibid.*
40. M.E. David, *Reform, Reaction and Resources*, NFER Publishing Company, 1977.
41. Roberts, *op. cit.*
42. David, 'Sexual Morality'.
43. *Guardian*, 15 May 1979, p. 2.
44. EOC Annual Reports.
45. Anna Coote, 'Equality and the Curse of the Quango', *New Statesman*, 1 December 1978.
46. EOC Investigation into Tameside LEA, 1977.
47. J. Coussins, *The Equality Report*, NCCL, 1976.
48. J. West (ed.), *Work, Women and the Labour Market*, Routledge and Kegan Paul, 1981.

49. C. Hakim, *Occupational Segregation*, Research Paper No. 9, Department of Employment, HMSO, 1979.
50. OPCS, *General Household Survey 1979*, HMSO, 1981, p. 77.
51. *Ibid*. p. 163.
52. Section 37 of the Income and Corporation Taxes Act 1970 states: 'A woman's income chargeable to income tax shall (for any year) during which she is a married woman living with her husband be deemed for income tax purposes to be his income and not to be her income.'
53. *The Taxation of Husband and Wife*, Cmnd 8093, HMSO, 1980, p. 24.
54. *Ibid*. p. 27.
55. *Ibid*. p. 29.
56. *Ibid*. p. 31.
57. *Ibid*. p. 32.
58. Lone parents can claim a larger child benefit, worth £3 more than the normal child benefit in 1981.
59. *Ibid*. p. 42.
60. The Law Commission, *The Financial Consequences of Divorce*, HC 68, HMSO, 1981, p. 11.
61. The Law Commission, *The Financial Consequences of Divorce: The Basic Policy, A Discussion Paper*, Cmnd 6599, HMSO, 1979.
62. EOC, *Who Cares for the Carers*, 1982.

A Caring Community
by Alan Walker

The remarkable accord between the two main political parties on the policy of 'community care' has existed for virtually the whole of the post-war period. Moreover, whereas the consensus on economic policies was broken by the fiscal crisis of the mid-1970s, the parties continue to agree on the importance of community care. The last Labour Secretary of State for Social Services, David Ennals, in 1977 announced that:

The present government was elected on policies which included protection of the weak and vulnerable in society . . . the progress of these policies is dependent on . . . how far [the public] will by their own efforts contribute to 'community care'. All of us, politicians or social workers, have an educative role here.

Four years later, the Conservative Secretary of State, Patrick Jenkin, argued along similar lines: 'The government's approach to the personal social services is founded on the simple fact that the frontline providers of social care always have been, are, and will continue to be, the family and the community.'

Thus, for different reasons, community care appeals to a wide variety of political values. It promotes independence, reflects an idealist model of social relations and is thought to be cheaper than residential care.

Examination of the reality underlying this consensus reveals a sharp contrast between political rhetoric and the day-to-day experience of giving and receiving care in the community. Far from there being care by the community, the bulk of care is provided within families, by female kin. Community care policy has taken the role of women as primary carers for granted. But in recent years this assumption has been questioned increasingly by women themselves, and serious doubt has been cast upon the future of a policy based, implicitly or explicitly, on the unequal sexual division of labour in family and society.[1] As Lesley Rimmer and Malcolm Wicks show in Chapter 3, the changing age structure of the population, the increased labour force participation by married women, as well as the divorce rate, raise questions about the future of community care as currently defined. The policy, however, has been subjected to surprisingly little critical attention. The purpose of this chapter is to contribute to a reappraisal through an analysis of the

development, practice and assumptions underlying community care. It
is suggested that, at best, care is provided *in* the community, by female
kin, and not *by* 'the community' and that, on grounds of social justice
and equality, this practice is untenable. At the end of the chapter are
some proposals that would begin to develop a form of *shared care*
between state and family and between men and women.

The development of community care policy

The notion that care should be provided in the community in preference to institutions developed in the early part of this century alongside
a growing awareness of the effect of institutions on people. At the turn
of the century the Local Government Board recommended 'more
homely' accommodation than the workhouse. The Mental Deficiency
Act 1913 provided for voluntary and statutory supervision of the
mentally handicapped in the community.[2] The Royal Commission on
Lunacy and Mental Disorder (1924–6) and the annual reports of the
Board of Control added weight to the pressure for the appointment of
almoners (psychiatric social workers) to help keep families together and
to assist patients and their families.[3] The development of services
proved to be painfully slow. By the end of the Second World War only
twenty-six psychiatric social workers had been appointed. Community
care policy became more explicit in the immediate post-war period
when the Curtis Committee recommended, in 1946, that preference
should be given to the care of deprived children in private homes or in
small groups. The 1948 Children Act established this principle.

The term 'community care' was first used in the field of mental
health. The Royal Commission on the Law Relating to Mental Illness
and Mental Deficiency (1957) recommended a shift in emphasis from
hospital care to community care for the mentally ill and mentally
deficient. It was argued that the term 'community care' should be
substituted for 'supervision' because the latter term suggested 'enforcement of control' over the mentally handicapped. According to the
Royal Commission, 'community care' covers 'all forms of care (including residential care) which it is appropriate for the local health or
welfare authorities to provide'.[4] One aim of the Mental Health Act 1959
was to establish a comprehensive community care service to meet the
needs of mentally disordered patients not requiring hospital treatment.
According to the Minister of Health, 'One of the main principles which
we are seeking to prove is the reorientation of the mental health services
away from institutional care towards care in the community.'[5] A similar
shift in policy was also proposed for the care of elderly people. In 1958
the Minister of Health stated that the 'underlying principle of our
services for the old should be this: that the best place for old people is in
their own homes, with help from the home services if need be.'[6]

The principle of extending community care for the elderly, the mentally ill and the physically and mentally handicapped was firmly established by the *Hospital Plan* and its sister report *Health and Welfare*, sometimes referred to as the 'community care blue book'.[7] The hospital plan was said officially to rest on the expansion of community care services for its success. The community care blue book contained central guidelines and details of local authority provisions and proposals for provision in ten years' time. But, as Jaehnig has pointed out, 'to propose a community care service is one matter, to make it a practical reality is quite another'.[8]

In fact the history of community care policy has been one of painfully slow progress towards very limited and misleading goals. Leaving aside the question of progress for the moment, it is important to establish that the policy of community care was compromised from the outset. In the first place, it was precarious because it was never clearly and consistently defined and, partly as a result, neither the political support, the planning machinery nor the necessary resources were ever mobilised to achieve it. Community care was and remains primarily a political slogan which, as Titmuss warned, employs idealist terms to describe limited public action.[9] The term 'community' is misplaced, and as we shall see, formal and informal provision usually takes the form of practical help and support or tending rather than 'care'. No doubt the term as well as the policy's lack of clarity are significant reasons for its survival – the words have succeeded politically even if the policy has failed.[10]

In practice, it merely meant the provision of domiciliary services by local social services departments to help people with disabilities to continue to live in their own homes. But even this limited goal was not applied consistently to all groups. For example *Health and Welfare* described the community care needs of elderly people in terms of domiciliary support, including home help, meals and laundry services and, in severe cases of disability, home nursing and night care; but, in the case of the mentally disordered, it redefined the concept of community care to include residential care.

Secondly, the principal rationale for the proposed expansion of community care in the early 1960s was economic – the official desire to reduce the cost of replacing the large number of Victorian hospitals and other institutions which were nearing obsolescence. Thirdly, the policy was primarily concerned with formal services, provided by local authorities, and paid very little attention to those members of informal networks of family and neighbourhood, and especially female kin, who provide the bulk of care. It was, in other words, concerned with care *in* the community and not care *by* the community.[11] Fourthly, there was no consensus about the precise amount of the formal provision that was required, or how it might be achieved. There was and remains a wide divergence between local authorities in their provision of services. The report *Health and Welfare* revealed massive geographical disparities in services but contained no proposals to counteract them. The question of how to ensure local compliance with national guidelines within a democratic framework was not faced squarely. Moreover figures presented in the report showed that local authorities were totally un-prepared for the proposed expansion in community care. Their plans forecast a rise in home helps of 45 per cent between 1962 and 1972 compared with a rise in residential staff of 87 per cent.[12]

Subsequent developments have confirmed the ambiguity and pre-cariousness of community care policy, the absence of strategic planning and of political determination to translate even limited policy into practice. The main events can be summarised briefly. The Seebohm Committee regarded the 'limitation' of the concept of community care to 'treatment and care outside hospital or residential homes' as 'un-fortunate'.[13] Discussion of domiciliary services was principally in relation to elderly people. Also it was only in relation to this group that the need to support families caring for dependants and for *shared* responsibility between the family and the personal social services was recognised. The commitment to community care in the White Paper on mental handicap also was ambiguous.[14] It set a target increase of 15 per cent in the number of mentally handicapped persons in residential care but omitted any planning forecasts for domiciliary services. Similarly with the review of services for the mentally ill, public opinion and resource constraints were presented as the major barriers to the achievement of a community based psychiatric service.[15]

The twin documents on priorities in health and personal social services in the mid-1970s also reaffirmed the state's commitment to community care services 'which aim to help people live an independent life in their own homes as long as possible'.[16] The latter document defined community care in remarkably broad terms:

In this document, the term 'community' covers a whole range of provision, including hospitals, hostels, day hospitals, residential homes, day centres and domiciliary support. The term 'community care' embraces primary health care and all the above services, whether provided by health authorities, local authorities, independent contractors, voluntary bodies, community self-help or family and friends.[17]

With the concept of community care so enlarged as to include all types of formal care and treatment, even the limited goal of the pro-vision of domiciliary services in preference to residential care was effectively abandoned. Planning for community care thus became primarily directed to coordination between services, not major shifts of resources from one to the other, or to closing residential institutions. The Merrison Commission on the NHS recommended that the policy of phased mental illness hospital closure should be reversed[18] and, despite its support for the Jay Committee's model of community care for people with mental handicaps, the government has refused to make a firm commitment to the closure of long-stay hospitals and to the expansion of community services.[19]

Then as public expenditure constraints tightened and the predicted expansion in the population of very elderly people came closer, the state discovered the informal sector.[20] Government's attention switched increasingly to emphasise the role of family, friends, neighbours and volunteers so that, in Abrams' term, 'nowadays neighbourhoodism is all the rage'.[21] Most recent official statements on community care reflect this stress on informal care.[22] The community care blue book (1963) described policy towards the elderly purely in terms of formal care services. The first Green Paper on policy towards the elderly, issued by the 1974–9 Labour Government, noted that 'There is no doubt that, as time goes on, growing demands will fall on the relatives of elderly people,' and where the family cannot cope we may need 'to look increasingly to the wider community to give more support of the kind traditionally expected of the family'.[23] (The launching of the national 'Be a Good Neighbour' campaign in 1976 by the Secretary of State for Social Services, David Ennals, was a specific reflection of this desire to increase community involvement in the care of the elderly.) The White Paper issued by the present Conservative Government underlined the new direction in policy by asserting that 'Care *in* the community must increasingly mean care *by* the community.'[24]

The failure of policy

The very timid goals for domiciliary support established in the 1950s and early 1960s remain unmet, let alone the political rhetoric. As Table 11.1 demonstrates, there is no evidence of a shift of resources from residential to community based care – indeed the reverse.[25]

A number of factors underlie this maintenance of the *status quo* which require more detailed analysis than is possible here. They include powerful professional interests within the hospital and residential sectors. Whilst not being opposed to community care in principle, they resist any reduction in resources in their own specialism. There is an administrative and political interest in the continued primacy of residential care where results can be clearly established in the form of bricks and mortar. Then there are trades unions' interpretations of the interests of their members working in residential institutions. In the legitimate pursuit of better conditions of service for their usually low paid and overworked members, trade unions such as COHSE have equated the continuance and expansion of the residential sector with future employment prospects. In doing so they have overlooked both

Table 11.1   Distribution of Gross Expenditure within English Local Authority Personal Social Services 1974/5–1980/1

Type of care	1974/5 %	1975/6 %	1976/7 %	1977/8 %	1978/9 %	1979/80 %	1980/1 %	1980/1 £
Residential care	49.6	51.0	50.8	50.5	51.9	51.7	51.5	974
Day care	11.3	11.4	11.8	12.3	12.4	12.2	12.4	234
Community care	22.7	21.7	21.0	21.7	20.6	20.2	19.8	375
Other	16.5	16.0	16.4	16.4	15.2	15.9	16.3	309
Total	100	100	100	100	100	100	100	1,892

Source: A. Walker, *Community Care*, Blackwell/Robertson, 1982, p. 21.

the potential for employment in alternative forms of care and the interests of those who will have to live in institutions unless alternatives are developed. In particular there is a great deal of evidence showing that residential institutions enhance dependency.[26] Finally there are administrative barriers to change, notably the 'damaging' division between health and personal social services and the qualifications and preferences of staff[27] which have not been resolved by the new joint care planning machinery between the health and personal social services.[28]

A succession of official and independent reports have documented the deficiencies in these services.[29] Table 11.2 shows the extent of the shortfall in the provision of community care services in relation to DHSS guidelines.

Three points must be made about the figures in Table 11.2. The

Table 11.2   Community Care Services in Relation to DHSS Guidelines

Service	Places per 1,000 population	
	DHSS guideline	Provision 1978/9
Day care		
Elderly (over 65)	4.0	1.1
Mental handicap	1.5	0.8
Mental illness	0.6	0.1
Domiciliary services		
Home help (over 65)	12 wte*	6.3 wte*
Meals-on-wheels	200 per week	112 per week

* Whole time equivalent.

Source: E.M. Goldberg and S. Hatch, *A New Look at the Personal Social Services*, PST, 1981, p. 6.

guidelines were established in the early 1970s and are now out of date, especially those relating to services for the elderly and very elderly. For example, the DHSS target of twelve home helps per thousand elderly by 1983 was laid down in 1972, before the projected expansion in the very elderly who are likely to need greatest support. In 1962 Townsend suggested that the ratio of home helps to elderly people should be increased to meet outstanding needs, to fifteen per thousand and then to twenty per thousand by 1973.[30] On the basis of the official guideline the shortfall in 1978/9 was 29,800 home helps. Secondly, the picture is likely to have been worsened by recent cuts in public expenditure. While projected capital expenditure has proved the easiest to cut, current community care staff and equipment have also been reduced.[31] A cut in gross current expenditure on the personal social services of 8.9 per cent was planned between 1979/80 and 1981/2 and an increase of 17 per cent in capital expenditure.[32] These cuts in expenditure have been made despite the need for more resources simply to cope with the increase in the numbers of very elderly people. Thirdly, within the national figures there is considerable variation between local authorities. For example, in 1979/80 the provision of personal aids to people with disabilities varied from 3.5 per thousand population in West Yorkshire to 7.6 per thousand in the West Midlands.[33] There is a similarly wide variation in the provision of home helps and other services.

To take stock then, the policy of community care is as precarious today as it was in 1961 when Titmuss questioned the official commitment to carry it out. The concept has never been established in statute and there is no right to services. Even the very modest goals for the provision of domiciliary services have not been achieved and are currently receding. Public spending constraints have resulted in a drive to increase the role of informal, especially voluntary, carers and so privatise the costs of care.[34] The meaning of community care has been diluted to mean care by family, friends, neighbours – anyone but the State. The preferences of individuals have been overtaken by the desire to reduce public spending. There is a danger that domiciliary care 'will be increasingly economic simply because the level of care provided becomes increasingly inadequate'.[35] Community care is overwhelmingly care provided by female kin. The development of formal community care policy has not only taken this social division of care for granted, it has positively supported and maintained it. As a result the social and economic costs of providing care continue to fall predominantly on women. A postal survey of carers by the Equal Opportunities Commission found that there were three times as many women carers as men.[36] Moreover, the independence of those requiring care rests to a large extent on the availability of female relatives. Elderly people, for instance, are much more likely to be admitted to hospital or residential care if they are single or if their children are sons rather than daughters.[37]

What is euphemistically referred to as 'care' is usually practical help and support or 'tending'.[38] These tasks include physical work such as lifting – for example a young person with a disability or an incontinent elderly relative – extra washing, cooking, cleaning and shopping. As well as physical fatigue there is often mental and emotional strain resulting from supporting a mentally handicapped or confused person. Finally, there is the burden of bearing the total responsibility for the provision of care with little or no help from other relatives or formal services. Listen to the mother of a teenage daughter with a muscle disability:

I get up at 6 o'clock and by the time I get her down stairs and have attended to her, it takes two hours. It is a full time job for me. . . . She is at her worst morning and night. We have to take it in turns to watch over her at night in case she wants us. The muscles in her throat are also affected, I have to cut up her food very fine and I have to make different food for her. I do all the washing, I couldn't afford to go to the launderette. Well she wets the bed because she can't get up.[39]

Although many caring tasks are similar to ordinary housework it cannot be assumed that they overlap with this other work. For example, the person being cared for may not live with the carer or, if they do, many require special help, such as a diet. Moreover all caring and other household work may require greater time and effort because of the need to keep an eye on the person being cared for all the time.[40] Providing care often has a disruptive impact on family life and on other members of the family. Thus caring is usually accompanied by tension between members of the nuclear family. As well as anxiety, physical and mental stress and inter-personal conflict, the provision of care often results in a lack of privacy and strained relationships with children because less time can be devoted to them. For example, moving an elderly relative into the family home in order to care for them can result in cramped accommodation for everyone, lack of privacy and increased tension between family members.[41]

For the principal carers, women – often married women with children – giving care to other dependent relatives can entail considerable costs. Some costs, such as mental stress, physical fatigue, tiredness and worry, are difficult to quantify, but can have a deep and lasting impact on women and their families. The impossibility of taking paid work is the more frequently reported and quantifiable cost of providing care. A recent official study of elderly people living in the community concluded that 'this survey therefore provides further evidence that the burden of caring for sick or elderly relatives most often falls on women and makes it impossible for them to work.'[42] Those who do manage to combine work and caring usually do so with great difficulty, their caring responsibilities causing them to be late for work or to worry constantly about leaving the dependent person at home. Some women have to change jobs or forego promotion because of their caring role.[43] It is rare for a husband's work to be disrupted. It has been calculated that the direct cost of the time spent by women caring for elderly relatives comes to £2,500 per annum and that the opportunity cost of earnings foregone because of caring activities is £4,500 per annum.[44] To this must be added the extra financial costs, such as extra heating, transport, food, bedding and so on which are usually associated with caring.[45] It is not surprising, therefore, that carers often suffer from financial difficulty. In contrast to the constant public debate about expenditure on the social services the privatised costs of caring to the family are rarely discussed publicly.

It should not be concluded that caring is all a matter of 'cost', but neither should it be assumed that all of the costs of care are borne by one side of the caring relationship. The person being cared for shares the worry and anxiety that can be associated with caring and the receipt of care from a son or daughter may be as difficult as the provision of it. If the principal carer can no longer cope, the person being cared for will probably end up in some form of residential care, a fate which neither party is likely to consider desirable. In other words, *both* suffer from the underdevelopment of formal community care policy and *both* share a common interest in the provision of alternative forms of care.[46]

Social policy and dependency

The dependency of both carers and those being cared for derives in large measure from the state. A consideration of the central role of the state in the social division of care is, therefore, essential in any reassessment of community care policy. Although there has been an explicit policy of community care for well over thirty years, the direct involvement of the state in the caring functions of the family is still relatively small. For example, there are three times as many bedfast and severely disabled elderly people living in their own or their relatives' homes as in all institutions put together.[47] Those people with disabilities living with their families are very unlikely to receive support from the social services. If the state is reluctant to assist in the care of adult dependants, it is positively opposed to the provision of services to families with young children. The dependency of children is viewed differently to other forms of dependency – as something to be 'enjoyed' – and it is firmly believed that the proper place for the care of young children is the nuclear family with the mother providing the bulk of care.[48] Thus while recognising in recent years the primary importance of informal relationships in the provision of care the state has, in fact, done very little to *support* these caring efforts. It has for the most part remained passive and legitimated this passivity by proselytising the twin ideological assumptions that it is 'natural' for family members (and women in particular) to care for their dependants and that state intervention in family life would be positively harmful to these natural caring relationships. As a result, community care services have been confined to a residual system of casualty intervention which, effectively, penalises families for caring. As we have seen, in recent years the state has attempted to reassert the primary duty of 'the family' to care for disabled members. According to the Prime Minister:

it all really starts in the family, because not only is the family the most important means through which we show our care for others. It's the place where each generation learns its responsibility towards the rest of society . . . I think the statutory services can only play their part successfully if we don't expect them to do for us things that we could be doing for ourselves.

By presenting traditional family responsibilities for dependants and the division of labour between the sexes and between the generations as 'normal' or 'natural', 'the state supports and sustains these relationships without appearing intrusive, thus preserving the illusion that the family is a private domain.'[49] So women and families continue to bear the social cost of dependency and the privatisation of family life protects 'normal' inequalities between family members.[50]

As well as giving implicit support to the sexual division of caring the state operates more openly to sustain it by the differential distribution of social services. Social policy, as Land has shown, assumes that men are not expected to look after themselves as much as women are and that men are not able to look after elderly infirm relatives.[51] So, for example, elderly men are more likely to receive home help support than elderly women. In social security too, the exclusion of domestic tasks from the attendance allowance, and married women caring for their husbands from receiving the invalid care allowance, reinforces the social division of care and ensures that many carers do not receive any payment for doing so. The influence of social services on the pattern of caring within families has until recently been underestimated. Not only do they confirm the 'covert' division of labour in care within the comparatively small number of families with whom they are in direct contact, but also indirectly, within the majority of families. In other words, the principle of non-intervention in caring relationships has an important bearing on how families and women in particular perceive their role and duty in the provision of care.

The norm of non-intervention in some aspects of family life reinforces itself by preventing demand for the social services and by ensuring that the family performs certain social functions, such as child-care. In this way the limits to the role of the state are firmly established, not in statute but through the normal pattern of family life. State involvement in, or help with, child-care or housework seems inconceivable at present. So the 'right' of families to self-determination is a myth for most families: 'the family, in practice, serves the need of the state rather than the more commonly held belief that the state is the servant of its people.'[52]

At the same time as the state has sought to maintain the strict division between formal and informal care and the primacy of the family in the provision of care it has actually increased the burden of such responsibilities on the family and has weakened its ability to provide care. It is impossible to consider policies on community care in isolation from other social and economic changes which have a direct or indirect bearing on the need for as well as the provision of care. Various social policies have tended to increase dependency. Some of these developments are explored elsewhere in this volume, but the main ones can be summarised here. The institutionalisation of retirement and early retirement and the official failure to recognise disablement in old age, for example, have increased the likelihood of economic and physical dependence in old age.[53] Cuts in social security benefits and reductions in real wages have deepened family poverty.[54] Faced with the harsh pinch of poverty families are less likely to be able to provide care. State employment and economic policies have increased long-term unemployment[55] which is not conducive, economically or psychologically, to the provision of care. Such policies have contributed to the decline in prosperity of inner cities and the consequent impoverishment of community life and break-up of informal networks. Then there are public expenditure policies which have not only reduced employment, but also the resources for formal care. Cuts in domiciliary services, such as home helps and aids and adaptations for people with disabilities, reduce the capacity of people to care for themselves and to support others and increase calls on relatives to provide care. Despite the importance of formal care services in supporting independence and the fact that many of those in need of domiciliary services do not have living relatives (for example, one third of those over sixty-five have no children), the presence of informal care for some people has been used by the last Secretary of State for Social Services as a *justification* for cuts in the personal social services. In a remarkable statement, not least for the ignorance it displays about the need for and distribution of community care services, Patrick Jenkin argued that:

The personal social services provide only a small part of the totality of care in the community for . . . the elderly, the old and frail, the physically handicapped and the mentally ill. . . . When one is comparing where one can make savings one protects the Health Service because there is no alternative, whereas in personal social services there is a substantial possibility and, indeed, probability of continuing growth in the amount of voluntary care, of neighbourhood care, of self-help.[56]

Contrary, then, to the myths that the family is protected by the state and that the family is a private domain, policies such as those reviewed here show that the state has had a major adverse impact on the family's ability to care for its dependents. In other words, the prosperity of families and therefore local communities, and their ability to provide care, rests to a large extent on the activities of the central and local state. This means that the provision of care *by* informal networks in the community depends on the degree to which the state cares *for* the family and the community.

Planning for shared care

It should be clear from the preceding analysis that the whole basis of community care policy is in need of a radical reappraisal. It reinforces the unequal division of labour in caring between the sexes. It reduces the independence of those being cared for. It implies a fundamental misconception of the needs of carers and cared for, who *both* require help and support in often difficult circumstances in order for them to retain a substantial degree of independence. Many carers are engaged in tasks which, perhaps because of their personal nature, are not readily shared with other informal carers:

You see the neighbours shy away from the incontinence . . . no one will sit with an incontinent grandma. Never. They'll babysit my grandchildren. If I am looking after my grandchildren they'll say 'do you want to go and do so and so? I'll look after the children.' But nobody will look after grandma.[57]

Policies which piously hope for a growth in 'natural' caring networks are likely to end up imposing further burdens on women.

Demographic change is increasing the population most likely to require care (see Chapter 3). For example, more than one half of those over eighty-five are unable to bath themselves without help – and at the same time social changes, such as the increase in the divorce rate, are reducing the availability of kin able to provide care. Who will care for the step-grandfathers and step-grandmothers of the next century is at the moment a matter of speculation. Policies which continue to assume that care, including care for children, will be provided within a conventional nuclear family are not likely to succeed. Secondly there are long overdue changes taking place, albeit slowly, in the status and aspirations of women, particularly in relation to the labour market. Unless policy is redirected towards sharing and supporting the caring activities of families rather than simply substituting for them, these two developments are likely to collide.

'Community care', in the romantic sense used by both Labour and Conservative politicians, probably never occurred and is most unlikely to be realised in advanced capitalist societies. Further, to assume that it can mean continuing to place an unacceptable burden on women as principal carers. The task for local services and families is to *share* care more effectively. On what basis might this happen? First, the conditions in which care occurs are determined in large part by state policies in spheres other than the personal social services, especially in employment, health, housing, social security, and day care, therefore action in these sectors is a necessary starting point, especially sex equality in the labour market. Equality in family caring roles or parity in their negotiation is only likely to follow from equal access to the labour market. Then income can be provided collectively for home responsibility. The payment of such an allowance without concerted action in the labour market would simply legitimate the inequalities in work and caring roles between the sexes.

Secondly, there is a danger that a moral imperative will be imposed on women to provide care. Thus an essential feature of this plan for community care is that it should not put women under a greater obligation than men to provide care and, as far as possible, it should actively encourage men to do so. Also, where possible, it should facilitate free choice.

Thirdly, there is a need to expand the scope and coverage of statutory domiciliary services, but in less rigid forms, using innovations like lay home carers who help families out and foster care for elderly people.[58] (These services could contribute significantly to the pursuit of full employment.) It is also necessary to consider the payment of income in lieu of services.[59] Such payments would include an improved attendance allowance scheme, intended to cover all tasks, domestic as well as nursing. Its scope should also be extended to cover less severe disabilities by the introduction of a third rate. The invalid care allowance should also be increased and enlarged to cover all carers, including married women. In the future this might be merged with a home care or home responsibility allowance paid to the partner of a couple who looks after children or any other person in need of care. In addition a comprehensive disability income would enable many people with disabilities to continue to care for themselves.[60]

The necessary increase in resources for the expansion in domiciliary services will come in part from the concomitant shrinkage of the residential sector and the redeployment of staff. The income maintenance measures can be phased in according to severity of disability, and in the planning of spending priorities, it is important to concentrate on those proposals which reduce dependency among both carers and cared for.

Changes such as those suggested here require a reorientation of professional and other values in the social services, away from dominant 'indoor relief' perceptions of need and pathological models of social problems, and most importantly towards a greater willingness to share care with the family and other informal carers. This sharing is essential if formal carers are to support and not just substitute for informal care. It requires a more flexible approach by social services and most problematic, a willingness on the part of social service professionals and planners to accept informal carers' and dependants' definitions of need.[61]

In sum, policies to promote community care must include care *in* the community, in the individual's own home or in group or sheltered housing; care *by* members of the community, including families, friends, neighbours and locally based formal carers, and care *for* the community, including measures designed to increase the caring capacity of the community. The goal should be full availability of domiciliary services or a financial substitute, and the right to such services for those who require them.

The difficulties of sharing care between kin and the state should not be underestimated.[62] But there are various initiatives which suggest that it is possible. These include the Crossroads care attendant schemes, the Hampshire care attendant schemes and the Kent community care project.[63] Sweden (as is so often the case) has done most to implement these ideas and provides some indication of what can be done.[64] In this country the restrictive notions of community care, and the assumptions they increasingly make about the duty, availability and willingness of families, especially women, to undertake care regardless of its cost are a wholly inadequate basis on which to form policy.

Notes and references

1. See for example, H. Land, 'Who Cares for the Family?', *Journal of Social Policy*, vol. 7, no. 3, 1978, pp. 257–84; J. Finch and D. Groves, 'Community Care and the Family: A Case for Equal Opportunities', *Journal of Social Policy*, vol. 9, no. 4, 1980; A. Walker, 'Community Care of the Elderly in Great Britain: Theory and Practice', *International Journal of Health Services*, vol. 11, no. 4, 1981, pp. 541–57.
2. K. Jones, J. Brown and J. Bradshaw, *Issues in Social Policy*, Routledge and Kegan Paul, 1978, p. 114.
3. S. Londale, J. Flowers and B. Saunders, *Long-term Psychiatric Patients: A Study in Community Care*, PSSC, 1980.
4. Report of the Royal Commission on the Law Relating to Mental Illness and Mental Deficiency, Cmnd 169, HMSO, 1957, p. 202.
5. House of Commons, *Hansard*, 1959, col. 719.
6. Peter Townsend, *The Last Refuge* (abridged version), Routledge and Kegan Paul, 1964, p. 196.
7. Ministry of Health, *A Hospital Plan for England and Wales*, Cmnd 1604, HMSO, 1962; Ministry of Health, *Health and Welfare: the Development of Community Care*, Cmnd 1973, HMSO, 1963.

8. Walter Jaehnig, *A Family Service for the Mentally Handicapped*, Fabian Society, 1979, p. 3.

9. R.M. Titmuss, *Commitment to Welfare*, Allen and Unwin, 1968, pp. 104–9.

10. M. Edelman, *Political Language*, New York, Academic Press, 1977.

11. M.J. Bayley, *Mental Handicap and Community Care*, Routledge and Kegan Paul, 1973.

12. Cmnd, 1973, *op. cit.*

13. Seebohm Committee, *Report of the Committee on Local Authority and Allied Personal Social Services*, Cmnd 3703, HMSO, 1968, p. 107.

14. DHSS, *Better Services for the Mentally Handicapped*, Cmnd 4683, HMSO, 1971.

15. DHSS, *Better Services for the Mentally Ill*, Cmnd 6233, HMSO, 1975.

16. DHSS, *Priorities for Health and Personal Social Services in England*, HMSO, 1976; DHSS, *The Way Forward*, HMSO, 1977.

17. *The Way Forward*, *op. cit.*, p. 78.

18. Merrison Commission, *Report of the Royal Commission on the National Health Service*, Cmnd 7615, HMSO, 1979, p. 138.

19. A. Wertheimer, 'People with Mental Handicaps', in A. Walker and P. Townsend (eds), *Disability in Britain*, Martin Robertson, 1981, pp. 156–84.

20. A. Webb and G. Wistow, 'The Personal Social Services: Incrementalism, Expediency or Systematic Social Planning?' in A. Walker (ed.), *Public Expenditure and Social Policy*, Heinemann, 1982, pp. 137–64.

21. P. Abrams, 'Social Change, Social Networks and Neighbourhood Care', *Social Work Service*, no. 22, 1980, p. 12.

22. See for example, DHSS, *Care in Action*, HMSO, 1981, p. 21.

23. DHSS, *A Happier Old Age*, HMSO, 1978, p. 6.

24. DHSS, *Growing Older*, Cmnd 8173, HMSO, 1981, p. 3.

25. Treasury, *The Government's Expenditure Plans to 1979–80*, HMSO, 1978; Treasury, *The Government's Expenditure Plans 1982–83 to 1984–85*, vol. 2, HMSO, 1982.

26. A. Walker, 'Dependency and Old Age', *Social Policy and Administration*, vol. 16, no. 2, 1982.

27. Paul Wilding, *Socialism and the Professions*, Fabian Society, 1981, p. 4.

28. T. Sargeant, 'Joint Care Planning in the Health and Personal Social Services', in T. Booth (ed.), *Planning for Welfare*, Blackwell/Robertson, 1979, pp. 173–86.

29. A. Hunt, *The Elderly at Home*, HMSO, 1978; I. Topliss and B. Gould, *A Charter for the Disabled*, Martin Robertson, 1981.

30. P. Townsend and D. Wedderburn, *The Aged in the Welfare State*, Bell, 1965.

31. A. Shearer, 'A Framework for Independent Living', in A. Walker and P. Townsend (eds), *op. cit.*, pp. 73–90.

32. DHSS, *Care in Action*, p. 5.

33. A. Shearer, *op. cit.*, p. 78.

34. K. Wright, 'The Economics of Community Care' in A. Walker (ed.), *Community Care*, Blackwell/Robertson, 1982.

35. L. Opit, 'Domiciliary Care for the Elderly Sick: Economy or Neglect?' *British Medical Journal*, 1, 1977, p. 33.

36. EOC, *The Experience of Caring for Elderly and Handicapped Dependants: Survey Report*, EOC, 1980, p. 9.

37. Townsend, *op. cit.*

38. R. Parker, 'Tending and Social Policy', in E.M. Goldberg and S. Hatch (eds), *A New Look at the Personal Social Services*, PSI, 1981, pp. 17–32.

39. EOC, *Caring for the Elderly and Handicapped*, EOC, 1982.

40. EOC, *Experience of Caring*, p. 15.

41. *Ibid.* pp. 32–3.

42. A. Hunt, *op. cit.*, p. 63.

43. EOC, *Experience of Caring*, p. 20.

44. M. Nissel, M. and L. Bonnerjea, *Family Care of the Handicapped Elderly: Who Pays?*, PSI, 1982, p. 56.

45. S. Baldwin and C. Glendinning, 'Children with Disabilities and their Families', in Walker and Townsend (eds), *op. cit.*, pp. 119–41.
46. Walker, 'Community Care of the Elderly in Great Britain', p. 557.
47. P. Townsend, 'Elderly People with Disabilities', in Walker and Townsend (eds), *op. cit.*, p. 98.
48. P. Moss, 'Community Care of Young Children', in Walker (ed.), *op. cit.*
49. R.M. Moroney, *The Family and the State*, Longmans, 1978, p. 213.
50. Land, *op. cit.*, p. 213.
51. *Ibid.* p. 268.
52. Moroney, *op. cit.*, p. 28.
53. A. Walker, 'The Social Creation of Poverty and Dependency in Old Age', *Journal of Social Policy*, vol. 9, 1, 1980, pp. 49–75.
54. J. Coussins and A. Coote, *The Family in the Firing Line*, CPAG/NCCL, 1981.
55. A. Sinfield, *What Unemployment Means*, Martin Robertson, 1981.
56. Social Services Committee, *The Government's White Papers on Public Expenditure: The Social Services*, vol. 2, HC702, HMSO, 1980, pp. 99–100.
57. EOC, *Caring for the Elderly*, p. 12.
58. Leeds City Council, *A Short Term Placement Scheme for the Elderly*, Leeds Social Services Department, 1979.
59. Shearer, *op. cit.*
60. Walker and Townsend, *op. cit.*
61. Barclay Committee, *Social Workers: Their Role and Tasks*, Bedford Square Press, 1982.
62. Parker, *op. cit.*, pp. 22–6.
63. A. Bristow, *Crossroads Care Attendant Schemes*, Association of Crossroads Care Attendant Schemes, 1981; R. Lovelock, *Friends in Deed*, Portsmouth Social Services Department, 1981; D. Challis and B. Davies, 'A New Approach to Community Care for the Elderly', *British Journal of Social Work*, vol. 10, no. 1, pp. 1–18.
64. S.B. Kamerman and A.J. Kahn (eds), *Family Policy*, New York, Columbia University Press, 1978, pp. 19–48.

12 Local Diversity without Local Neglect
by David Townsend

Mixed feelings

Imagine in a wild moment you join the Labour Party. Your first practical difficulty is over when you find out where the meetings are held. Not long afterwards you will discover one of your first theoretical difficulties. Labour Party members have never really made up their minds about whether they are 'centralists' or 'localists'. They are, of course, both. The strength of the mix is a matter of personal conviction and political pragmatism.

Remember the arguments in your ward party when Conservative local authorities refused to introduce comprehensive education? Outrageous behaviour – on a simple show of hands. Remember when Labour local authorities refused to sell council houses? Heroic behaviour and a defence of local rights. It is not an ambivalence unique to British socialists. The French Socialist Party has much the same problem. President Mitterrand, a centralist, has Rocardian decentralists in his party. The President has, with Gallic charm, agreed that greater power to regions and towns is essential. He has appointed a Minister for Decentralisation to see to it. History will not wait on the Labour Party to make up its collective mind. After the last war, and subsequently, there was a shift to greater central involvement in local service provision. Mrs Thatcher's government has greatly tightened financial controls. As Professor J.A.G. Griffith put it: 'To the extent that the interests of the two groups inevitably conflict there can be no partnership but only a decision.' To talk of partnership was a 'pleasant and comforting evasion of the problem'. Professor W.A. Robson in 'Local Government in Crisis' is even crisper: 'Everyone knows where the whip-hand lies and acts accordingly.'[1]

Income from central government was only 12 per cent in 1913–14, 27.4 per cent[2] at the beginning of the Second World War and 36 per cent in 1974–5. A year later it was nearly 40 per cent of total income. If capital expenditure is excluded the figures show even more starkly the extent to which central government has increased its financial control over local government. In the ten years from 1966–7 to 1976–7 rates moved from 33.8 per cent of income to 23.8 per cent whilst government grants rose from 37.1 per cent to nearly 50 per cent. There are a wide range of central controls and statutory limits whose logic is none too clear. Nor was this altogether unpalatable. Rates are unpopular; exchequer money enabled services to grow relatively painlessly. Local authority members had someone else to blame when their plans were thwarted. The personal social services provide an example. Quarterly meetings were inaugurated between chairmen of Social Services Committees, directors of social services and ministers by Barbara Castle in 1974 and continued by David Ennals from 1976–9. At the meetings chairmen would complain, quite reasonably, that the available cash would not meet the targets the ministers set. Directors gave professional assessments in support of that view and, in response, ministers offered joint finance, a sum of money taken from the NHS budget to finance the growth of community services. The chairmen often then expressed some resentment of these Greeks bearing gifts, because they said the money could only be used for certain national priorities and tied the hands of local authorities.

Nor does 'voluntarism' provide a way out of these difficulties. Whatever the merits of fostering more informal means of support within the community which Alan Walker discusses (Chapter 11), it is unrealistic to imply, as some recent authors have, that the voluntary sector is efficient, idealistic or competent enough to take over a substantial part of local authority provision. Most 'voluntary' services depend heavily on local government for cash and are more at risk from central government cuts and controls. Peter Beresford raises other issues. Such services, he argues, tend to be 'patchy, ill-distributed and poorly co-ordinated. Voluntarism replaces paid with pittance or unpaid work. The new voluntarism of so-called informal helping networks is more often advocated than to be found operating effectively in areas with the greatest problems. Even more than more formal approaches to voluntary action, it places the greatest burdens on women, perpetuating their social and economic dependence in sexist, subordinate, caring roles.'[3]

The alternative to this 'pittance' work is the growth of non-statutory services staffed by NALGO members paid from 9 am to 5 pm which, apart from the difficulties of achieving accountability, are little different in organisation and aim from local government services.

Unless we stop the present slide into financial centralism, Britain's local services and control over them will be emasculated. In the past it was argued that the small size of local authorities meant that central government *had* to intervene. That is no longer valid. For the Labour Party, an inability to revive local government as an active vehicle for change in local life will cause its own death at its grass roots. Make local authorities not worth fighting to win and the Labour Party is on the slide at local level. In a letter to the *Guardian*, Professors Jones and Stewart (respectively Professors of Government, LSE, and Local Government, Birmingham University) succinctly sum up what has happened since the 1979 general election:

In the Parliamentary session 1979–80 the Government introduced the local government Planning and Land Bill in the House of Lords. It later withdrew that Bill and a new reduced local government Planning and Land (No. 2) Bill was introduced in the House of Commons. This Bill was eventually carried into legislation, transforming the financial framework within which local authorities operated.

Within less than a year a new Local Government Finance Bill was introduced into the Commons, containing proposals for referendums on the budgets of local authorities. This proposal was withdrawn within a month. Then a new and different proposal was introduced, as the Local Government Finance (No. 2) Bill to abolish supplementary rates; and dangerously coupled with it was a provision to enable the Secretary of State to impose grant penalties after a local authority's budget was set – a means of direct central control over local government expenditure and rating. The Government is now to amend that proposal, although it is not yet certain that all the dangers of mid-year hold back penalties have been resolved.

The record is amazing; four Bills in two years; two Bills withdrawn, three major changes in intention; and a grant system that is not merely complex beyond belief but contradictory in purposes.

Local authorities have been given two targets and face a relationship between grant and expenditure that varies in shape from authority to authority. For some of them, as expenditure goes up grant comes down, then down, then up, then down.[4]

The Conservative opposition to public spending in whatever form, whether voted for by local voters or not, explains this otherwise extraordinary saga. That and their attitude to welfare services require that local choice be denied if local choice means more services.

New life for local government
The first and overriding priority must be to accept local democracy and provide it not with a life support system, but a new heart. Independence for local authorities is worth a few Bromleys, Norfolks or North Yorkshires, authorities whose political pretensions will always outmatch their generosity and compassion. Socialism must be built from below.

Revenue raising ability is the key to greater freedom for local authorities. Without that freedom, local diversity will tend to vanish and local neglect become the norm. In the last ten years the issues and the practical problems have been studied in exhaustive detail and options presented for public debate (see for example the Layfield Committee report of 1975 and the Conservatives' 1981 Green Paper) New sources of revenue are feasible, though they may for technical reasons take time to introduce. The problems lie not so much in the practical complexities of an income tax or sites tax – other countries have coped with these adequately enough – but in the reluctance of central government, not least the Treasury, to see local authorities possess greater financial freedom, and in the problems of geographical equity.

The first is overplayed. The Treasury and the present government believe that the centre must be able to control both the level of public capital expenditure and local authority revenue or current spending if macro-economic policy is not to be endangered since local spending is such an important part of the economy. There is a case for central government controlling capital spending *in total* since borrowing to finance it affects interest rates. The case for central control over locally funded self-balancing revenue spending seems spurious, as Foster and his colleagues have argued.[5]

The problem of local inequalities that could derive from more local independence in revenue seems a major problem at first sight. It was one of the things the Poplar councillors campaigned about long ago. 'Westminster gets £29,000 for a penny rate; Poplar gets £3,200.'[6] Even today a 1p rate in the London Borough of Camden raises over £1 million; a 1p rate in the London Borough of Lewisham raises less than half that. Camden receives no rate support grant from the government. It was always less dependent on that source of income than Lewisham which receives over 50 per cent of its income from the rate support grant.

We have to be realistic. There is no possibility of abolishing central grants, but they could be simplified and related to the income and age structure of different areas. The primary aim would then become one of geographical equity. This will not be achieved quickly. The crucial decision is to accept the case for a new source of revenue.

It is a myth that central services necessarily provide geographical equity. The health service's record until 1976 was just one example. Equally central politicians' attempts to force 'national solutions' in housing produced some of the worst advertisements for public sector activity. Dick Crossman in November 1964 confided in his diary that: 'We have to concentrate on six or seven places, Liverpool, Manchester, Birmingham, Glasgow, London, where the problem of housing is so bad that the local authorities simply can't grapple with the job. . . . A Labour minister should impose central leadership, large-scale state intervention in those blighted areas of cities.' In 1965 he wrote: 'I tried to indicate how important industrialised building is to us. Since I wrote that, the Prime Minister has committed us to industrialised building and I see nothing to lose if we make the local authorities turn over to it; since conventional architecture is so terrible it couldn't be worse.'[7] Of course everyone now knows (and many, not least the occupants of high rise flats, knew then) that it could indeed be worse. The Ronan Point Flats disaster provided a fitting memorial to that.

At least Tony Crosland learned from that mistake. In 1973 he wrote:

I am therefore adamantly opposed to a *national* house building target. It may have made sense in the earlier post war years when the evident need was to build and build still more. It makes no sense in the far more diverse and complex conditions of today. The national housing programme should be the sum of a series of local decisions; and the function of government is to create the conditions in which local needs and demand can be met.[8]

This statement, which shows some awareness of past failures, might be taken as the key to other local authority services and their relationship with central government.

A measure of greater independence in terms of revenue and financial control is not all that is needed to put new heart into local government. The personal social services illustrate the problems of encouraging local diversity without local neglect particularly well. There were over twenty separate Acts of Parliament referred to in the 1970 Social Services Act, which set up the present local authority social services departments. Each of those Acts conferred different personal social services functions on local authorities over a period of forty years. Here, then, opportunities exist for all kinds of diversity and neglect.

Central government has made various attempts over the last twenty years to persuade local authorities to establish some degree of conformity with central government intentions. Declaring target numbers of places per thousand for particular groups of people has been a well tried formula for ministers. But the use of averages may be more effective with England test selectors than local authorities.

Common standards for services have emerged more from the decisions of local authorities than from the interventions of central government. National minimum standards . . . are in fact rare. Most mandatory obligations laid on local authorities are general . . . They have discretion *about the level and extent of the service, its frequency and intensity*. The standards which have emerged are not nationally determined . . . they are common standards that have evolved.[9]

In 1962 the Conservative Government tried to establish a basis of information on which to assess local services. The results, published in 1963 as *Health and Welfare: the development of Community Care*, bear out the *New Society*'s authors' opinion. The exercise, repeated in 1964, 1965 and 1966, made little impact except in revealing the unequal quantity of provision in different parts of the country. 123 local authorities in 1965, for example had no hostels for mentally ill people. In 1966, forty of those authorities had no plans for any by

1976. Nationally the figures for local authorities' mental health homes and hostels still show 58 per cent of authorities without recorded provision for mentally ill people; and for mentally handicapped people the figure is 49 per cent. Elderly people have done better in some respects than mentally ill or handicapped people (see Tables 12.1 and 12.2). There are more of them and they excite greater and easier compassion and more political commitment. They also exercise their voting rights.

The Chronically Sick and Disabled Persons Act 1970 is not permissive. Individual rights to services may finally be supported by recourse to law. (The recent Wandsworth case in 1981, in which the Secretary of State insisted on improved telephone provision for disabled people in Wandsworth, shows that, however reluctantly, the law can be invoked.) Under this Act, a person has the right to a telephone as soon as need is established under the legislation; but a similar right is not extended to an old person who needs residential care nor to a mentally ill person who needs hostel care.

There was a major increase in provision for the disabled and the numbers on registers in the early 1970s, but little decrease in the diversity; central government restraints on spending are probably increasing that diversity now as some authorities comply and others resist the cuts.

Specific cash grants do however get results. There is no doubt that the introduction of NHS joint finance money, earmarked for use by local authority social services departments, has given impetus to better services for mentally ill, mentally handicapped and elderly people. (Amongst the last group are the greatest number of physically disabled

Table 12.1   Numbers of Day Centres and of Places

	Day Centres	Places
Elderly people		
1974	206	9,270
1979	393	18,889
Mixed physical handicap and elderly		
1974	103	5,818
1979	205	12,307
Mentally ill people		
1974	102	3,598
1979	128	4,622

Source: Local authority returns to DHSS, 1974–80.

Table 12.2   Day Care Places by Area

	Mental illness		Elderly (over 65)		Physical h. (under 65)		Mixed	
	no.	places	no.	places	no.	places	no.	places
1975								
Barking	I	50	I	25	3	125	Nil	
Shropshire	I	30	Nil		Nil		Nil	
Derbyshire	I	25	I	40 .	4	345	Nil	
Newcastle	I	100	I	40	I	150	Nil	
Bradford	I	25	I	50	2	136	Nil	
Coventry	I	100	Nil		I	100	Nil	
1980								
Barking	I	50	Nil		2	131	I	50
Shropshire	I	50	Nil		Nil		Nil	
Derbyshire	I	40	2	80	4	345	I	90
Newcastle	I	140	I	100	I	150	Nil	
Bradford	I	25	I	50	I	150	Nil	
Coventry	I	100	Nil		I	100	Nil	

Source: as Table 12.1.

people.) On a national scale, the sums involved are relatively small: £40 million in 1978–9. But their application, which David Ennals widened in 1977 to include voluntary organisations working with local authorities, has been successful. Roughly one third of the cash went on each of the three groups. The money, with tapering arrangements, is negotiated with local authorities. They bear the costs from their own funds in later years. Where central government holds certain developments crucial, short-term specific funding to achieve those ends is compatible with local independence. It should be flexible though. Joint finance cannot at present be devoted to housing projects. Yet sheltered housing schemes are every bit as relevant to the purposes of the scheme.

Table 12.3   Numbers of People on Handicapped Registers

	1974	1979
All	497,158	848,790
Very Severe Handicap	15,580*	55,024
Severe or Appreciable Handicap	59,564	321,663

* 1975.
Source: as Table 12.1.

Urban aid, by contrast with joint financing, is much more of a lottery. There is little local control, over the choice of schemes at least. Programmes covering everything from ethnic minority services or mentally ill people's needs to unemployed teenagers may be agreed by a local authority. Those priorities may be subsequently overturned by Department of the Environment officials. Joint financing, on the other hand, is an integral part of joint planning at local level where complete freedom to choose schemes lies. Inner city partnerships introduced by the Labour Government in 1977–9 were an improvement on urban aid for the same reasons.

Confusion at the centre

Central direction might be less harmful if it were less fragmented and conflicting. The DHSS is really three ministries. Two are concerned with national services; social security and health. The other is headless and responsible in part for the personal social services. No one speaks for them. In the 1974–9 Labour Government there was a minister with responsibility for disabled people. He covered all three parts of the department. There was a Minister of Health who dealt with certain aspects – for example mental handicap – of the personal social services. There was a Parliamentary Under-Secretary who tended to get alcoholism, battered women and elderly people. At times in meetings with local authority representatives, four of the five ministers attended. This was good for public relations but not so good for direction. The present Conservative Governnent is no differently organised, except that it does not pretend to be interested in disabled people. There is no separate minister with responsibility for them.

Combining responsibility for *all* the personal social services in one minister, below the Secretary of State, is long overdue. The minister would act as the focus for negotiations with local authorities about minimum standards, and be in a better position to represent the services' views in discussions with the Department of the Environment, the Treasury and voluntary agencies.

To accompany that development should go a revised, strengthened social work service. The concomitant to more local financial independence should be a strong critical professional system of quality control and advice, backed by national research on standards, and the power to publish reports, such as the HMI for schools possesses. In the days of the local authorities' children's departments, the inspectorate – operating from the Home Office – had a far more influential role than the present small social work service. They cover all services but without real sanctions, at least ones they use. It is true that Secretaries of State intervene occasionally in the affairs of a local authority social services department. They generally have done it to ensure services are maintained – that cuts proposed are not too severe. But they have done it as often in response to political pressures as at the promptings of the SWS. There is no reason to believe that local authorities would be resistant to such a change. They accept the schools inspectorate as valued defenders of standards as well as advisers.

Diversifying local services
These proposals may enhance the relationship between central and local government, but there are other considerations which bear on the nature of local government itself and how far it is, in its present form, the best or only vehicle for the delivery of services. The development of housing associations answers particular needs in what is often a more humane way than local housing departments. Diseconomies of scale operate in human agencies. A small organisation can manage more easily and with a concern for individuals. If that is true in housing is it not more plausibly the case in social services? Is a wider mix of private, municipal, voluntary and family care in the personal social services possible and desirable? In country areas, meals-on-wheels services are almost always at a lower level than in city areas. In the counties there is a higher proportion of meal deliveries by organisations like WRVS; a municipal service probably delivers all meals in cities, apart perhaps from special ethnic services, such as a Jewish service.

Do highly unionised staff employed by a council department give more for the ratepayers' money than a group of voluntary people acting on an altruistic basis? Questions like these form the basis for the increasingly legalistic attitude taken up by ratepayer action groups in challenging some local authorities. (The role of District Auditor and the state of the law in local government is not something to occupy one corner of a chapter in a book on social policy, but nevertheless it should be mentioned as an issue which has to be reconsidered by central government.) It is important that councillors do not treat the question as one of dogma. Where voluntary help is available a municipal core service, with neighbours cooking meals for the person next door or down the road, can be encouraged or arranged.

The London Borough of Camden has, for example, invested in the care of elderly and disabled people by placements in private house-holds. Those initiatives have been based on local experience and local response to requests for such accommodation. It may not be possible elsewhere, but a future Minister for the Social Services could make it his business to promote those kinds of ideas.

There are restraints on how responsive a municipal social services department can be to changing needs. If alternatives to residential care (and each place may cost up to £10,000 per year per person) are found, then staff can easily feel threatened. The resistance to change may cost money. The service itself can be prevented from shifting its priorities. An example is in the demography of care. Older children are now more likely to be in residential care. As a result of the falling birth rate, together with the conclusion (reached after long discussion) that foster care or day care may be better for many children, some children's homes may become redundant. They should be closed and precious cash and personnel transferred to meet newly identified needs. Trade unions do not always see it that way any more than do professional staff.

There are a number of other ways in which diversity will not easily be translated into national plans. 'Privatisation' of services administered for private profit, an idea overtly attractive to many on the political right and covertly to some on the left, has gained credence in the last few years. This panacea has arrived for some with the emptying of dustbins by private enterprise in Southend. In the personal social services its application is a bit more complicated. Would it be so easy in other local authority services – more private architects? More private builders? But it is a possibility and there may be advantages. An indication of the balance of advantage can be obtained from consideration of the 'privatisation' which is full-bloodedly applied in some parts of the USA. There, the equivalent of a local authority, with federal funds, can 'buy' services; agencies sub-contract themselves to provide major services to authorities. Some are profit-making concerns; some are not. The limits of this system are not hard to envisage and are soon reached. They tend to take on the 'easier' parts of the job. Quality controls are difficult to maintain; administration costs are higher.

But there can be a place for 'private' parts in a local authority social services department. They cannot be prescribed by central government. The provision of facilities for ethnic minorities is a fruitful area. For example, elderly members of ethnic minorities may wish to have luncheon services of their own, not only from a nutritional and cultural point of view, but for social reasons. Luncheon vouchers or financial arrangements with local ethnic restaurants can provide a cheaper, more sociable and more enjoyable meal.

It would be foolish, however, to think that a greater proportion of work done by volunteers will solve many of the problems of large-scale authorities. The large urban areas have the lowest pool of voluntary effort to draw on. Some volunteers are working from parallel bureaucracies. They too are unionised so that costs may be the same and working practices similar. The accountability of voluntary workers is to no one but the people they work with and their consciences. For the local authority worker, it is to both of those and also to an employer who must be accountable for public money spent. The kind of local neighbourhood organisation discussed by David and Land in Chapter 10 may do more than promote flexible community based services, though the two ideas are compatible.

The question of legislation embodying individual rights to services, or of legislation laying duties on local authorities to provide them, is one that cannot be avoided. It may assist better working relationships between local authorities and non-statutory agencies. Qualification for benefit under the Chronically Sick and Disabled Persons Act 1970 is more likely to obtain service than under most other legislation. Should the principle be extended? The 1977 NHS Act gives an indication of what might happen if it were. A recent case in Enfield brought by the families of patients who were in need of psychogeriatric care resulted in the creation of such a service. The Area Health Authority (AHA) was obliged to provide it. But there is a drawback; the AHA announced that it would have to reduce services somewhere else to pay for that development. The same could be true for local authorities. In changed legal circumstances the role of the local government ombudsman would not only be altered but could be more effective.

For some mentally ill people discharged, let us say, from a psychiatric hospital, the prospect of an immediate hostel place or group home by right, and not at the discretion of the local authority, would be a real change. A cost-conscious social services director will tell you the financial outlay would be immense. For mentally handicapped people a 'Bill of Rights' rather on the lines of what Sweden provides for its mentally handicapped people could provoke major changes, but it would be useless and unwise unless authorities have the financial capacity to respond.

The Barclay Committee on the future of social work might have considered some of these themes but it failed to do so. 'It is not our functon,' the Report announces, to offer any judgment on the level of socal services which in present circumstances can or ought to be the aim'.[10]

In brief

Reform on this scale will only come about with a change in national government policy. The freeing of local government forms part of a generous and compassionate approach to the nation's problems. Within that freedom, local diversity can grow and provide seeds for new developments in a whole range of local services. This chapter has suggested ways in which that can come about. There will still need to be considerable central government involvement, but it will not be of a dictatorial kind. There will need to be greater co-ordination amongst government ministers; there may need to be new legislation – for example empowering local authority social services departments to license and inspect private nursing homes. Establishing priorities means redistribution in cash and kind, through the identification of groups of people and needs which have been neglected. A positive response to them can be provided within that framework. With these aims there can be an imaginative diversity in local affairs without local neglect.

Notes and references

1. J.A.G. Griffith, *Central Departments and Local Authorities*, Allen and Unwin, 1966. W.A. Robson, *Local Government in Crisis*, Allen & Unwin, 1966.
2. Layfield Committee, *Local Government Finance*, HMSO, 1975.
3. P. Beresford, 'Power to the People', *Social Work Today*, 30 March 1982.
4. *Guardian*, 18 February 1982.
5. C.D. Foster, *et al.*, *Local Government Finance in a Unitary State*, Allen and Unwin, 1980.
6. Noreen Branson, *Poplarism 1919–1925*, Lawrence and Wishart, 1979, p. 47.
7. R.H.S. Crossman, *Diaries of a Cabinet Minister*, 1975, p. 144 and pp. 81, 131.
8. C.A.R. Crosland, *Socialism Now*, Jonathan Cape, 1974, p. 140.
9. 'Making Local Government More Local', *New Society*, 25 February 1982.
10. Barclay Committee, *Social Workers: Their Role and Tasks*, Bedford Square Press, 1982.

13 Learning and Democracy at the Workplace
by Tom Schuller

Social policy and paid employment are most often seen as instrument-ally rather than integrally connected. Efficient health and education services are needed if the workforce is to be physically and intellectually fit to work. Conversely, a productive economy is needed to generate the cash required to provide social services. Yet the workplace is a social institution where most men and women spend a major part of their lives, and whose influence reaches beyond the physical boundaries of the office or factory. It therefore demands attention as a vehicle and expression of social policy.

There are two reasons for the title. The first is to show that the focus will not be confined to formal education and training. One aim of this chapter is to discuss how life can be breathed into cliches about the importance for learning of the organisational environment. The second is that discussions about learning are usually focused either on the individual or on the industry. These are certainly important, but they have tended to squeeze out reflection about how learning can be developed at the level of the workplace. I shall argue that it is important for people to be involved in defining their own learning needs as members of a collective enterprise. This should form a vital link between individual opportunity and educational and training policy.

The chapter has two parts. First, there is a summary look at the general background of education and training in this country. This includes its crude quantitative deficiencies, its unequal distribution and some brief policy suggestions. Secondly, I argue that adequate learning opportunities are a *sine qua non* of people's ability to develop at work and to exercise some sort of control over their own working lives, whether collectively or as individuals. I suggest a four-pronged approach to achieving this: specific attention to the workplace as a learning environment; major steps towards paid educational leave as a general right; serious measures of positive discrimination; and a strengthening of the rights of union representatives to time off for training. Underpinning this is a premise that the organisation of learning must itself be brought under democratic control. The setting up of work environment committees as joint union and management decision-making bodies is proposed as one means of achieving progress towards the several objectives.

An unskilled society

An ugly phrase for an ugly fact. There is no doubt that at almost every level provision is inadequate in quantitative terms, and that its distribution is inefficient and inequitable. Some 65 per cent of young people in England and Wales (slightly fewer in Scotland) leave school at sixteen and do not go on to any form of full-time further education. The vast majority of these have no qualifications, or ones that are virtually worthless. Perhaps less well known is that only about one in four or five of this group – 14 per cent of all sixteen-year-olds – go into jobs involving part-time further education. Once people have entered the labour market without qualifications, their chances of getting out of the lowest stratum are minimal. As the 1980 CPRS Report on Education, Training and Industrial Performance observed: 'Upgrading later on is very hard and upgrading from unskilled can be almost impossible in some occupations at any age.'[1]

Comparisons with other countries are fraught with difficulties. It is difficult to pinpoint exactly corresponding levels of qualifications, and the way they mesh with the employment structure may vary significantly.

Nevertheless, a recent careful comparison between Britain and West Germany yields some striking results.[2] The study concentrated on three levels of qualification: university, intermediate and none. In the rather distasteful vocabulary of 'human capital', the 'current stock' position is as shown in Table 13.1.

The significant difference is not at the level of university qualifications. The crucial and dramatic difference is at the intermediate level – that of craftsmen and technicians. For every person with a degree qualification, there are nine in Britain with some form of intermediate qualification and seventeen in Germany. But as the author of the study

Table 13.1   Qualifications as Percentage of Labour Force

		University	Intermediate	None
All	Britain	5.5	30.0	64.4
	West Germany	7.1	59.9	33.0
Manufacturing	Britain	3.3	28.7	68.0
	West Germany	3.5	60.8	35.7
Non-manufacturing	Britain	6.5	30.7	62.8
	West Germany	8.9	59.4	31.6

Source: see text.

observes, it is probably even more important to stress the second ratio which derives from the overall pattern: for each person with an intermediate qualification, there are 2.4 in Britain without any qualifications but only 0.6 in Germany. Whatever the methodological crudities, the pictures conjured up both of average skill levels and of work organisation in the two countries are strikingly different. Inadequate overall training provision reinforces steep and narrow authority structures at the workplace. Without a broader skill base we are unlikely to achieve less hierarchy and more flexibility – both crucial components in the quality of work.

In 1977, 146,000 passes were achieved in Germany in manufacturing skills (Berufschule and factory trainees combined), compared with 62,000 in equivalent British terms (City & Guilds Part II). But perhaps even more significant than the crude statistics is the following observation: 'As a result of a division of responsibility when the training boards were established, it was decided that the latter should provide practical training, and City & Guilds should provide the theoretical foundations and background; the division has unfortunately been so thorough that no-one in Britain knows how many have satisfied both requirements. Indeed, no awarded qualification hinges on any such joint requirement.' The wry tone of the comment should not disguise its significance. We have no proper integration of theory and practice in the development and exercise of skills at work. The overall haphazardness in British training policy is illustrated by the Manpower Services Commission's inability to go beyond listing the names of organisations with whom it was 'in dialogue' on training; it simply did not possess, in its 1980 review, *Outlook on Training*, information on trainees reaching specified skill levels.[3]

Though this situation has developed over a long period, it has been sharply aggravated by the present government's policies, which are barbaric in the literal sense, incoherently articulated and directly opposed to a learning society. Higher education has been thrown into confusion as polytechnics, colleges and universities respond to cuts. Adult education has been all but eliminated in many areas at precisely the time when people have most need of it to cope with major changes in their personal and occupational lives. Training is being decimated, as sixteen out of twenty-three industrial training boards have been scrapped and training places drastically reduced. The Engineering ITB, for instance, reports the lowest annual intake for craft and technician training since records began fifteen years ago. All of this sets us even further behind our neighbours and competitors.

General guidelines for the reconstruction of post-school education and training have already been established by the Labour Party. They are based on the need to allocate resources more fairly between sectors and over the individual's life cycle. They comprise the following basic elements: the provision of a unified system of education, training and employment for the sixteen–nineteen age group, including a guarantee to all sixteen- and seventeen-year-olds of a right to a student traineeship; the development of a comprehensive training and retraining system for adults, including the introduction of an educational entitlement which can be drawn upon at any time or times throughout the individual's life; the provision of more open access and more flexible course structures in educational institutions to encourage 'unorthodox' student clienteles; a strengthening of the co-ordinating role of the Manpower Services Commission and of the services advising organisations and unions on the development of training policies at the place of work.

It is the last aspect on which I wish to concentrate since it is by far the least developed. What are its aims? In the most general sense they are to promote social prosperity, generated by a more equally educated and confident populace. British capitalism appears to have a uniquely *short-sighted* view of investment, in training as elsewhere. The capacity to adapt, to control and respond to social and technological change is strangled by a 'bottom line mentality'.

Even when they are discussed, education and training are talked of solely in terms of equipping people with the skills required by the economy, or by particular sectors of the economy. The CPRS report is quite explicit: 'This report deliberately looks at education and training from the limited perspective of the needs of the economy.' These needs are taken as given, determined by technological developments, market pressures or organisational constraints. What is significant, however, is not the focus on economic requirements but the way this focus is interpreted:

Although the report attempts to look at education and training issues from the point of view of the employer, it recognises the difficulties that are involved in identifying employers' needs. These are far from uniform; there are inconsistencies between what employers say they want and the values implicit in their selection process; their conception of their needs, present and future, is frequently not explicit and clearly formulated.[1]

In other words, even when the needs of the economy are wholly identified with the needs of the employers, it turns out that they themselves often do not know what they are.

One critical reaction has been to suggest we should avoid discussion of education and training policy altogether on the premise that to argue for more and better skills is to bind workers more firmly into exploitative relations of production. The authors of a trenchant analysis of the politics of British education include a condemnation of the MSC as 'Labour's paradigm for capitalist training', exemplified in the way it has tightened the links between the needs of employers and state provision. They conclude:

> It is indeed not education that should conform to industry, but industry that should conform to the needs of human development. We need educational critiques of work, in factories and in homes, of the kind that some researchers, attentive to workers' experiences, are now beginning to supply. The longer (but not *that* much longer) term aim is not to meet the needs of capitalist industry as currently constituted in Britain in a weak and dependent form but to develop a form of social organisation, linked to changes in the relations of sexes, which would actually produce more real wealth than a capitalist and patriarchal social order.[4]

This is almost a postscript to a detailed and subtle analysis, and it would be unfair to present it as a major conclusion. Nevertheless the bracketed phrase and the emphasis within it (their own) hint at a sense of vulnerability to the riposte: what skills *should* we try to help people acquire, so that they can develop their critical awareness, safeguard themselves from exploitation, and at the same time earn a living? The tension between subservience to the needs of capital on the one hand and unemployability and irrelevance on the other is not squarely faced. The crucial political question is not the simplistic, dichotomous one of whether or not to meet the needs of capitalist industry, but what is the *scope* for change and how can this be achieved?

One way forward is to focus on how people can learn at their place of work to control their working lives. They do need to develop occupational skills which will secure them employment but at the same time there are major steps which can be taken in the workplace to increase their ability to transform the quality of that employment.

New directions

1 Work environment
(a) Job content

> The worker . . . does not follow the general process of labour and production. He is not a point that moves and so creates a line, he is a pin stuck in a particular place, and the line is made up of a succession of pins that an alien will has arranged in accordance with its own ends. The worker tends to carry this mode of being of his into every aspect of his life. At all times he adjusts easily to the role of material executor, of a 'mass' guided by a will that is alien to his own. He is intellectually lazy; he cannot and does not wish to look beyond his immediate horizon.[5]

This may be unduly sweeping. But far more attention must be given to the *content of work* as a crucial influence on learning. For professional people, learning is an in-built part of their work. Formal in-service training may or may not be adequate, but the actual work itself allows, encourages or demands learning. The opposite is true for the majority of workers.

Some boring jobs will always be with us (though fortunately we have varying conceptions of boredom). But it is not at all naive to suggest that we should take seriously the establishment of a general principle: that the specification of 'decent working conditions' should include the implications of the job for the employee's intellectual health and development. This has already been done in Scandinavia. Learning and a good work environment are explicitly linked and promoted in the activities of the Swedish Work Environment Fund, established in 1972 with a budget of 400 million S kr per annum – an astronomical figure if converted to UK equivalence. Its objectives are to support research, development, training and information in the improvement of the working environment. It therefore helps both to make jobs safer and healthier and to develop employment which satisfies certain positive intrinsic needs.

Organisational initiatives such as job rotation and job enrichment should be considered for their value as learning devices. They have often been touted as solutions for alienation and boredom. The superficiality of this approach has long been exposed, most pithily by the celebrated Chemco worker's comment: 'I don't feel enriched, I just feel knackered.'[6] A greater experience of jobs within a given enterprise should give employees a chance to learn more skills. More importantly, given our focus on control, it is a step towards a clear understanding of the overall context of the enterprise and of their own employment conditions.

The Department of Employment's Work Research Unit has laid down certain principles for the organisation of work, all of which derive essentially from the concept of the worker as a thinking autonomous person. Tasks should combine to form a coherent job and contribute significantly to the eventual product; there should be variety in working methods, and feedback on performance; discretion on the job should be promoted, and workers should control their own jobs. One can of course be sceptical about how far all, or any, of these can be achieved under existing relations of production. The fact remains that guidelines have been established which imply that choices are made about the nature of production, and that the writ of the technological imperative does not run in every corner of the world of work. To operationalise these guidelines is difficult and will raise questions about power relationships at work. But that merely confirms our focus on the enterprise as the point of change.

(b) Knowing one's workplace
The idea of understanding one's own work processes provides the

bridge to the specific educational proposals which follow. Standard textbooks on good industrial relations procedures urge the employer to organise a proper system of induction for their employees. The recent ACAS advisory booklet defines induction as 'helping a new employee to settle down into a new job as soon as possible, by becoming familiar with the people, the surroundings, the job, the firm and the industry.'[7] How seriously are the latter elements taken, I wonder? At the most mundane level it presumably includes some information on the structure of the particular department within which the employee works, and the names and functions of immediate superiors. But how much information is provided on how decisions are made, at departmental, plant or company level? What assumptions are made about the limits of people's interest in understanding their working environment? Proper information should be available statutorily if necessary to enable employees to understand the functioning of their workplace. It should cater for their specific needs. It must be organised in such a way as to encourage people actively to assimilate and use it.

One specific example illustrates the general theme. Workers in the Swedish social security system were faced with the prospect of computerisation leading to radical changes in the nature of their jobs and the skills demanded. In particular, the changes involved a centralisation of the system, and the replacement of knowledge of social security and social insurance arrangements by familiarity with electronic data processing techniques. The combination of these changes would mean that workers in the local offices would essentially be transmitters of information and finance in a system of which they had little understanding and no control. Instead of understanding the goals of social security and the rules to be applied, they would be required to know how to feed input data into the computer and which transaction codes to use. The relevant union (FF) responded to this by organising some 700 study circles to help in the formulation of a programme of action. The result of this initiative, together with head office research, was a programme which dealt with: the *content* of work, in terms of the maintenance of skills, the preservation of personal contact with those to be served and the continued decentralisation of responsibility; *non-fragmentation* of work, such that staff would as far as possible handle cases individually, without responsibility for it being split up between several people; *training*, so that staff have an overall view of the different sectors of social security and an understanding of clients' problems.[8]

(c) Committee power
In the MSC's review of the 1973 Employment and Training Act, directors, training specialists and line managers from thirty firms were consulted about the most important factors influencing their decisions

on training. Of the twenty-one factors mentioned, 'shopfloor views', 'company union representatives' views' and 'national union policies' came respectively nineteenth, twentieth and twenty-first.[9]

How might this be changed? The 1974 Health and Safety at Work Act gave statutory backing to the establishment of joint health and safety committees. Such committees existed before, but are now very much more widespread as a result both of the Act and the interest which accompanied it. Their actual impact is difficult to assess precisely.[10] Although 'health' is included in their title, they concern themselves primarily with safety matters, and their effectiveness on that score varies considerably. In many cases their activities are tightly constrained by the unwillingness of employers to commit significant resources. Nevertheless they have beyond reasonable doubt had a beneficial effect on accident rates. They have served to raise consciousness about workplace safety dramatically. They have also established the important precedent of statutory employee rights to joint decision-making. They have therefore laid the basis for discussion on how the right of workers to influence their own working conditions can be extended to include the quality of the workplace as a social environment.

Committees are not always the best instrument for making decisions. But statutory support for the setting up of Work Environment Committees would be a major step forward. It would bring under joint control company policies on both training and working conditions. More important, it would promote the idea that organisations can be deliberately structured to foster rather than stunt human development. There are of course variations in the extent to which this can be achieved, and trade unions will take time to build up the necessary competences. Neither are good reasons for not beginning. Work Environment Committees are one major instrument.

2   Paid educational leave (PEL)

If it is accepted that we should attempt to organise work itself so as to encourage learning, there is an obvious case for accompanying this by formally building the time off for learning into the general conditions of employment. This is, it should be remembered, common practice in some of the professions, most obviously the academic.

The British Government is a signatory to the 1974 ILO Convention on PEL which divided education into three categories: general, vocational and trade union. Since then some concrete progress has been made on the third category, but none at national level on the other two. Other countries have, in various ways, taken legislative initiatives, either at national (France, Sweden) or regional (West Germany) level to establish PEL as an individual right. It is always tempting to glorify achievements elsewhere in order to belabour our own failings, and we should not be disingenuous about what has in fact been accomplished. In France, for instance, implementation of the right has been fairly tightly restricted, control resting firmly with the employers. In Germany, the distributional impact is almost certainly regressive since it is largely younger civil servants – a category with above-average educational experience already – who have benefited. Nevertheless, the examples illustrate the scope for potential action.

Piecemeal advances have been made in the UK. Unions are beginning to show greater interest in the idea of negotiating sabbaticals, whether for education or more generally. Since 1976, the Ford manual workers have included in their annual pay claim a demand for three months paid leave after every ten years service, and the Society of Post Office Executives is now calling for paid sabbatical leave for all members. We can expect this to proliferate as the whole movement towards shorter working hours gathers momentum. Some organisations already have some form of agreement on sabbaticals but the leave is generally discretionary and almost invariably restricted to non- manual employees.[11]

It is not possible to put forward here a scheme for the general introduction of PEL. Even if it were possible it would not be appropriate other than in broad terms. The logic of my previous argument, and the structure of collective bargaining in the UK, mean that detailed agreements should on the whole be reached at industry or company level. All I wish to do is suggest general principles on which PEL should be based.

(a)   It should maximise employee choice. There is bound to be some conflict of interest over the uses to which the leave may be put. Conditions may be set either on the take-up of the leave itself or on whether it is accompanied by financial support. Employers are likely to press for the training to be vocational and firm-specific. Yet the distinction between general and vocational, enshrined though it is in the ILO Convention, is often difficult to uphold in practice, especially in a world of rapidly changing technology and labour mobility. Maximising choice is not only a matter of classification of what type of education the individual should be permitted. Adequate and varied provision must be there in the first place. Evidence from elsewhere suggests that formal educational institutions are often slow to respond to – let alone anticipate – the needs of those on PEL. But if they were faced with customers with cash to pay for courses they would no doubt respond.

(b)   It should incorporate the principle of positive discrimination.

There is a danger, as with other fringe benefits of this kind, that PEL will be granted to the better educated. The Italian trade unions, in negotiating their agreements on 150 hours PEL, established as a priority the need to help those who had not completed basic education. The Swedes make specific provision for immigrant workers to be able to learn Swedish.

(c)   It should strengthen educational provision for workplace representatives. This is dealt with below. The established right to time off for recognised representatives must not be eroded.

(d)   It should be democratically organised and administered. This is not just a pious wish. Article 6 of the ILO Convention requires states to involve the various interested parties in the development and application of a policy on PEL. Broad participation is an essential way of drawing in people who would otherwise have remained uninterested. It is a sound educational principle to involve students as early as possible in the formulation of learning programmes. This principle is in fact enshrined in the 1976 Norwegian Adult Education Act, which requires any institution wishing to qualify for public assistance for its courses to demonstrate that it has made significant attempts to democratise its decisions on course content and structure.[12]

I have already proposed the establishment of work environment committees along the lines of health and safety committees. If these are set up, training should form part of their remit, and PEL along with it. If work environment committees are regarded as too ambitious, committees specifically concerned with training and manpower development could be constituted on a joint basis to promote and monitor company policy. The crucial point is the one of principle: that people should be entitled to influence the scope for their own development. If this sounds too airy-fairy, we should remind ourselves that the rights to codetermination over training are recognised, to varying degrees, in many other industrialised countries: France, Denmark and Finland, to name but a few.[13]

The financing of education and training at the company level depends in part on government activity. I have already referred to the macro-economic arguments for devoting resources to further education on a national level.[14] Within individual organisations, the amount and the distribution of expenditure on training cannot but reflect a variety of factors: the industry within which the organisation operates, its market and cash flow position, technological developments and prevailing personnel policy, to name only a few. The government should provide the right framework, public support and a developed network of incentives and facilities.

3   Postiive discrimination: not just more for some

The dismal pattern of educational inequality, deep rooted within formal education, repeats itself at the workplace. The CPRS sum up the current distribution of training resources:

> The concentration of training into apprenticeships has been largely at the expense of unskilled workers and female workers (there is of course a large overlap between the two groups). Many girls undertake training before entering employment by attending vocational courses at FE colleges, paid for by their families and LEAs. But once in employment, both unskilled and female workers receive a very small share of the training by the ITB system.[15]

Table 13.2 provides powerful evidence, which speaks for itself.

Entry qualifications are only part of the story. Not only do about a third of those who leave school at sixteen get virtually no training at the time – they are unlikely ever to get any subsequently. The MSC's review revealed that under half of the firms interviewed (47 per cent) maintained any policy for training *all* grades of worker.[16] Seven per cent of them had no plans for training anyone at any grade; details of the plans of the remaining 46 per cent are not given, but we can be fairly sure that the excluded grades are the workers already lacking in skills. I could find one reference only in the document to the specific training needs of disadvantaged groups.

Similar, if less plentiful, evidence exists in relation to ethnic minorities. It demonstrates the cumulative effect of educational disadvantage on the conditions and prospects of specific categories of workers. But the problem is not a mere logistical one of how to provide for certain groups more of the opportunities currently available to their more favoured colleagues. It is a question of who controls both access to training and the definition of what counts as skill.

The issue has been clearly put:

Table 13.2   Sixteen and Seventeen-year-old Entrants into Employment: Distribution by Length of Training Received (%)   (*England and Wales 1979*)

	All	Male Apprentices	All	Female Apprentices
No training	31.1		42.2	
1–26 weeks	23.2		43.1	
27–52 weeks	3.5		3.8	
53–104 weeks	6.1	7.1	4.5	19.5
Over 104 weeks	36.2	92.9	6.5	80.5

Source: *Department of Employment Gazette*, September 1980.

To suggest that the remarkable coincidence between women's labour and unskilled labour in our economy is solely the result of discriminatory training programmes, or even of home responsibilities, is surely naive, since it implies that with educational upgrading and the provision of more day nurseries women would take their place alongside skilled men workers, and gender-ghettoes in waged work would disappear.[17]

The authors back up their argument with specific illustrations from the paper, clerical and clothing industries to reveal the complexities of the relation between skill and sex. The definition of skill is not a neutral operation, determined by the objective nature of the work to be done. In fact skill is not even defined by the specific machinery employed, concrete and non-arbitrary though that may seem. It is often the result of socially constructed categories which prejudice the status and opportunities of certain groups.

Obviously this raises some rather fundamental questions which go well beyond the scope of this chapter. They can only be resolved – even partially – by more generalised developments than those at the level of the individual workplace. Nevertheless, the issues can be dragged down from the level of pure abstraction. The pursuit of positive discrimination in learning by unions and management should embrace the following: a review of job content, to improve the quality of work of disadvantaged groups; regrading of jobs where required both through comparison with other jobs (redressing straight inconsistencies in grading differentials) and directly encouraging the promotion of the disadvantaged; a review of recruitment and promotion policies. Given this combination of policies, specifically educational policies will have a chance of being effective.

4   Training for representatives

The 1975 Employment Protection Act established the right for official union representatives to take time off with pay for recognised training purposes. This was an important principle to establish, and due advantage was taken of it, with an expansion in TUC training from 16,461 students in 1975 to 39,051 in 1979–80. Individual trade unions also conduct their own training. Although systematic evaluation of this training is difficult, there can be no doubt that in a general sense it has resulted in a more confident and competent corps of lay representatives. Some regard this enhanced capacity to know and follow their agreements as reformist bureaucratisation but that is a matter of political taste. If knowledge is accepted as at least a potential asset, there remains a powerful case for extending these rights – and not only because employers are demonstrably using the recession as a reason for chipping away at the right to time off.[18]

There are two chief reasons why expanded training opportunities for workplace representatives is an important issue. In the first place, the nature of collective bargaining is changing. It would be oversanguine to talk of a continual extension of collective bargaining such that more and more decisions were being brought under joint control. There is an unevenness in the development of company decision-making and of union organisation which may even have resulted in a broadening of the 'gap', such that union organisation is weak at the very points where crucial decisions are taken.[19] The collapse of large segments of British industry has knocked the stuffing out of many negotiators, leaving them with little to talk about other than the size of redundancy payments. Nevertheless, the number of issues which have been brought under the remit of collective bargaining has increased substantially if patchily: recruitment, pensions, working hours, new technology. It is recognised by many organisations as legitimate for these at least to be raised for discussion. This places enormous demands on lay representatives and indeed on full-time officials, even where they are well supported by a central research office. The point does not need labouring – how many of us would be confident of interpreting our own organisation's books, even if it were open to us to 'read' them?

The second, related, reason is that the growth of representation, allied with the increasing complexity of both the issues involved and the corporate structures within which they are debated, places great strain on relations between representatives and their members. If we are to have a flourishing and democratic workplace organisation, representatives must be given the opportunity to learn how to establish and maintain good links with their members. Here again I am not talking solely about formal learning, although this may well be an important component. I am arguing that serious thought needs to be given to enabling representatives to develop *and exercise* communication skills both as individuals and as part of a collective organisation.

In short, then, we do not need to give life-long tenure to union representatives, but we do need to give them adequate opportunities to learn how to do their job and to keep good relations with those they represent. The corollary of this – and the final proposal in this chapter – is that there should be a substantial expansion of membership education within trade unions. The TUC is already planning this, and rightly so.[20] In the first place most of the same arguments concerning comprehension of new bargaining issues apply as much to the shopfloor as they do to their representatives. Secondly, the tasks of the representatives will be much assisted if their members understand what they are trying to achieve, and provide them with positive support. Thirdly, an alert and informed membership is the best check on unrepresentative behaviour.

Does all this rightly fall under the rubric of social policy? I would argue that it does. In the first place, one of the reasons why education has had only limited success as a social policy instrument for equality is that it has too often been restrictively interpreted in terms of formal schooling, divorced from the realities of power relations at the workplace. Secondly, people's experience of work affects their behaviour in the community at large, however hard it is to specify the exact relationship. Enabling them to learn to work should encourage a more positive approach to learning generally. Finally, the workplace is very much a social unit; equipping people to share in the control of its character and organisation is of exactly the same order as providing housing, hospitals and schools to enable them to participate generally in a democratic society.

Notes and references

1. Central Policy Review Staff, *Education, Training and Industrial Performance*, HMSO, 1980.
2. S.J. Prais, 'Vocational Qualifications of the Labour Force in Britain and Germany', *National Institute Economic Review (98)*, NIESR, 1981.
3. Manpower Services Commission, Outlook on Training, HMSO, 1980.
4. Centre for Contemporary Cultural Studies, *Unpopular Education*, Hutchinson, 1981, p. 264.
5. A. Gramsci, *Selections from Political Writings 1910–1920*, Lawrence and Wishart, 1977.
6. H. Benyon and T. Nichols, *Living with Capitalism: Class Relations and the Modern Factory*, Routledge and Kegan Paul, 1977.
7. ACAS, *Induction of New Employees*, Advisory Booklet 7, HMSO, 1982.
8. B. Göranzon, 'Job Design and Automation in Sweden', paper presented to International Symposium on Co-determination in the Public Sector, Abetsliventrum, Stockholm, 1981.
9. Manpower Services Commission, *op. cit*, p. 44.
10. P. Beaumont, R. Coyle, J. Leopold and T. Schuller, *The Determinants of Effective Joint Health and Safety Committees*, Centre for Research in Industrial Democracy and Participation, University of Glasgow, 1982.
11. Labour Research Department, *Bargaining Report No. 16*, September/October 1981.
12. O. Skard, 'Recent Legislation and the Norwegian Pattern of Adult Education', in T. Schuller and J. Megarry (eds), *Recurrent Education and Lifelong Learning*, Kogan Page, 1979.
13. E. Cordova, 'Workers Participation in Decisions within Enterprises: Recent Trends and Problems', *International Labour Review*, vol. 121, no. 2, ILO, Geneva, 1982.
14. M. Peston, 'Recurrent Education: Tackling the Financial Implications', in Schuller and Megarry (eds), *op. cit.*
15. CPRS *op. cit.*, p. 19.
16. Manpower Services Commission, *op. cit.*, p. 47.
17. A. Phillips and B. Taylor, 'Sex and Skill: Notes Towards a Feminist Economics', *Feminist Review*, no. 6, 1980, p. 80.
18. T. Schuller (ed.), *Is Knowledge Power?*, Aberdeen People's Press, 1981.
19. P. Cressey and J. MacInnes, 'Modern Capitalist Enterprise and the Structure of Control', in D. Dunkerley and G. Salaman (eds), *The International Yearbook of Organisational Studies 1981*, Routledge and Kegan Paul, 1982.

20. D. Gowan, 'Membership Education', *Trade Union Studies Journal*, no. 4, WEA, London, 1981.

14 Planning Social Priorities – Nationally*
by Tessa Blackstone

The need for priorities

Governments rarely have much idea what their social priorities are. It is important that future Labour Governments should be clearer about this than they have been in the past. One reason for the rather disappointing overall performance of recent Labour Governments in the social policy field has been the lack of a clear set of priorities. This has sometimes led to individual policies which are mutually contradictory and not surprisingly lead to perverse outcomes. The Labour Party now has a large accumulation of new policies, together with unrealistic expectations about the chances of getting them enacted. There is a danger that the same mistakes will be made again. Neither the present machinery of government nor the party's policy-making process seems likely to get to grips with the issue. The problem begins in opposition. This ought to be the time when social priorities are identified, considered and broadly ranked according to their importance. Unfortunately this does not happen. There is some effort by political parties whilst in opposition to work out their priorities *within* particular parts of their programme, for example within health or within social security, although even here they are often left vague and muddled. However, there is little or no attempt to draw up a list of priorities across the whole range of social policies.

In the Labour Party, policy-making in opposition takes place through two main mechanisms. The first is Party Conference. The second is through the committee structure of the National Executive Committee (NEC).

The Party Conference can hardly be said to embody a carefully thought out method for determining priorities. What gets on to the agenda is fairly arbitrary. It is largely based on the number of resolutions on different issues received from constituency parties. The debate takes place in an atmosphere unconstrained by reference to the likely cost of new policies or how they will be paid for, or to the problems or consequences of implementing them. As a consequence, a whole range of highly laudable goals are adopted with little reference to

* I would like to thank Nicholas Deakin, William Plowden, Tom Schuller and the editor of this volume for comments on an earlier draft of this chapter.

the realities of financial constraints, and with no attempt to attach priorities to them.

The NEC has a number of specialist committees in different areas of policy onto which it co-opts trade unionists, local authority members, academic experts and others, whose task is to work out policy initiatives. The work of these committees interacts with Party Conference in two ways: it takes into account decisions made at Conferences; and policy papers which are produced and endorsed by the NEC may go to the Party Conference as NEC statements.

Whilst the sub-committees and their working parties may go into much more detail than debates at the Party Conference, they often also fail to take a tough and realistic view of resource implications, and, more important, there is no effective mechanism for deciding how to allocate priorities between areas or even to resolve conflicts of aims. Neither the Home Policy Committee nor the NEC itself does this. Thus when it comes to drafting the Manifesto there is a mass of commitments to be sorted out, some of which may conflict.

Manifestos are of necessity very general statements of purpose and contain little detailed working out of priorities. What is needed is a series of back-up papers which do this, and which ministers in a new government can take with them as a basis for immediate action. If not, the civil service will inevitably impose its view on what social priorities should be, if only by asserting the departmental line.

The political difficulties of achieving an agreed view of this kind should not be underestimated. There will be enormous pressures to fudge matters. In so doing, potential conflicts between shadow spokesmen fighting for their own areas of policy are avoided. Moreover the electoral consequences of deciding 'across the board' priorities may be considered damaging. Some interest groups are going to discover before an election rather than after it that they are not first in line for more attention. The exercise may have to be done but not published.

Failing a clear set of priorities formulated in opposition, social priorities must be defined as soon as the government takes office. A collective ministerial discussion should take place, preferably under the chairmanship of the Prime Minister, to outline the government's broad strategy for social policy in its first and subsequent years in office. There should also be a mechanism for reviewing progress at the end of each year and for making any adjustments required as a result of changed circumstances, for example higher unemployment. The discussion should try to reach agreement about those policy proposals formulated in opposition which are of the highest priority, those which rank as medium priority and those which are of lower priority. Only when a political ranking of this kind has been done can progress begin on working out the details of the strategy, including the timing of policy changes. Some might criticise such a procedure as dangerously 'irrational' because over-dependent on the respective power of new ministers in arguing the case for their own department, or on the effectiveness of different pressure groups in pleading for their client groups and their services. However, in a properly briefed collective discussion it is more likely that inevitable effects of this kind can be taken into account. The alternative danger, that the decision-making process may become too technocratic, seems fairly remote. All the pressures are in the other direction.

Criteria for choosing priorities

Although the difficult choices depend in the end on political judgements, there should be some agreement on what kind of criteria should be used in trying to reach decisions. These might include:

(a)   Likely distributional effects;
(b)   Public expenditure implications;
(c)   Possible employment effects;
(d)   Demographic pressures;
(e)   International comparisons;
(f)   Information about the public's priorities from opinion polls.

Nearly all of them pose technical difficulties and some are controversial.

For a Labour Government committed to greater social equality, the criterion of *distributional effects* ought to be central, as Le Grand illustrates in Chapter 6. To work out the likely distributional consequences of new policies is, however, more difficult than simply costing them. It is particularly difficult if we try to examine the combined impact policies have not just on income groups but also on age, sex, regional and racial categories. Assumptions have to be made about the nature of take-up as well as its extent. Information is often not available on which income, age or ethnic minority groups are using existing services, which makes such assumptions somewhat unreliable. Even rough and ready estimates of the various distributional effects of policies may be helpful. Raising the issues can be more important than the precise figures.

Though *public expenditure implications* are often ignored in opposition, few would argue that the potential costs of any policy innovation should be ignored and these rapidly become crucial. The Treasury sees to that. What is frequently left out of such discussions are the scale and distributional impact of tax expenditures (see Chapter 6). Changes in tax allowances are a crucial part of social policy but get treated as Inland Revenue matters and left to the Chancellor.

Employment effects are also controversial. Whether additional jobs are created for groups suffering from high unemployment is not relevant to identifying where the most serious gaps in provision exist or where the greatest social needs are, and it may also distort the outcomes of the analysis, giving some labour-intensive new programmes greater priority than they otherwise deserve. However, if there is a pool of unemployed skilled labour, whether bricklayers or primary teachers, both the resource and public expenditure implications will be altered in favour of, say, building programmes or nursery education. Where unemployment is as high as in contemporary Britain, it probably places additional demands on a variety of social services as well as being economically wasteful.[1] Thus the reduction of the numbers of un- employed people has a valuable indirect effect in releasing some resources which can be used for other groups as well as direct ad- vantages to the unemployed. On balance therefore it seems right to include employment effects in the list of criteria.

The inclusion of *demographic pressures* is uncontroversial. An increase in the projected number of old people and a declining birth-rate leading to fewer children must mean some reallocation of resources.

International comparisons may help to put our own priorities into perspective. There is no reason why priorities in Britain should be the same as in some other country or indeed why they should adhere to some European average. The technical difficulties of international comparison mean that care must be taken in interpreting some of the data that emerge. However the study of different patterns of provision elsewhere often helps to clarify possible alternatives for Britain.

What British *public opinion* considers to be important has only been investigated on a haphazard basis. In spite of their limitations, and the danger that if badly done they may be neither valid nor reliable indi- cators of the public's views, polls can provide valuable information which helps to balance the claims made by the growing number of pressure groups. In a democracy they are not the only way of discover- ing what the public most wants to see changed or developed, but they are a source of additional information which should not be completely ignored. The usual objection is that people do not know enough about possible alternatives but the government can contribute to public edu- cation on these issues. The *Priorities* documents[2] published by the last Labour Government on the health and personal social services were im- portant in educating professional and interested lay opinion on the consequences of an ageing and dependent population, on trends in costs and the constraints imposed by public spending limits. It is not impossible to envisage a wider-ranging document discussing broader social priorities.

Machinery for setting priorities

Even if priorities are clear, the construction of a 'blueprint' social plan would neither be feasible in the departmental structure of British central government, nor would it be sensitive enough to new needs that may emerge. Nevertheless, if 'ad hocery' is to be avoided there is a need for some kind of central planning *capacity* to develop a flexible strategy and to plan its implementation. Whilst individual departments have to varying degrees set up planning machinery, the only system that exists at the centre of government is the Treasury's Public Expenditure Survey Committee (PESC).[3]

However, even PESC has not lived up to early expectations as a system of planning and controlling public expenditure. The Treasury, seeking to contain public spending more tightly, has shifted the emphasis *away* from planning to control and restraint. As Wright argues, any rationality that PESC now has is largely 'spurious'.[4] He lists some of the reasons which include: a progressively shorter planning period; the abandonment of any attempt to survey prospective resources; the use of cash limits which restrain rather than control public expenditure; and the growing use of public expenditure as a tool of short-term economic management.

From the beginning, PESC was concerned with inputs rather than outputs and has failed to build in any monitoring or evaluation of expenditure programmes. Finally, the PESC process is largely incremental, with small additions and subtractions being made to programmes rather than there being any fundamental replanning.

If planning, defined as 'an attempt to determine policies that relate to some future time period'[5] is to be both rigorous and radical (in the sense that it reviews a wide range of possible options, including some that are quite new), then new machinery is required. The classic central government response to problems which cross departmental boundaries is to set up an inter-departmental committee. However, it may be too weak a device, because its members are all departmentally based and its secretariat is too small and insufficiently well qualified for research and information gathering.

One alternative might be to strengthen the CPRS. This may have certain disadvantages. If the CPRS is to continue to perform the functions for which it was originally set up it must continue to advise ministers on all the main areas of policy. Asking it to take on the specific role of social planning has the slight danger of distorting its effort by over-concentrating on social policy, unless it were to grow in size. That has the danger that it may lose its cohesiveness as a unit. Another alternative might be to set up a social planning unit in the Cabinet Office. Two or three units (although of a slightly different kind) already exist there, including the assessment staff, which analyses intelligence and other information on foreign countries, and the European unit, which co-ordinates policy towards the EEC. A social planning unit might be staffed by a mixture of civil servants on secondment from the relevant departments, economists, statisticians and social policy experts from outside government. It should not have more than about half a dozen staff and would have to rely to a large extent on departments and to some extent on institutions outside central government to provide it with the necessary information. The disadvantage of such a unit is that it creates yet another small organisation at the centre which could find itself duplicating some of the work of the CPRS or the Number 10 policy unit. It might also be less powerful than a revitalised CPRS, whose head has Permanent Secretary status and ought to be someone who is politically close to ministers under the next Labour Government. The new Manpower and Personnel Office in the Cabinet Office might also work with a social planning unit *within* the CPRS on social service manpower. Whatever the exact location of a social planning unit or group, and the CPRS is probably the right one, the planning of social priorities cannot be left entirely to individual departments. There is a need for some central impetus to look across the whole range of social policy and to encourage improved analysis within departments.

Thus the unit's tasks should include:

(a)   Co-ordination of programme development work of different central government departments in related areas, taking into account manpower and capital requirements;

(b)   Improvements in the data base to aid the above;

(c)   Establishment of a research programme on key issues of cross-departmental and policy importance;

(d)   Development of efficient consultation procedures about possible new plans and programmes;

(e)   Links with the Treasury and PESC, to monitor tax and spending decisions to ensure that agreed social priorities are adequately reflected in the PESC allocations and tax policy;

(f)   Collection of information about the possible problems of implementing policies at local level;

(g)   Devising proposals for monitoring and evaluating new policies, including client satisfaction and dissatisfaction.

These tasks are easier to list than to carry out. For the unit to be effective, the backing of ministers – particularly the Prime Minister – would be essential, especially in dealing with the Treasury. It should be seen as ministers' instrument for planning their agreed social priorities.

Indeed one of the tasks of the unit should be to provide the briefing for ministerial discussion of priorities.

There will be powerful constraints on social expenditure and the unit would have to have close contact with the Treasury. Once overall limits were set by Cabinet the unit's task would be to secure a set of consistent priorities within and between social programmes and tax policy. Redistribution and family policy should be high on their agenda.

The central task is that of programme formulation and development. All the others are necessary adjuncts. It would be difficult for a social planning unit to draw the boundaries between its work and that of departments in this central task. Clearly the details of new programmes (or for that matter cuts in existing programmes) would continue to be worked out in the spending departments. There would therefore need to be close contact between departmental policy planning branches and the new unit. The latter's special contribution would be to try to assess different aspects of departmental programmes against the background of social policy priorities generally.

Capital programmes can serve as an illustration. One of the characteristics of public spending in the last decade has been the extent to which these have been cut in comparison to current spending. Whether such savage slashing was desirable is highly questionable. In some cases the effectiveness of the service may be severely reduced by the failure to invest in capital. A classic example of this is the BBC external services where, until recently, recurrent expenditure had been maintained but there had been little capital investment. A direct consequence was that programmes were being produced which in some parts of the world could barely be heard at all and in others had only poor audibility, which discouraged tuning in. The whole purpose of the enterprise is thus defeated. Facilities for surgery in the health service, the teaching of science in education, rehabilitation and training programmes in prisons can all be cited as areas where there is likely to be a fairly direct link between capital expenditure and outcomes. In the personal social services or social security they may be much less closely related. Yet even in the last example capital may not be unimportant: the take-up of certain benefits may be smaller if the social security offices are extremely uncomfortable and depressing places in which to wait.

We need then to increase our understanding of the relative effects of the quality of the capital stock on the quality of the services provided. This is one of the activities that a central social planning unit might pursue. Where it identifies insufficient priority being given to capital programmes, it should provide some counterweight to the current inbuilt tendency of the Treasury and the spending departments to cut these programmes.

Work of this kind – and similar work on manpower requirements covering such issues as the desirable relative balance between professional and non-professional and paid and voluntary personnel – requires both an improvement in the data-base on which such judgements can be made and the expansion of research. Some improvements were made by the 1974–9 Labour Government, which accepted the need for good social statistics, but some of the advances have been reversed by the present Tory Government which has cut the government statistical service. Apparently it does not believe that decision-making should be well informed by good statistical information. More recently it has reduced the funds available for social scientific research. These cuts will inevitably mean that some research which would have been useful in planning social priorities does not get done. The social planning unit would need to work closely with the Central Statistical Office on the collection and analysis of social statistics. It should also have a small research budget of its own, which would allow it to commission studies directly, rather than relying on the research programmes of departments which are likely to be confined to departmental interests and to ignore those that cut across departments.

A number of the issues identified so far were also identified by the CPRS when it formulated the Joint Approach to Social Policy (JASP).[6] Foremost amongst JASP's objectives was the need to co-ordinate better the work of different departments concerned with social policy. In fact its effort at improving co-ordination by such mechanisms as a Cabinet Committee on long-term social policy and an official committee at Under-Secretary level were less successful than some of its other initiatives.[7] Success in co-ordinating programme development in different departments in related areas has escaped most people. The failure of the DES and the DHSS in doing so in the area of services for pre-school children, in spite of some ministerial effort to achieve this, is just one example.[8] Because of the jealously guarded autonomy of departments, there will certainly be opposition to attempts which constrain departments' freedom to pursue their own objectives. However, interdepartmental co-operation has become generally accepted as necessary, even if only lip-service is sometimes paid to it, and to some extent it already does act as a constraint on departmental autonomy, as do the procedures required by the Treasury in PESC. The fact that previous attempts at the co-ordinating aspects of planning have not been very successful does not mean that greater success in the future can never be attained. The best way to proceed may be by a combination of centrally imposed initiatives and the encouragement of various forms of reciprocity between departments at departmental level. These might include shared information-gathering and monitoring on particular client groups and particular services which cut across departments.

Monitoring policy

It is important that there should be some consideration of and feedback about possible problems of implementation at the policy planning stage. However good the social planning process in other respects, it will fail if encapsulated in some remote vacuum at the centre of central government without reference to the main bodies directly responsible for implementation, in particular the local authorities and the National Health Service. The social planning unit will need to consult on an informal basis with the local authority associations and regional health authorities, and with the professionals who run the services. Departments which have to relate to particular professional groups such as teachers or doctors are sometimes too ready to accept the professions' interpretations rather than those of their clients. Being a little more distanced from the professionals may help a central social planning unit assess priorities more critically. For instance, it is noteworthy that planning for preventive medicine is virtually non-existent.[9]

It is even more important to develop methods for monitoring and evaluating the effects of programmes once implemented. First, it is important to ensure that priorities do not get lost at the implementation stage because resources that were originally designated for one thing such as extra teachers to meet the needs of minority group children get used for something else, such as generally smaller class sizes. Secondly, it is necessary to find out more about whether programmes which are being applied in the right places are effective in meeting their objectives; for example, are the extra teachers working with minority group children in ordinary schools actually helping to improve their educational attainment and reduce the numbers being sent to special schools?

Programme Analysis and Review (PAR) was the first major attempt to try to monitor the effectiveness of particular programmes, in social and other areas of policy. PARs were meant to be boldly radical in selecting subjects for analysis (no sacred cows) and in the range of options which they explored (no holds barred). The central departments of the Treasury, Civil Service Department and CPRS contributed to them, as well as the departments directly concerned. The report resulting from a PAR was considered by ministers collectively. PARs were selected by an official committee chaired by the Treasury which received proposals from individual departments as well as suggestions from the central departments. This committee also reviewed the progress of the PAR programme as a whole. The system was introduced in 1971 and finally collapsed in 1979, after several years of ill-health; during its short life some eighty PARs were produced on a wide range of subjects. The reasons for its demise are complex and cannot be gone into at any length here. But there are one or two lessons that can be learnt and that should be taken into account before any new system is introduced from the centre for evaluating the effectiveness of policies. First, it is essential that ministers should be involved at the outset in deciding what should be included in the monitoring programme. They were not in PAR, which served to reduce their interest in its outcomes. Second, there should be no secrecy about what is being monitored. The ludicrous cloak-and-dagger approach PAR meant there was no one outside central government to speak up for it or for the need for particular studies under its auspices; it also allowed some departments to shelter behind the argument that they did not want to do a particular PAR because they could not consult their constituencies. Third, all teams undertaking particular PARs should include as consultants one or more outside experts who might bring fresh ideas into a department's view about possible alternative ways of achieving particular ends. This would not guarantee a radical approach but might help to get it. Most PARs failed to achieve this.

In any future monitoring system, consideration could be given to studies being carried out jointly by central and local government in those areas for which local authorities have the prime responsibility. Inputs from voluntary organisations and pressure groups to the monitoring process would also be valuable. Particular attention ought to be paid to how far programmes are responsive to clients' expressed needs and both voluntary bodies and pressure groups may be able to provide valuable evidence of this.

At the beginning of this chapter it was suggested that the distributional impact of social policies should be a crucial factor in setting priorities. We have a fair amount of information already about the likely distributional impact of increasing resources in some areas. We know, for example, that expanding higher education with more full-time provision for eighteen- to twenty-one-year-olds is not likely to benefit low income groups. There are many other areas, though, where our knowledge of the effects of policies on different income groups, ethnic groups, age and sex groups is incomplete. New policies should all be monitored in this respect.

One of the most difficult problems to be faced is how to define and measure the output of social policies. In spite of the fact that during the last twenty years we have greatly improved our capacity to measure outcomes, little actual measurement takes place. The problems stretch far beyond technology. There can be no agreement about outcomes until there is a measure of agreement about objectives. It is not sufficient to say that our objectives are that people should be healthier, better housed, or better educated. We must have some idea about what it means to be healthier, better educated or better housed. Thus is a family in a high-rise flat, with hot running water and an inside lavatory, better housed than a family in a terraced house without these amenities, but with a garden? Or is a child who has spent time at school learning about how to make a film, doing creative writing, and understanding the family structure of the Nayar, better or worse educated than the child who has read Cicero and Ovid, learnt grammar and syntax, or understood the way ox-bow lakes are formed?

There are three main problems in measuring 'outputs':

(a)   Defining what we think the outputs should be (the objective problem);
(b)   Finding ways of measuring them (the technical problem);
(c)   Interpreting the findings from the point of view of future policies (the response problem).

Problems of this kind indicate the immense amount of time and effort required to monitor social programmes effectively. However, if we are to go on improving the quality of life of the population we must not shrink from this challenge.

The assessment of performance unit in the DES is one example of what can be done. Better use of the various inspectorates and bodies such as the health advisory service are another way forward. Finally there must be some overall monitoring of the government's social policies to ensure that its priorities are adhered to and it is not blown off course. There should be an annual ministerial review for this purpose.

Conclusion

Social planning in Britain is still in its infancy. Nevertheless there have been some advances in spite of the justified criticisms of commentators like Peter Townsend, who advocates a somewhat utopian vision of social planning as the provision of a complete blueprint which would enable the restructuring of society.[10] There is for example more awareness of the need to plan in the light of regional differences in needs and information about the present distribution of resources. The Resource Allocation Working Party for the health service (RAWP) is probably the best example of an attempt to quantify carefully what has to be done to get rid of regional inequalities in provision. Under the present government, where cutting expenditure has been the dominant obsession without too much regard for some of the consequences, little progress has been made. Under a Labour Government with a very different political ideology there will still be a great need to make clear decisions about priorities, however hard this may be, to review them regularly, to plan carefully how to develop social policies in future years in the light of these decisions, and to try to discover the consequences of our actions.

Notes and references

1. Adrian Sinfield, *What Unemployment Means*, Martin Robertson, 1981.
2. DHSS, *Priorities for the Health and Personal Social Services in England*, HMSO, 1976.
3. Hugh Heclo and Aaron Wildavsky, *The Private Government of Public Money*, Macmillan, 1981.
4. Maurice Wright, 'From Planning to Control: PESC in the 1970s', in Maurice Wright (ed.), *Public Spending Decisions*, Allen and Unwin, 1980.
5. Howard Glennerster, *Social Service Budgets and Social Policy*, Allen and Unwin, 1975.
6. Central Policy Review Staff, *A Joint Framework for Social Policies*, HMSO, London, 1975.
7. W.S.L. Plowden, 'Developing a Joint Approach to Social Policy', in Kathleen Jones, Muriel Brown and Sally Baldwin (eds), *The Yearbook of Social Policy in Britain 1976*, Routledge and Kegan Paul, 1977.
8. Central Policy Review Staff, *Services for the Children of Working Mothers*, CPRS, 1978.
9. Howard Glennerster, 'From Containment to Conflict? Social Planning in the Seventies', *Journal of Social Policy*, vol. 10, part 1, January 1981.
10. Peter Townsend, 'Social Planning and the Control of Priorities', in Peter Townsend and Nicholas Bosanquet (eds), *Labour and Inequality*, Fabian Society, 1972. Peter Townsend, *Sociology and Social Policy*, Penguin, 1975. Peter Townsend, 'Social Planning and the Treasury', in Nicholas Bosanquet and Peter Townsend (eds), *Labour and Equality*, Heinemann, 1980.

Local government has passed through a series of traumatic changes over the past decade. The effects of these changes are clearly visible in the behaviour and attitudes – morale, indeed – of those members and officers who have lasted the full distance. Consideration of the potentiality for developing a new approach to planning social priorities in local government must take account of these events – which is why this essay begins with a short catalogue, more or less in chronological order.

First in the sequence comes the territorial reorganisation of local government outside London in the Walker Act of 1972. In longer perspective, this legislation takes its place as one of a group of initiatives taken by the Heath government, designed to secure more effective management in government through modifications in its structure and machinery. This flavour is also detectable in the internal reorganisation that followed. The Bains apparatus of corporate management and PPBS, administered by a policy and resources committee, supported by a chief officers' board and informed by the creation of new facilities for research and intelligence, was intended to provide the new authorities with the capacity to discharge the new responsibilities laid upon them in planning, social services and housing. The benign approval of central government for this process was indicated through publications like the management studies from the Six Towns series.[1] The same process also ushered in the brief heyday of management consultants in local government, who perished like mayflies in the next phase, with the solitary exception of those flexible enough to obtain work advising on dismantling the structures they had helped to create.

By the mid-1970s local government had begun its dizzy ride down the switchback of resource allocation. The brief affluence of the new authorities in the early 1970s came to a sudden halt after the IMF fiasco of 1976.[2] Then cuts began to bite more deeply, first into capital schemes and then increasingly into service provision. At the same time, public discontent about the cost of local government and the quality of the service being provided also began to rise. Local government found itself caught between two fires.

As David Townsend showed in Chapter 12, the changing face of central government has been the single most important factor in setting the policy context within which local government has to function. Alongside general restrictions, Whitehall has shown an increasing appetite for using control over resources to impose changes of policy emphasis. Hence, the Shore tilt has been followed by the Heseltine lurch, first in the opposite direction (urban to rural) and then, in the case of some favoured authorities, back again. The once unthinkable is now in plain view – housing relegated to the end of the queue of spending priorities.

Under these new pressures, local government has itself passed through a series of changes. 'Test-to-destruction' radicals in both major parties insist on the fundamentally political character of the role of local authorities. Out-and-out opposition to any set of policy objectives set by ministers, on the basis of the local counter-mandate, has provided the recipe for a whole series of clashes between centre and locality, many of which have ended up being arbitrated by the courts. In the process, what once separated technical issues from overtly political ones has been swept away.

The social policy agenda

Against this background of turbulence, it is striking that there should have been comparatively little emphasis on defining priorities for social policies. On the Labour side, the preoccupation has been with the selection of members and the means by which they are made accountable to the group and the party outside, not on equipping them to do a better job once elected. The party's programme has more often than not consisted of a narrow range of actions more or less arbitrarily defined as 'socialist', to be implemented come what may by a head-down kamikaze charge designed to make some impact within the space of a single term. While on the other side of the widening political divide, to identify any set of activities as 'social' is to mark them down for an early cut, if not complete elimination.

Yet developments have not all been on one side of the balance sheet. The demonstration that a wide range of issues are relevant to the policy debate hastened the end of the old baronial system, in which chief officers reigned undisturbed over large areas of policy-making. The past decade has seen the arrival in local government of a number of younger staff who are anxious to act, in Ken Young's useful phrase, as 'policy entrepreneurs'.[3] This involves taking up issues and using access to other centres of power both inside and outside the authority to try to push them along. Such entrepreneurs are not inhibited about forming alliances with like-minded members to speed the process up, and sub-specialisms have developed in response to new policy initiatives on employment and race relations. More about them later. They have been helped by the existence of an instrument for which there is no precise equivalent in central government – corporate management. Politicians of all parties tend to view corporate management at officer level as a means of excluding them from debates at the crucial stage, and eliminating inconvenient dissenting opinions. Concern on the Labour side was heightened by the perceived origins of the technique and by the cold technical language of 'rationality' that it employs. Yet corporate management serves a vital purpose by imposing a discipline on officers where none existed before, by seeking coherence in policy aims and co-ordination between different social services. Corporate management can also serve an important second-order purpose in providing the means by which policies can be reviewed and essential mid-term mid-course corrections can be made. There is a parallel here with similar needs experienced in central government, which Tessa Blackstone discusses in Chapter 14.

Some obstacles to progress

The main danger, in present circumstances, is not that posed by the existing machinery, as such. It is that corporate planning has been diverted to serve as a device for managing the effects of the cuts that have been imposed by central government on local authorities since 1976. Thus the meetings to which chief officers attach first priority are not those designed to review the council's strategy for the next five years: they are emergency gatherings at which a sequence of ever deeper cuts are prepared. The outcome of episodes like this is that in many authorities corporate management is now regarded by members and officers alike – though for diametrically opposite reasons – with acute suspicion.

This is unfortunate. Corporate planning does provide a means of assessing priorities across different programme areas, though the precise forms adopted can differ between authorities and there are problems associated with identifying priorities and co-ordinating programmes between different agencies. These can apply with as much force to the issues arising from overlap of responsibility between the upper and lower tiers of local government as they can to border areas between local authorities and other government agencies (quangos and local arms of Whitehall like the National Health Service).

Two examples can stand for a multiplicity of problems. The first is the GLC's attempt to draw up a strategic housing plan for London, based on a set of agreed objectives for house construction and rehabilitation. The process of negotiation between the thirty-five different public agencies responsible for housing in the metropolis proved so complex, the divergence of interests so substantial, and the fragmentation of power between the various agencies so total that a complete term (1973–7) of Labour control at County Hall proved insufficient to reach full agreement. The Tories used their subsequent term of office

(1977–81) in the precisely opposite sense, to withdraw the GLC from the housing field. The issue of gross inequity in provision and practice has been allowed to go into abeyance. The second case is that of the under fives (also cited by Tessa Blackstone in her parallel chapter). Here services are split between different statutory agencies which function in different areas under different systems of control; while the whole is complicated by the importance of the role of the voluntary sector. In a period of expansion, like the one initiated in the White Paper of 1972, increased resources from government served as a device for setting priorities and co-ordinating activity. In a period of contraction, the weaknesses of devices like joint circulars from the central government departments stand exposed. In the disputes between the various agencies about the division of responsibility for funding it is the voluntary sector, which provides the largest part of the actual service but has the least share of power, which runs the largest risk of going to the wall.

The second major problem is the assembling of relevant information on which a set of clearly defined priorities can be based. Here again, the tools are available, at least in theory. The Institute of Local Government Studies' investigation of the distribution of research and intelligence units shows that nearly all authorities in England and Wales have some capacity for the collection and analysis of social data.[4] In the late 1960s, several of the larger authorities embarked on ambitious programmes for co-ordinated action covering a range of policy areas for which local government is responsible, drawing upon elaborate exercises in the analysis and projection of trends in the local population and economy (such as Tomorrow's London, 1969). Few, if any, of these ambitious schemes actually led to any significant action. Latterly, the reviews, even those of the larger units, have tended to be less ambitious (GLC Review of Social Issues, 1980). The weakness of even these exercises have tended to be that they are not directly linked to political objectives. This is not entirely surprising, since the political priorities at local level have become increasingly dominated by the struggle between local and central government. This even extends to quarrels about data.

The GLC's persistent attempts to persuade the Department of Employment to endorse the presentation of unemployment statistics at Employment Exchange level were based on an important disagreement over the emphasis of central government policy, the council maintaining that to present statistics at regional level, on the basis of travel-to-work areas, was to conceal the presence of double-digit unemployment at a number of inner city exchanges. The stereotype of low unemployment rates in London in turn affected levels of resource allocation through special programmes, in the same way that RAWP allocations were influenced by the factors chosen in identifying regions as 'over-provided'.

The main factor inhibiting the development of local social pro-grammes has been the all-embracing character of the economic crisis. The distance travelled over the course of the decade can be appreciated by referring back to the contempt with which the Layfield panel of inquiry into the Greater London Development Plan (GLDP Inquiry 1969–71) turned aside the attempts made by the GLC to define a positive role for local government in stimulating the local economy. Now, ten years later, any urban local authority worth its salt has an economic regeneration programme, with associated projects and em-ployment promotion officers to implement them. Where a decade ago the proof of a council's constructive energies lay in the scope of its social services, now the acid test of success is the number of new jobs created – or, in the more difficult areas, saved.

The importance of economic priorities

The range of activity covered by the employment initiatives of local authorities has expanded impressively over the decade.[5] This is an area where the lines of demarcation, both professional and between authorities, have not yet had time to establish themselves as a serious obstacle. But the field is already becoming congested, as the competing advertising programmes of the larger authorities imply. Central gov-ernment had its attention attracted to this area of activity by a number of successful local experiments (Rochdale, Tyne and Wear), and began to interfere and impose items: mandatory co-operation with the private sector and the withdrawal of local government from a whole range of traditional activities in a number of experimental areas (the enterprise zones). The likelihood is that central government will intervene through the restriction of resources – or possibly by challenging the use of relevant powers – in order to curb the more ambitious of local government's recent initiatives. If it did so, that would generate yet another wasteful conflict.

While any attempt to isolate local social policy from these economic concerns would be rightly dismissed as utopian nonsense, it does not seem unreasonable to try to devote some special attention to social policy issues. As Tessa Blackstone points out in the preceding chapter, the job generation criterion for priority, if applied without regard to the nature and location of the jobs generated, is far too crude a device by which to judge the worth of new developments in policy. At the same time, it has to be recognised that if social policy initiatives are to be given some degree of priority in their own right, it will have to be on grounds that are defensible in the special circumstances of a major depression.

The assumption made so far is that such a process is compatible with – may even be assisted by – the present machinery of corporate management, introduced into many authorities after 1974. Some criticisms of this system have already been cited: the more fundamental objection, voiced among others by Cockburn,[6] is that the system reflects its origins in the American business world and is deliberately intended to exclude the views and interests of client groups, in part through the use of a 'filter' of technical language and in part by isolating the decision-taking process from political and community pressures. Without accepting this criticism in its undiluted form, it is fair to say that corporate management has made little allowance for the representation of consumer interests, in part because it was assumed that this would be the province of members. How far they, in turn, choose to exercise such a watchdog function on behalf of their constituents is largely a matter of local practice. In some authorities, it must be said, the Labour Group and its deliberations are just as remote from the electorate (not to be confused with the party faithful) as any chief officers' board. It is part of the argument of this paper, however, that it is possible to provide some opportunities for the discussion of substantive decisions about policy through a structured consultation process involving representative groups from within the local authority area. The experience of structure plan consultation[7] and the GLDP Inquiry suggest that to obtain a response on complex issues requires very careful preparation. In the GLC case, the sole focus for public involvement was the motorway issue, which accounted for virtually all the objections lodged,[8] and public interest dribbled away in a series of large formal meetings dominated by formal discussion of technical issues. The alternative of social surveys, enthusiastically embraced by some authorities as a means of reaching the 'real public', was largely discredited by low response rates. Street-level consultations on issues of direct local relevance gained in quality and response but fragmented the broader issues. Experiments in the co-ordination of local opinion through the activities of 'umbrella' organisations standing slightly apart from the statutory sector, as in some of the inner city partnerships, lend some weight to the notion that a process of consultation could be genuinely helpful, on both sides.

Towards social programmes for local government

To launch on the preparation of a programme outlining priorities for social policy suggests that we have the equipment to define such priorities and are broadly clear what the options are. However, to embark on any seriously intended programme of consultation is usually to upset any preconception on either of these scores. In particular, any attempt to categorise need groups by priority ranking – a potentially helpful line of advance – runs into the basic difficulty that priority allocations are likely to differ radically as between different interests in the community. Even so basic a proposition as trying to achieve some degree of priority for education or more broadly still for children may run into problems in a highly deprived neighbourhood with a disproportionately large number of single people, old and young, and childless couples. This might have mattered less when programmes were still incremental and resource decisions were about where to distribute the additional expenditure; but in a situation like the present where real cuts are being made all round, priority for (say) the disabled can only be achieved at the expense of other groups in need. Remembering Donnison's account of the letters of protest he received about supplementary benefits rates from the working poor,[9] it is difficult to exclude the possibility of a backlash affecting local government services equally strongly.

Periods in opposition can be helpfully employed in a review of programmes across the whole range of social policies. Some useful models are already in existence (see, for example, the Fabian Society's *A Radical Agenda for London* or the 'Socialist Programme for Islington'). Such an exercise necessarily involves forming a clear concept of what is politically possible – not abstracted from the political debate any more than from the economic imperatives. Equally, its authors should be prepared to be open-minded about some of the issues that have acquired totem significance in the social policy field in some sectors of the labour movement (council house sales, comprehensive school sixth forms and, rapidly assuming the same touchstone status, cheap fares). Against this background, the outline of an agenda might look something like the following.

First proposition

A review should be undertaken of all existing services on a need group basis, involving all the activities of relevant agencies. (One model for such an exercise would be the review of policy for the under fives and adolescents at risk undertaken for the Lambeth inner city partnership in 1978.) This approach has subsequently been developed by the race relations unit at Lambeth.[10] The objective is to establish at the outset the effects of current policies on the position of the groups identified. It is capable of being extended to other groups besides ethnic minorities – for example, it should almost certainly now be accepted that the long-term unemployed form a distinct group of this kind. Consequences of existing policies for the young family could also be explored in the same way.[11] Once the distributional effects of such policies for the elderly or the mentally handicapped have been established, a set of priorities for action become feasible, if three further conditions can be satisfied:

(a)   The record needs to incorporate the activities of all agencies with relevant responsibilities, not only in the statutory sector but also voluntary bodies;

(b)   There needs to be a parallel process of identification of resources available for possible new initiatives – not only those immediately available to local authorities in main programme areas, but also special grants (particularly relevant in the case of ethnic minorities) and possible sources of funding in the private sector;

(c)   Serious attempts should be made to obtain the views of the consumer groups for whom the services are intended. This should cover not only the introduction of new programmes but modification in existing provision.

Second proposition

The decentralisation of the machinery of service delivery to the maximum extent feasible should be an intrinsic part of any social policy programme. This has already been attempted on a substantial scale in a number of social service departments[12] as part of the so-called 'patch' approach, which decentralises administration to small area level and provides a unified range of services operating out of a single office (East Sussex is one authority currently restructuring its services on this basis). A similar approach is being pursued by a number of housing authorities, notably Walsall (before the recent change of political control). By extension, an attempt could now be made to cover a variety of services, both locally and centrally run. The pedigree of proposals for 'miniature town halls' is admittedly rather mixed; it goes back to the early 1970s and the initial attacks on 'centralised bureaucracy' associated with the community development projects.[13] The experience of CDPs was not a happy one, either for the immediate participants themselves or the host agencies,[14] but some of the ideas first developed in the CDP context, notably their work on equipping neglect groups with the resources needed to assert their claims, deserve another airing. The possibility of associating local budgets with decentralised multi-service centres would also repay further examination. There are major problems of accountability here but the idea is explored elsewhere in this volume.

Third proposition

Any programme or series of plans for particular groups must be subject to periodic review in the light of the best evidence that can be obtained about its effectiveness. The essential first review of any programme would be at the hustings, in the election at which it is 'presented'. However, the view that this is sufficient in itself does not survive closer scrutiny. The mandate theory of government, weak enough in all conscience at the national level, fades almost to vanishing point in the local context. If the test is to be free consent of the majority to a line indicated in advance, the Apathetic Tendency have commanded a majority in most local authority areas for the past decade. More seriously, the mandate theory allows no scope for mid-course correction, in circumstances which are likely, if the past decade is any guide, to be exceptionally volatile. The importance of establishing measures of the effectiveness of policy that go beyond a simple record of money spent or political objectives met is therefore central. One of the Tory Government's rare virtuous deeds in its dealings with local government has been its insistence on the wider availability of information on local authorities' affairs. The social accounting movement that this initiative has helped to get back on its legs is a thoroughly healthy development and should be extended as rapidly as possible to cover similar assessments of the local performance of the agencies of central government.

Conclusions

These propositions have been sketched out very broadly. They are intended as sketches, adaptable to local circumstances. The question of new machinery has, by design, been left to last. The importance of using existing machinery to the full has already been sufficiently stressed. The option of drastic change, either in the internal structure of individual authorities or in the system as a whole, should certainly not be excluded, but would necessarily be a long haul.

More important, in many ways, than machinery – at least in the short term – are people. If new policies are to be introduced and implemented in the single term that all but a fortunate few authorities can expect these days, the right sort of officers are essential – people prepared to use their skills but also to shake off the restraints imposed by traditional local government professionalism.

In some larger authorities, the creation of a social policy unit, responsible direct to the chief executive and through him to the chairman of the policy and resources committee, may be an expedient worth trying out; but in general the temptation to create new machinery that duplicates existing structures ought to be resisted. Rather it is a question of allowing full play to the initiative of those who have shown that they can make good use of it and encouraging them to develop the widest possible network of contact within and outside the authority.

A series of clear political priorities, set out with supporting argument in a public document open for public comment, the opportunity to explore the implications of policy initiatives or policy change before implementation with those who will be most directly affected, and a system of monitoring and review sufficiently effective to enable policy changes to be made in good time will not, in themselves, bring about the immediate construction of the New Jerusalem District Council; but they would be a useful step in the right direction.

Notes and references

1. Department of the Environment, 1972.
2. Sir Leo Pliatsky, *Getting and Spending*, Blackwell, 1982.
3. K. Young and N. Connolly, *Policy and Practice in the Multi-Racial City*, PSI, 1981.
4. E.M. Davies, *The Central Research Function in Local Government*, INGLOGOV, 1979.
5. J. Mawson, 'Local Economic Planning in the 1980s', *Local Government Studies*, 7, 4, 1981.
6. C. Cockburn, *The Local State*, Pluto Press, 1976.
7. W. Hampton, *The Individual Citizen and Public Participation*, Department of the Environment, 1978.
8. David Eversley, *The Planner in Society*, Faber, 1972.
9. David Donnison, *The Politics of Poverty*, Martin Robertson, 1982.
10. H. Ouseley *et al.*, *The System*, Runnymede Trust, 1981.
11. See Howard Glennerster, *Social Planning: a Local Study*, Martin Robertson, forthcoming.
12. R. Hadley and S. Hatch, *Social Welfare and the Failure of the State*, Allen and Unwin, 1981; and the Barclay Report, *Social Workers: Their Role and Tasks*, Bedford Square Press, 1982.
13. See also David Donnison, *The Micro Politics of the City*, CES, 1972.
14. J. Higgins *et al.*, *Government and Urban Poverty*, Blackwell, forthcoming.

Towards a Larger Concept of
Citizenship
by Howard Glennerster

The social legislation discussed in this volume, so much of it passed
shortly after the Second World War, embodied what T.H. Marshall
was to call a third level or dimension in citizenship.[1] From the time of
Magna Carta onwards Marshall argued, British people have won certain civil rights – the freedom from arbitrary arrest and prison without
trial, free speech, freedom of worship, equality before the law – at least
in theory. In the nineteenth and twentieth centuries, they won a second
element of citizenship – one person, one vote. The Second World War
and its aftermath were to add the third dimension: 'The right to a
modicum of economic welfare and security, to share to the full in the
social heritage and to live the life of a civilised being according to the
standards prevailing in society.'[2]

Those capable of a productive contribution to society and all dependent people in the community had a right to a minimum standard of life
even when affected by ill-health or other social and economic reasons
that interrupted their earning power. As we have seen even Beveridge
and Marshall's ideal has yet to be fully accomplished, notably for the
unemployed and families with low income earners.

Nevertheless, one common theme of all the contributors to this book
is that the whole notion of citizenship now needs to be extended and
enriched. Some liberal commentators, including Marshall himself,[3]
have been uneasy about the inherent tendency to extend the ideal
of citizenship in modern society. They see the implied extension of the
social market beginning to challenge and undermine the private sector,
overloading government institutions with a range of activities they are
unsuited to manage. Piachaud and Davies have discussed the economic
constraints in their chapter and there is undoubtedly point in the
argument that our political institutions have not adapted sufficiently to
carry the weight of new responsibilities social policy has brought them
in the past thirty years. The positive response to both positions is,
however, to adapt our social and political institutions to a new and more
inclusive idea of citizenship that reflects the interconnected social
world we live in, rather than to halt that development because we have
not the wit to change our political and legal systems. Such an ideal rests

on a concept of citizenship that derives from a sense of shared obligations and common rights to be full members of society in terms of work, living standards and the capacity to share our common living and working environment.

Local citizenship

David and Land and Walker argue for a new lower tier of political control for personal social and environmental services, comprising perhaps no more than a ward or two in present local government terms, in which the smaller electorate with some source of revenue of its own and support from the local council could run day care schemes, family support and community care in the true sense. With representatives on school governing bodies and community health councils they could provide a much more accessible focus of interest for many members of the community, including mothers who do not want to be involved in main-line party politics. The extended use of ordinary families in mutual helping arrangements could make local citizenship a reality, one that involved giving and not merely the receipt of a guaranteed cash minimum from the central state.

It is a great pity that the Barclay Committee got bogged down in arguments about 'the right way' to develop the professions' use of such support.[4] Individual departments and individual workers are best left to devise their own strategies.

Local independence

As Townsend argues, if central government seeks to take upon itself the whole function of providing social welfare or regulating it, the results often bring social welfare into disrepute. Hence, the virtue of giving local authorities wider discretion to do what their electors will vote for. This must mean a reform in local government finance. The notion that this will breed fiscal irresponsibility on the one hand or extreme neglect on the other is not born out by past events. Redistribution built into the grant formula and sufficiently vigorous central inspecting of standards are, however, necessary. In the end though, local people must be the judge of the social standards and institutions they use. They cannot forever be protected by central government.

Full citizenship for discriminated-against groups

In very different ways both racial minorities and women have been denied full participation in the activities and market earning power of our society because of social custom, values and prejudices. To give them full access and rights of citizenship will involve changing our laws which, by changing behaviour, may begin to modify built-in, barely appreciated prejudices. Bindman and Carrier, Rimmer and Wicks and

David and Land have set out a series of immediate steps to be taken along this road.

Bindman and Carrier argue for changes in the law against both direct and indirect forms of discrimination. They suggest that any practice or situation that gives rise to a discriminatory impact on minorities should be sufficient to prove indirect discrimination and that substantial compensation should be available to injured parties. In direct discrimination the burden of proof should be on those who treat individuals less favourably to prove that the reason was not racial. They also propose measures in housing, education and employment services designed to promote special provisions for the distinctive needs of minority groups and an overall monitoring of government policy in this field by a Cabinet sub-committee.

David and Land are also concerned with measures to strengthen the law relating to women's rights but are anxious lest too direct a copy of American legal approaches prove counter-productive.

Rimmer and Wicks suggest ways in which there can be greater flexibility between working and family life so that no members of the family are inevitably excluded from paid work or caring. They argue that all aspects of policy should be examined with respect to their impact on the family.

David and Land argue for a shorter working day, for cash benefits to meet the loss of earnings involved in caring for sick or dependent relatives or others, irrespective of the sex of the carer, and for extended eligibility to the invalid care allowance, covering married or cohabiting couples. Day care and other services for working mothers, not necessarily in formal institutions, are also on their list. This ties in with the use of local community support we discussed earlier.

Workers and the workplace

Schuller has argued that the concept of full citizenship must extend to the factory and office floor, to the control people have of their working environment and their capacity to acquire and change their working skills. He argues for work environment committees to oversee work and training opportunities in each firm, paid educational leave incorporating the principle of positive discrimination, and training for worker representatives.

Adapting universality to the least advantaged

As Le Grand has argued, the original Marshallian concept of citizenship implied that so long as services were free and universally available, access would be equal. It has been more equal than in the private market, but removing the cash barrier in an unequal society is not enough. The National Health Service, for example, can distribute money to poorer areas, deliberately develop preventive work with workers at risk, and improve antenatal care in poorer areas, but there are practical limits to what can be achieved. Where services disproportionately benefit the higher income groups, subsidies can be withdrawn and the proceeds used to expand services that reach the poorest. The necessity to do this is heightened by the dramatic worsening in Britain's long-term economic fortunes which Piachaud and Davies chart so forcefully. It is crucial the Labour Party does not adopt unrealistic spending goals and avoid the issue of priorities.

Setting social priorities

Determining how large a social policy sector we can afford is in the end a political decision. The limits are ones of democratic consent. In any period there will be costs to 'private' living standards, especially if the underlying growth rate is small, and there will be other trade offs that Davies and Piachaud discuss. Economies that are very similar in economic structure and levels of income vary widely in the extent to which they decide to tax themselves, as Abel-Smith showed. Many tax themselves more than we do. But if tax rates are not simply to provoke more inflation and if inflation is to be contained other than through paying a cruel price in unemployment, some mechanism has to be devised to reach some agreement, tacit or explicit, on the level of private incomes and social benefits year by year. To develop such a means of setting social priorities may take many years but it would have to encompass the kind of immediate issues that Piachaud and Davies raise. Unions and the wider public would have to be involved in the process of debating and deciding social priorities.

This is where a sense of social responsibility has to be created at a national level. It is the most difficult extension of citizenship of all those we have discussed but it underlies all the rest. It will also entail an improved machinery for translating social priorities into departmental policy and practice, nationally as Blackstone argues, and locally in ways Deakin discusses.

Fairer shares in taxation

Probably the major reason why social policy has not had a more equalising effect in Britain is that the taxes which finance it are levied in such a way that the burden falls heavily on the poorer earners, far more so after over three years of Conservative tax reforms. Greenaway discusses the options that would be open to a new government. Fairly sharing the burden of dependency and shouldering the cost of benefits for the disabled is the other side of the coin of citizenship. People who wish to live in a civilised society must pay a price. The simpler the tax structure and the fewer the allowances and exceptions, the less room there is for the rich and sophisticated to avoid paying their membership fee.

An acceptable range of rewards

Pond and Popay argued that the post-war strategy of achieving a socially acceptable range of living standards through a combination of social benefits and taxation has been ineffective and that it is necessary to collectively determine the range of rewards that can be tolerated in a society that has any pretensions to common citizenship. The lower levels we currently tolerate preclude full participation in widely acceptable standards of living and at the other extreme some rewards are so gross as to cause resentment and preclude any form of collective agreement to contain aggregate incomes within non-inflationary parameters. They argue that we should work towards a statutory floor and ceiling to incomes. Pond and Popay argue that the present range of high earnings are not economically functional.

Full employment

Underlying all else must be an economic strategy that will ensure employment opportunities. Sinfield sees this as central to all other social policies and to any conception of citizenship. An individual denied the right to earn a living for herself or himself and their dependants can never be a full citizen, however generous the unemployment compensation. If governments really accepted that principle, full employment would again become possible. Davies and Piachaud, however, point out that for those with jobs, still the majority, reducing inflation will continue to have a high political priority. If this can only be achieved by trading less job security for others they may well be prepared to pay that price. Once again then we see the importance of some collective determination of incomes, benefits and a full employment strategy and an appreciation that they are interdependent.

Will there be a future for the Welfare State?

Almost exactly five months after the Fabian seminar at which the papers in this volume were presented, Mrs. Thatcher held her own seminar on the future of the Welfare State – the Cabinet meeting of September 9th 1982. If we are to believe the leaks to *The Economist* (18 Sept. 1982) a Central Policy Review Staff paper was discussed which suggested that under current policies public expenditure would take a growing share of the nation's resources and that if this were to be reversed in line with the Government's declared intentions major policy changes would have to be made which would effectively destroy the Welfare State as we know it today – an end to state funding of higher education, a reduction in the real level of social security benefits and replacing the National Health Service by private insurance. The report seems to have been officially shelved but the impression remains that social spending is rising uncontrollably and that it is the fault of the Welfare State. It is also clear that if the Conservatives were re-elected for a second term these proposals would be reconsidered and could stand a strong chance of being introduced.

The reported contents of this paper suggest a very different scenario to that presented at the seminar by Davies and Piachaud. How is that? David Blake's analysis of the document in *The Times* (8 Nov. 1982) gives us some clues. The widely leaked scenario seems to be a 'worst case' position that embodies some fairly extraordinary assumptions, with much of the real blame for rising expenditure falling not on improvements to the social services but on defence spending and on the outcome of the government's own economic policy. Even the worst case does not involve a substantial rise in the share of the GNP going on public spending.

About 40 per cent of the projected extra spending was evidently taken by defence, both to keep to the target of a real 3 per cent per annum rise in spending, and to take account of the tendency for defence costs to rise faster than other costs. Both entail policy decisions by the government, and are in no sense irrevocable. Indeed it seems the Defence Department has been told to keep its costs in line with other departments. Spending on housing is apparently presumed to double which seems improbable. The bulk of social programmes, it is argued, would take a smaller share of national spending if there were no policy changes because of the underlying demographic position. The exceptions are services for the very elderly. This confirms what previous contributors have said. Finally, the most pessimistic assumption of all seems to be that the present recession and levels of unemployment last. If that were true it would be a condemnation of the Government's own economic policy, not of the social services. The scenario has all the hallmarks of an attempt to scare people into accepting major surgery which Mrs. Thatcher and other Conservatives want for ideological reasons.

Over the long run as contributors have argued elsewhere in this volume, social spending has risen faster than total domestic output for basically four reasons: the increasing number of dependent people below and above working age, the rising price of services relative to other prices, the rising standards of services, benefit levels and the numbers covered, and the long run rising levels of unemployment. Some of the factors causing this rise are relenting or being reversed while others are dependent on the policy of governments. The basic age structure, with the exception of the very elderly, is not going to produce the same additional burdens as it has done in the past. If there is a rise in

productivity in the rest of the economy which results in rising private
sector earnings and these then push up public sector pay this does
increase the 'price' of public services, but it also increases the scale of
incomes that people have out of which to meet taxes. If growth in
productivity slackens, so should the tendency to pass on pay increases.
Levels of benefit, coverage and we would hope levels of unemployment, in the long run, should be susceptible to government policy.

While the Labour Government expanded social spending overall *and*
reduced public expenditures' share of the national income the present
Conservative Government have increased its share and increased the
tax burden. Housing and education spending have fallen in real terms as
did current spending on personal social services after 1980/81 (House of
Commons Social Services Committee Second Report HC. 306–I July
1982). Social security spending has risen sharply because of the rising
levels of unemployment. The GNP itself has fallen. Their failure to
reduce taxation is the fault of their own economic policy and the world
recession not the social services. The future of the Welfare State is
being called into question on false premises.

A move forward
There is a long new agenda here and much else that could be added. But
many have come to despair of being able to move our society forward
again. Many did in the 1930s, but others found the courage and the
conviction to apply themselves to thinking through what a new society
might be like. We have enjoyed the fruits of that courage and we have
no right to despair. We have a duty not to.

Notes and references
1. T.H. Marshall, *Sociology at the Crossroads*, Heinemann, 1963.
2. *Ibid*. p. 72.
3. T.H. Marshall, 'Value Problems in Welfare Capitalism', *Journal of Social Policy*,
    vol. 1, no. 1, 1972.
4. *Social Workers: Their Role and Tasks*, Bedford Square Press, 1982.

Index

LIVERPOOL POLYTECHNIC LIBRARY

3 1111 00233 7374

Glennerster, H
The future of the welfare state: remakin
T M 361.6 GLE 1983